**ASTOUNDING TRUE OCCURRENCES
THAT STARTLE THE MIND
AND EXCITE THE IMAGINATION!**

THE WORLD'S STRANGEST MYSTERIES is a breathtaking collection of amazing people and incredible events that have challenged the understanding of expert and layman alike.

Here are enigmas of science and history that defy explanation, unfathomable puzzles that have never been solved by the world's greatest minds.

For the wide audience that is fascinated by true accounts of nature at her most freakish, THE WORLD'S STRANGEST MYSTERIES will be an unforgettable reading experience.

THE WORLD'S STRANGEST MYSTERIES

by RUPERT FURNEAUX

ace books

A Division of Charter Communications Inc.
1120 Avenue of the Americas
New York, N.Y. 10036

THE WORLD'S STRANGEST MYSTERIES

Copyright © 1961 by Rupert Furneaux

An Ace Book by arrangement with
Odhams Press Limited

Printed in U.S.A.

CONTENTS

FOREWORD

EVERYONE loves a mystery, as long as it remains a problem to be solved. But where to find the Great Mysteries, the World's "Strangest"; those which have puzzled us, some for centuries? All of mine have been told before, some by myself, but here they are all together for your investigation.

No collection can be absolutely complete: here I have tried to bring together the most intriguing and unusual mysteries, those that still live in an age of scepticism.

THE MONEY PIT

THE GREAT work was finished, the last spadefuls of earth thrown back into the pit which had taken so many months to dig. When the grass grew again in the spring all trace of it would be lost. No one would suspect that beneath the giant oak a pit thirteen feet wide and a hundred and seventy feet deep had once been dug. If anyone stumbled upon it, it would avail them little, for deep down in the earth a trusty and timeless guardian protected the treasure these nameless men had hidden.

At their leader's orders the men combed the ground around the tree; nothing must be left to betray their presence, not a spade or musket, buckle or button to give the game away. While the men cleared up, the leader jotted on his chart the directions by which the pit could be found and the mighty guardian freed from its vigil.

"Seven by eight by four," he wrote, wondering when he would next stand upon that arrow of stones and plot the course to the tree.

The last boat pulled off to the ship anchored in the cove. Quickly the sails were set and the anchor weighed. Slowly she turned and headed for the open sea, her company unaware that never again would they set eyes on their treasure island.

Behind them they left a silent witness, the giant oak. Scored by ropes, its limb, cut off four feet from the trunk, and jutting out over a slowly sinking saucer-shaped depression in the ground, was to set off the world's most baffling and long drawn out treasure hunt.

Time passed: no man trod the little island in Mahone Bay, Nova Scotia. Uninhabited and unexplored, nature continued its cycle. The giant oak grew older, and the ground beneath it sank a little deeper as the earth subsided.

This is the story of one of the world's strangest mysteries. Mysteries are often intriguing but seldom rewarding! The solution of this one offers a fortune.

Since 1795 a number of private individuals armed with picks and shovels, and several syndicates equipped with the latest modern tools, have dug and drilled on that little island in Mahone Bay, Nova Scotia. Even the late Franklin Roosevelt in his youth had a try at finding the treasure and several men have spent their lives and their fortunes in the quest of wealth, the existence of which no one doubts.

So far nothing has been gained and thousands of pounds have been sunk in the Money Pit, as it is aptly named. Yet each individual and every syndicate would willingly tackle it again if they had the cash; and few summers pass without eager treasure seekers willing to risk their money.

The story of the Money Pit on Oak Island is the most intriguing of all the mysteries of buried treasure. Some time before the year 1795 a company of men dug a pit thirteen feet wide and one hundred and seventy feet deep on the southern promontory of the island and in the pit they placed a quantity of gold and filled it in. For most people that would have been protection enough, but these men were not content. To safeguard their cache from chance discovery they devised a system of subterranean water channels which have baffled treasure seekers for one hundred and sixty years. They were psychologists, too, for they thought out a further trick to deceive those who might overcome the powerful guardian they had harnessed for the protection of their treasure. These men were engineering geniuses yet we have not the slightest clue who they were. They came from nowhere. They must have worked on Oak Island for months. They buried a treasure, the origin of which there is no clue, and they sailed away into the oblivion from which they had come. Whoever they were these men must have died together for they did not dig up their wealth or pass on the secret of its hiding-place.

But, as we shall see, they *may* have left a chart of their secret island though no one can now find it. Behind them they left a mystery which even the unearthing of their treasure may never solve. One thing seems certain: these nameless men would have laboured as they did only to hide a treasure of vast value. The labour they went to and the work they did is so permanent that one is almost tempted to believe that they did not expect to return, for to dig out the pit again would have required months of hard work by a large and disciplined force. That anyone has come even to know of their work is owing to just one chance in a million.

The story starts on one October day in 1795. Three young woodsmen from the mainland, Jack Smith, Anthony Vaughan and Daniel McGinnis were out in their canoe in Mahone Bay, a sheet of water 20 miles long and 12 miles wide; a secluded anchorage containing 365 small islands, all un-inhabited and unexplored. One of these islands was notice-ably different from the others for it was covered with a magnificent growth of live-oaks, whereas on the others only spruce grew. Live-oaks are seldom found north of Virginia.

Deciding to investigate, the three men landed on the beach where, embedded in a great rock, they found a heavy iron ring-bolt similar to those by which ships are moored. Ex-ploring the island, which is a mile long and half a mile broad, they came upon a clearing in the centre of which stood a single giant oak tree. On it were marks and figures and one branch, 16 feet from the ground had been sawn off 4 feet from the trunk. Its bark was deeply scored by the marks of ropes. Immediately below this branch was a large circular depression in the ground, which looked as though someone had dug there.

Brought up on a coast which had once been the haunt of pirates, it did not take Smith, Vaughan and McGinnis long to smell treasure. Next day they were back with picks and shovels. Digging into the hard blue clay they found them-selves in a well-defined circular shaft 13 feet wide, of which the sides were scored by the marks of picks. Ten feet below the surface they came upon a platform of oak logs 6 inches thick. The ends of the logs were embedded in the sides of the pit. Hoisting them out and expecting at any moment to reach the buried treasure they were convinced lay below, they were disappointed to find still more hard-beaten clay. Digging on they came to another oak platform at 20 feet and still another at 30 feet.

Realizing that the task was too much for them and with winter approaching, they abandoned work and returned to the mainland, more convinced than ever that whoever it was who had dug the pit had done so to conceal a treasure of great value.

Knowing that they needed machinery to dig farther they tried to raise capital amongst their friends, but they met with a complete lack of response. They learned from some of the oldest inhabitants that the island was considered to be haunted, and they heard strange tales of long ago when bonfires had been seen from the mainland at night.

Both Smith and McGinnis married and settled on Oak Island, as they named it. When Smith's wife had to return to the mainland to have a baby she told the story of the pit to Dr. John Lynd. He became interested and raised a sum of money among his friends. In 1803 digging operations recommenced. With the help of buckets and pulleys for the removal of the earth a depth of 80 feet was soon reached, an oak platform being encountered at each 10 feet level.

At 80 feet the treasure-seekers came upon another obstruction, a layer of charcoal laid over a thick mat of coconut fibre; a strange tropical product to find in bleak Nova Scotia. At 90 feet they reached a layer of ship's putty, hard as brick. Below this putty they found a flat stone 3 feet long and 16 inches wide covered with strange markings, which neither they nor anybody else has been able to decipher.

Smith took the stone and built it into the wall of his house, where it remained for many years, until in 1928 it was taken to the mainland for the local experts to see. In or about that year it became lost, so it is unlikely that anybody will now be able to determine what it said. The discovery of this stone incited the treasure-seekers to fresh efforts. Surely, at last, they must be near their goal? Great was their excitement, therefore, when at a depth of 98 feet their picks struck another hard obstruction. As it was late on a Saturday night work was suspended for the week-end.

When the diggers returned on the Monday morning the pit was filled with 65 feet of water.

Unfortunately for Smith, Vaughan, McGinnis and their friends, they did not then sit down to try to work out from where this water came. If they had done so they might have solved the problems of the pit, or one of its problems at any rate. They might even have found the treasure, or part of it. They cannot be blamed, however, for their lack of perception; they did not know they were up against men who had prepared against the chance discovery of the pit.

Faced on that Monday morning with the pit, which had taken them so much hard work to dig, full of water, the 1803 syndicate attempted to bale it out by hand. After weeks of effort they succeeded only in lowering the level of the water by a few feet. They then went to the immense labour of digging another pit beside it with the object of draining the original pit. Reaching a depth of 110 feet, they tunnelled under the original pit. While they were digging the bottom of the old pit collapsed and they were lucky to escape being drowned. Overnight the new pit filled up to 65 feet level and the Money Pit itself remained full of water.

This catastrophe brought the first treasure hunt to an end; the syndicate went bankrupt. Smith and McGinnis continued to live on the island, part of which they farmed, but when a new syndicate was formed on the mainland in 1849 only Vaughan of the original finders of the pit was still alive. When he led the new treasure seekers to the site of the Money Pit they found it had completely filled in.

Although they found no treasure the new syndicate made two great discoveries.

They established, as no one really doubted, that the pit contained treasure, and they learned the secret of the powerful guardian that had been left to prevent people from removing the treasure.

The syndicate of 1849, which was made up of local business and professional men, decided on a new technique. Before embarking on costly excavation they would test the pit with a drill in order to see what lay beneath.

Digging down to the water level they set up a platform and installed a pod auger, a form of primitive drill used in coal mines. At 98 feet the drill encountered the hard obstruction reached by the 1803 syndicate. This appeared to be another oak platform. Passing through it the drill dropped to 108 feet, where it encountered a hard substance which was identified by the shavings brought up as oak. Put down again the drill went through a further 12 inches of oak and then it started to wobble about as though it was pushing through loose metal. This went on for 22 inches.

When the bit was brought up two tiny links of gold chain were found adhering to the end of the drill, so at last there was evidence that the pit was a treasure cache. Wildly excited the treasure seekers put down their drill again. It passed through another 22 inches of loose metal, the bit wobbling as before, and reached another layer of oak 4 inches thick. The drill was put down several times on different sides of the pit and each time it disclosed the same formation of oak and metal. It is clear that the drill had gone through two oak chests one on top of the other, each containing loose metal, probably gold, as shown on the accompanying diagram.

While the directors of the syndicate were examining the links of gold brought up, the foreman driller, James Pittbaldo, put down the drill again and when it came up he was seen

11

THE MONEY PIT

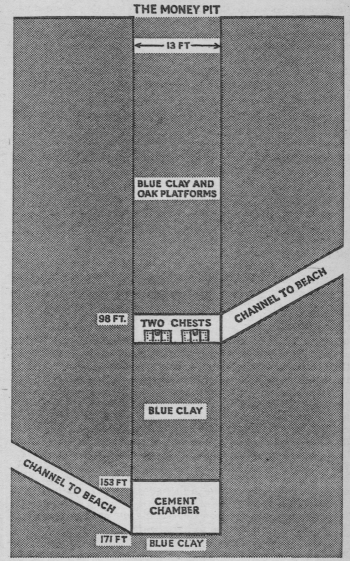

13 FT

BLUE CLAY AND
OAK PLATFORMS

98 FT.

TWO CHESTS

CHANNEL TO BEACH

BLUE CLAY

CHANNEL TO BEACH

153 FT

CEMENT
CHAMBER

171 FT   BLUE CLAY

to remove something from it and put it in his pocket. He refused to say what he had found and he disappeared next morning, but significantly within a few days he and a local coal mine operator tried to get control of the title to the island. Before Pittbaldo could be questioned he was killed in a mine accident elsewhere, so we shall never know what it was he found. It is said, however, that his drill brought up a jewel.

The new syndicate had at last established that what was previously a supposition was now a certainty. The pit was a treasure cache, but they were no nearer lifting the treasure than had been their predecessors, for the water level remained at 65 feet. After again trying baling they repeated the error of their predecessors by digging another pit alongside the original one. Reaching the depth of 118 feet, they tunnelled under the Money Pit with the object of draining it, but its bottom collapsed into a welter of mud and both pits were soon filled with water.

While working in the pits they learned a fact of major importance. The water in the pit was sea water and it rose and fell with the ebb of the tides. A careful watch showed that the water in the pit fluctuated one inch for each foot of tide. Sea water, they knew, could not have seeped through the hard blue clay. It must, therefore, be brought to the pit by a subterranean channel.

The source of the subterranean channel which brought the sea into the pit was easily traced, for it had been noticed, without anybody realizing its significance, that at low tide the sea appeared to run out of the sand at Smith's Cove, some 460 feet from the pit. Examination of the beach disclosed that an area extending from high- to low-water mark and 145 feet wide had been made into a vast sponge to absorb the tide as it came in each day. The beach had been dug out and filled with rocks and stones beneath which five drains, spread in a fan-like pattern, converged to a central channel. Over the rocks and stones had been laid a thatch of eel grass, a tropical vegetable fibre, which collected and held the water, turning the beach into a permanent reservoir. The central channel ran inland and from it the sea water drained into a subterranean pit, from where a channel led into the Money Pit.

How, then, did those who dug the pit expect to dig out their treasure when and if they came back to recover it? Although it has never been found, it is assumed that somewhere in the subterranean water channel there is a secret water gate, by which it would have been possible to cut off the sea water.

Apart from digging the pit itself, a tremendous feat without machinery, these men had run a long subterranean channel from the beach which must have required a vent to bring air to those working beneath. This was found by accident: a farmer on the island working near the Money Pit was ploughing with a yoke of oxen when his beasts suddenly disappeared into a hole that opened beneath them. This led to the channel itself which was found to be some three feet wide and high.

The treasure seekers now knew that in order to drain the pit it was necessary first to cut off the water from the sea. They attempted to do this by building a coffer-dam across the beach to prevent the reservoir from being filled at each high tide. This dam collapsed during a particularly high tide, and the 1849 syndicate went bankrupt.

Nothing was done between 1863 and 1893. Then a local business man, Frederick Blair, from whose son I have heard much about the Money Pit, formed a new syndicate to attempt the recovery of the treasure. Although Blair worked at the pit off and on for fifty years he achieved no greater success than had those before him, but early on he discovered something even stranger than what had gone before.

When Blair and his friends came on the island the original pit and the others which had been dug around it had all collapsed, and a fresh start had to be made. It was decided to make a complete investigation of the area beneath by drills before any attempt to dig was made. While the new syndicate explored they also investigated the possibility of cutting off the pit's water supply, and to this end they drilled five holes across the line of the supposed subterranean water channel, put down dynamite and blew them up. This had the desired result, for it was observed that the water no longer rose in the pit.

In the pit itself Blair put down first a three-inch pipe in which the drill could operate, pipe and drill passing through the area previously investigated and encountering blue clay again below the chests. Although there was no need to search deeper they allowed the drill to go on. At 112 feet and 126 feet it encountered both wood and iron, and then continued on through the blue clay until a depth of 151 feet was reached.

It should be said here, as will be seen on the diagram, that the natural level of blue clay on the island as disclosed by

14

drill holes finishes at 110 feet and below that brown marl is encountered. This is not the case in the pit itself, for the blue clay continued. At 151 feet the drill appeared to bite into soft stone. Some of this was brought up and was subsequently sent to a firm of chemists in London for analysis. They reported that it was man-made cement. This cement was two inches deep and below it the drill went through 1½ inches of wood, a few chips of which were brought up. What was then disclosed has been described in a sworn statement made by members of Blair's syndicate.

"When the auger passed through the wood it dropped from 1½ inches to 2 inches and rested upon a substance, the character of which no person has attempted to state. The material was apparently of soft metal that could be moved slightly thereby forming a crevice or space into which the drill would drop, and stick or wedge. This happened a number of times and it was often necessary to pry the drill loose. After working for two hours or more we managed to get the drill down four inches when it worked easier, but it would not go down under the ordinary method of drilling (raising and dropping the rods) but by a continuous twisting and turning of the rods under constant pressure we managed to get 18 or 20 inches deeper, a total of 24 inches of material bored through under the wood. The drill then struck a substance similar to that encountered immediately under the wood."

The statement continues:

"The conclusion was that the first four inches consisted of metal in bars which were pushed aside by the drill, enough to permit it to pass, and that the additional twenty inches consisted of coin or metal in small pieces that fell into the space left by the tool as it was drawn up, and also, that under the small pieces there was more metal in bars."

From this drilling and the analysis of the stone it is assumed that between 153 feet and 160 feet down there lies a cement chamber filled with metal, probably gold.

This cement chamber contains, probably, the bulk of the treasure in the Money Pit. Apparently the two oak chests between 98 feet and 104 feet, though in themselves a cache of great value, were put there as a blind, for most chance treasure seekers would have been content with the finding of the chests and would never have suspected the bulk of the treasure lay far beneath.

Underneath this cement chamber the drill disclosed two more secrets. A spout of water coming up the pipe at the rate of 400 gallons a minute revealed the existence of yet another subterranean water channel. The source of this second channel was traced to the beach on the other side of the island. When a dye was pumped down the pipe, water of that colour was found on the south beach. Drilling was continued below the 160 feet level and more blue clay was encountered. At a level of 171 feet the drill bit into a layer of iron, which has never been drilled through. As far as anybody knows, therefore, the pit finishes at that level with an iron obstruction.

All these facts were learned by 1897 but although so much had by then been discovered, no progress was made by the Blair syndicate, although some £20,000 had been spent, because when digging was commenced after the drilling had been finished, it was found that the whole area underground was so disturbed by the many different pits and tunnels which had been dug, that it was impossible to relocate the original treasure area. The area underground was a mass of waterlogged mud in which the original treasure chests and cement chamber had become lost.

Lack of capital prevented any other move until in 1935 an American named Gilbert Heddon who had plenty of money and considerable experience of mining brought into action the most up-to-date machinery, powered by an electric cable from the mainland. Electric pumps were set to work to drain the pit, but even they could not cope with the continual inrush of the sea. In the end Heddon and Blair, with whom he went into partnership, had to give up. Mr. Heddon, however, made a detailed investigation into the entire history of the pit, and of the island. He learned some strange things.

It will be recalled that when Smith, Vaughan and McGinnis tried to raise capital in 1795, they were told by the local inhabitants that the island was haunted, and very few people would go there. One particular woman had told them that her grandmother, who had lived all her life in the little town of Chester four miles across the channel from Oak Island, had said that when she was a girl she remembered seeing strange men and fires on the island, and that several local men who had rowed over to investigate had never returned. Heddon traced this story back to approximately the year 1720, or some seventy-five years before the pit was discovered.

About 1870, a man, apparently well to do and of Latin-American type, had turned up in the neighbourhood. He hired a boat and crew, and each morning of his stay had sailed out to sea and taken a course to the north-west, which, from the account of the men who had accompanied him, could have led only to Oak Island. One of the crew had said that each morning this man examined what appeared to be an old chart. He had never landed on Oak Island and after a few weeks he left the neighbourhood and never returned.

Very naturally Heddon thought about the people who could have dug the pit some two hundred years before. He made a study of many books about famous pirates. In one of these, a life of Captain Kidd, he found published a chart of the island on which Kidd is supposed to have buried his treasure. Looking at this chart it occurred to him that the island was strangely similar to Oak Island. Although it was not exactly alike, it conformed in general outlines. Checking the chart against a chart of Oak Island it was found that many details were similar. For example the elevations were the same. Ponds marked on the map conformed to places which once may have been ponds on Oak Island. Around the island the soundings were the same as on the chart, but even more extraordinary was a legend written on the chart which read:

"18 West and by 7 E Rock, 30 South-West,
14 North tree, and 7 by 8 by 4."

These figures presumably indicated a course which when followed would lead to the hiding place of Kidd's treasure.

Heddon and his associates decided to see if these figures and directions fitted Oak Island. Starting with the east-west line they found at Smith's Cove a white granite boulder, deeply embedded in the sand, in which a round hole had been bored 1¼ inches in diameter and 2 inches deep. Just as they found this stone, Blair, now a very old man, came to the island and, told of their discovery, exclaimed, "there is another stone on the island marked in exactly the same way", and he took them to a beach on the other side of the island where a second granite boulder was found to have an exactly similar hole. A line was run between the two stones and at the point recorded in the legend, a second line was run due south-west, it being assumed that the original directions were in rods. Thirty rods in this direction took the now excited treasure seekers to a point covered with a heavy growth of bushes. Clearing the ground they found embedded in the soil a 14-feet long triangle or arrow which pointed directly north at the Money Pit by which had stood the original tree. Everything pointed to the existence of a chart left by the original hiders of the treasure, presumably Captain Kidd himself.

Modern research has proved that the famous Captain Kidd was never a pirate. A privateer, he was probably the innocent victim of influential rogues who got him hanged at Wapping in 1701. This did not, however, overcome the belief that Kidd had something to do with the pit and that he had left behind him a chart which must have been of Oak Island, a place he might easily have visited some time about 1669.

To settle the problem Heddon came to England, where he found the author of the book who assured him that there could be no possible connexion between the chart he had published and Oak Island. Kidd's map, he said, related to an island in the China Seas. He had been allowed to see the original chart by its owner. There was no doubt that it was an authentic chart drawn by Captain Kidd, for it had been found in an old chest belonging to him. The owner had not allowed him to see the latitude and longitude on the chart and his reproduction of the chart in his book was only a freehand drawing of what he had been allowed to see. The original chart had not borne the legend which so exactly fitted Oak Island. The author told Heddon that he had examined thousands of charts in various museums and he could only assume that he had noted these directions from some other chart, which must have been of Oak Island, and had superimposed them on his Kidd map by chance.

Heddon had to return to Nova Scotia with the maddening knowledge that the men who dug the Money Pit and had devised the ingenious safeguard that had for so long protected their treasure, had left a clue for its rediscovery. It was clearly an impossible task to find the map again for there was no clue to its whereabouts. It might be anywhere in Europe. This original chart may have contained information showing how the water gates in the two subterranean channels could have been closed, thus permitting comparatively simple excavation of the treasure.

Although Blair's and Heddon's treasure trove rights granted by the Canadian Government were extended after the war, no further progress was made and none of the would-be fortune hunters who have come to Oak Island each summer since then have made any real progress.

I have had considerable correspondence with the present owner of these rights and with others in Nova Scotia and the general opinion is that any fresh start to the search for the treasure must commence with the re-location of the original pit. Borings would be needed to locate the chests and cement chamber. This does not sound difficult, but as usually happens in treasure hunts, it is handicapped by lack of adequate finance and proper equipment. Many treasure seekers come and go, wasting their money, when if the hunt was properly organized and fully financed it would seem likely that the pit would yield a profit. Whether or no anybody will succeed in re-locating the treasure and digging it out, a mystery remains. Who were these men who had treasure worth so much trouble to conceal?

Many suggestions have been put forward as to whom they may have been. The first choice is, of course, pirates, but against the pirates theory is the obvious inference that it is highly unlikely that any gang of pirates would have concealed their treasure in such a way.

The work involved in digging the pit and the channels must have taken months. It could have been accomplished only by a highly disciplined force of men, one of whom at least must have been an engineer of genius and a psychologist of no mean order. These qualifications hardly fit a gang of pirates. Obviously the diggers of the pit intended to come back, for all the wealth in the world was no good to them at a depth of 160 feet. To dig up their treasure they would have had to return with an equally disciplined force of men prepared to spend many weeks excavating the pit.

While we cannot discount the possibility that the Money Pit contains a pirate's hoard, it would seem necessary to look elsewhere for the men who dug it. There are several clues of a rather negative nature. In the first place we can put the period of the pit's construction somewhere between 1695 and 1740, for the tree would not have been strong enough to have been used as a hoist prior to the former year; then, too, there is the story of the strange happenings in or about the year 1720. Another clue lies in the coconut fibre or eel grass found both in the pit and in Smith's Cove. This must have been brought from a southern clime and we must not ignore the significance of the fact that Oak Island is the only island in the bay on which grew these live-oaks which are quite foreign to Nova Scotia. It is stated also that red clover, a weed found usually only far to the south, grows in profusion on the island.

If the directions printed on the chart found in the Kidd book have any authenticity it may be assumed that the original diggers of the pit were English, for the words are written in that language.

Another possible clue lies in the discovery of a particle of parchment brought up in the 1897 drilling. Microscopic in size, this parchment bears the letters "V.I." which, of course, may have been written in any language.

To decide who these men may have been, it seems necesary to think who, other than pirates, had treasure to hide in the eighteenth century. Little gold was in circulation before the conquests of Mexico and Peru, and it has been suggested that the treasure of the Money Pit may represent a consignment of gold being conveyed home by a Spanish galleon. The officers and crew may have decided to steal the cargo and hide it temporarily on the American coast.

Another theory is that the treasure represents the lost jewels of Marie Antionette. When she and her husband, Louis XVI, were captured on their attempted flight from France in 1791, her lady-in-waiting escaped with the royal jewels. This lady is supposed to have gone to Nova Scotia and no one has been able to trace what happened to the jewels.

A more feasible theory is that the Oak Island treasure represents a known store of gold reputed to have been two million pounds in value, belonging to the garrison of the French fortress of Louisbourgh on Cape Bretton Island. This island was captured by the British in 1745. In 1748 it was handed back to France and the French Government set about its re-fortification. For this purpose £2 million in gold was sent from France.When in 1758 the fortress was again taken by the British it was found that very little work had been done. It may be that the garrison made off with the gold and secreted it on Oak Island, which lies only some 250 miles to the south. That the engineers of the French garrison would have been capable of constructing the Money Pit supports this theory.

There the matter stands. We are no nearer a solution and no nearer the recovery of the treasure. It is now nearly twenty years since I first heard of the Money Pit, and I have spent many hours thinking about it.

One point seems to stand out clearly. It is the durable nature of the work that amazes us. Those who dug the pit seem to have presented themselves with a herculean task in its recovery. They must have felt certain that they would be able to return with sufficient force to dig it up.

The really amazing thing is that no one talked. This suggests that no one lived to tell the tale. Many men must have been involved in the concealment of the treasure and some at least might have talked of the story in some seaport tavern.

These men, or the majority of them, must have perished almost immediately after the treasure was hidden. They sailed away from Oak Island thinking themselves rich and wealthy men. Perhaps something like this occurred:

The ship's officers may have said to themselves: "If the crew are allowed ashore, the story will be out in a week." Upon them came not so much the greed of gold, the desire to acquire all the treasure for themselves, but the fear that they would lose it from some indiscretion. Anchoring near a mainland, they may have blown up the ship, rowing ashore themselves, while the crew slept. Then, one of the men, perhaps the "Man of Genius" himself, thought that the secret was still shared by too many, so he killed his confederates and became the sole inheritor of the secret. In his fear, he destroyed his own chance of recovering the treasure for now he had no ship and no crew.

For many years, perhaps, he tried to get back to Oak Island, until at last time ran out. Somehow the chart he had made reached Europe, and somewhere, in some museum's files, it lies awaiting a chance discovery which will at last solve one of the greatest of the mysteries of treasure trove.

THE MASKED MAN

For two hundred and fifty years curious enquirers have sought the identity of the mysterious masked prisoner of seventeenth-century France. First whispers about the individual, whose name was unknown and who had died there in 1703, percolated from the Bastille in 1711. In the next fifty years the story swept France and eventually over all the world. With no reliable information to go on, speculation grew into a legend in which myth was piled on myth, until in the end the unfortunate masked prisoner was described as wearing an unwieldy contraption of iron. In Alexander Dumas' story he was identified as the twin brother of Louis XIVth.

The secret of the man's identity was essentially a Royal

secret, one which Louis XIVth and his advisers were determined we should never penetrate. They went to great lengths to stop us, laying false clues and suggesting an audacious solution, but they did not bargain for the day when the Royal Archives would be thrown open to public inspection.

The identity of the "Ancient Prisoner", as he was called, the Man in the Mask, is history's greatest enigma. Modern methods of detection have solved it, partly at least. The mask has been lifted from the face it was intended to hide for ever. But why that particular face had to be masked so that it should not be recognized after thirty years is still a matter of speculation.

Those who knew the secret were all dead by 1721. Then the last Minister to be concerned, M. de Chamillart, implored to reveal the secret on his death bed, declared he had taken his oath never to reveal it. The mistress of the previous Minister, pressed for information, said the Masked Man was a son of Ann of Austria (the wife of Louis XIIIth) born in 1626 after the visit of the English Duke of Buckingham to her Court. For many years there had been rumours of an affair between the Queen of France and the dashing English Duke. The Minister's mistress said this illegitimate son was imprisoned and masked by Louis XIVth, to whom he bore a striking resemblance. While this woman may have known something, it seems more likely that she was fed with an impossible solution to the mystery, one which by its very audacity might serve to hide the truth.

Louis XVth, Louis XIVth's grandson and successor, when told the secret on attaining his majority, declared: "If he were still alive I would give him his freedom." In later years, when speculation about the masked prisoner was at its greatest, he stated: "No one has yet told the truth and all conjectures are false."

While the myths of Voltaire and Dumas, based on the story that the man was an illegitimate son of The Royal House, masked to conceal his likeness to the King, excited popular imagination, more serious investigators found little to go on.

The first clues to the identity of the mysterious masked prisoner came to light in 1761 when the Journals of Etienne du Jonca, the King's Lieutenant, at the Bastille, were published. He recorded for the year 1698:

"Thursday, 18 September at three o'clock in the afternoon, M. de Saint-Mars, Governor of the Chateau of the Bastille, made his first appearance, coming from his command of the Iles Sainte-Marguerite-Honorat, bringing with him, in his litter, a prisoner he had formerly at Pignerol, whom he caused to be always masked, whose name is not mentioned; directly he got out of the carriage he put him in the first room of the Baziniere Tower, waiting until night for me to take him, at nine o'clock, and put him with M. de Rosarges, one of the sergeants brought by the Governor, alone in the third single room of the Bertaudiere Tower, which I had furnished with all necessaries some days before his arrival, having received orders to that effect from M. de Saint-Mars: the prisoner will be looked after and waited upon by M. de Rosarges, and maintained by the Governor."

Five years later du Jonca recorded the prisoner's death.

"On the same day, 19 November, 1703, the unknown prisoner, always masked with a mask of black velvet, whom M. de Saint-Mars, the Governor, brought with him on coming from the Ile Sainte-Marguerite, whom he had kept for a long time, the which happening to be a little ill yesterday on coming from Mass, he died today, about ten o'clock at night, without having had a serious illness; it could not have been slighter. M. Giraut, our Chaplain, confessed him yesterday, is surprised at his death. He did not receive the sacrament, and our Chaplain exhorted him a moment before he died. And this unknown prisoner, kept there for so long, was buried on Tuesday at four o'clock p.m., 20 November, in the graveyard of St. Paul, our parish; on the register of the burial he was given a name also unknown, M. de Rosarges, Major, and Arreil, surgeon, signed the register."

And in the margin du Jonca has written:

"I have since learnt that they called him M. de Marchiel on the register, and that forty livres was the cost of the funeral."

The entry of the man's burial in the register of the Church of St. Paul was also found. It reads:

"On the 19th, Marchioly, aged forty-five or thereabouts, died in the Bastille, whose body was buried in the church-yard of St. Paul, his parish, the 20th of the present month, in the presence of M. Rosarge, Major of the Bastille, and of M. Reglhe, surgeon major of the Bastille, who signed, Rosarges, Reilhe."

For many years the name under which the masked prisoner was buried, "M. de Marchiel," was thought to provide a convincing clue to his identity. It seems far more likely, however, that this was a false clue carefully laid to deceive us.

Other clues were derived from the recollection of a prisoner in the Bastille, de Renneville, who, when he caught a glimpse of the masked prisoner, was told by the turnkey Ru, who had been with St. Mars at Pignerol, he had been a prisoner since 1672. As we shall see later on, when rumours of the masked prisoner's incarceration in the South of France were collected, it came to light, from the prison register, that the man had first been imprisoned in 1669.

Until the French Revolution, little more was known about the masked prisoner. It was hinted that he had always been treated with the greatest deference and that on his death all his possessions were burned. According to popular rumour he was always masked, even while he ate and slept. Even so, before more definite records were disclosed, a particular theory had taken root in the middle of the eighteenth century. It was widely believed that the masked prisoner was a man named Mattioli, an envoy of the Duke of Mantua, who had double-crossed King Louis XIVth of France, and had been imprisoned under the care of St. Mars in 1679. It was a convenient theory, because the name under which the masked prisoner had been buried might have been a French way of spelling an Italian name. This Mattioli theory, as we shall see, held the field until 1869. Then it was largely discredited when discovery of a private letter written by St. Mars in 1681 showed that Mattioli had passed out of his custody for thirteen years and the security of another prisoner was preferred to his.

The names of many other men have been put forward to account for the identity of the masked prisoner but all of them have been eliminated inasmuch that they have been found either to have been alive after 1703 or dead before 1669, the year in which the prisoner first came under St. Mars' care. Mattioli, however, is still seriously considered as a contender to the dubious title of the Man in the Mask by many enquirers, and there can be no doubt that the Masked Man was either Mattioli or one other particular person. All the evidence points to the fact that he was not Mattioli, the man who Louis XIVth and his advisers wished we should assume was the masked prisoner.

When the State Papers of France and the Archives of the Bastille were thrown open to public inspection in the French Revolution, they were immediately examined to see if they threw any light on the mysterious masked prisoner. Great was the disappointment when they did not appear to do so. Napoleon caused a careful search to be made, but it yielded no greater success than had the previous enquiry instituted by Louis XVIth to satisfy his wife's curiosity.

When the Archives of the Ministry of War came to be classified they were found to be in great confusion. Many years of cataloguing and research produced a mass of letters which had passed for over thirty years between the Minister and Monsieur de St. Mars, the Masked Man's gaoler. In some cases the actual letters, or their copies, still existed: in others the existence of a letter was known from the Minute in the Ministry's letter book. These letters disclosed that for thirty years there had been a continuous interest in the safety and well being of one particular prisoner who was guardedly referred to as "your prisoner", "the man who was sent to me", "the man of the Tower", the "Ancient Prisoner". Which prisoner was he? Many notable people had been imprisoned by Louis XIVth in the special care of St. Mars.

St. Mars, an under officer of Musketeers, a subordinate of the D'Artagnan immortalized by Dumas, the gaoler of France's most important prisoners, took command of the Keep at Pignerol in 1665. Rising in command he was transferred to another prison in 1680. The unknown man who died in 1703 must therefore have been imprisoned at Pignerol before 1680; we know almost certainly that the actual date was 1669. Of this mysterious prisoner we now have the following information. He was brought by St. Mars, masked and in a litter, to the Bastille from the island of Saint Marguerite, on 18 September, 1698. He had formerly been a prisoner at Pignerol. A story related after his death in 1703 stated he had been a prisoner for thirty-one years. He was buried under a false name, but in the register his name was given as Marchioly, which was probably a false clue designed to disguise his identity forever. From other minor clues we know that he was a tall man, well built and in good health, aged about sixty years at the time of his death. Other information discloses that he was a Frenchman and a Catholic, for there is no reference to an interpreter and he was allowed to hear Mass.

St. Mars had been at Pignerol, in charge of France's most important prisoner of state, Monsieur Fouquet, the disgraced Minister of Finance, for four years when in July, 1669, he received a new prisoner. The long and mysterious imprisonment of this man can be traced in the series of letters that continuously passed between the gaoler and the Minister of War, Marquis de Louvois.

Towards the end of July, 1669, St. Mars received a letter from Louvois, dated 19th of that month:

"The King has commanded that I am to have the man named Eustache Dauger sent to Pignerol. It is of the utmost importance to His service that he should be most securely guarded and that he should in no way give information about himself nor send letters to anyone at all. I am informing you of this in advance so that you can have a cell prepared in which you will place him securely, taking care that the windows of the place in which he is put do not give on to any places that can be approached by anyone and that there are double doors to be shut, for your sentries not to hear anything. You will yourself once a day have to take enough food for the day to this wretch and you must on no account listen for any reason at all to what he may want to say to you, always threatening to kill him if he opens his mouth to speak of anything but his necessities."

Louvois told St. Mars to prepare for the prisoner, "bearing in mind that as he is only a valet he does not require anything special." The term "valet" in seventeenth-century France implied a confidential secretary or servant rather than a menial. This is the real clue to the prisoner's identity. It seems possible that in these letters the King and his advisers made a slip. While it appears conclusive that the name of the prisoner stated in the *Lettre de Cachet* gave the true name of the prisoner, it is significant that the name was omitted in the Ministry of War Minute as a precaution to keep his name hidden from prying eyes. Either St. Mars failed to destroy the original letter, or it was forgotten that the man had been named to him in it.

On 28 July the King himself wrote to his representative in the town of Dunkirk, saying:

"I am dissatisfied with the behaviour of a man named Eustache Dauger and I want to secure him. I am writing to inform you that as soon as you shall see him you are to seize him and arrest him and to conduct him yourself in all safety to the citadel of Pignerol, where he is to be guarded by Captain de Saint-Mars, to whom I am writing the attached letters so that the said prisoner shall be received and guarded there without difficulty. After which you are to return from there to render an account of that which you shall have done in execution of the present order."

On the same day the King wrote to St. Mars informing him that the Captain of the town of Dunkirk was bringing to him a prisoner named Eustache Dauger. He was to keep him in good and safe custody, preventing him from communicating with anyone at all by word of mouth or writ of hand.

That the prisoner duly arrived at Pignerol in August is apparent from a letter from St. Mars to Louvois written on the 21st of that month.

"Monsieur de Vauroy has handed over to me the man named Eustache d'Auger. As soon as I had put him in a very secure place, while waiting for the cell I am having prepared for him to be completed, I told him, in the presence of M. de Vauroy, that if he should speak to me or to anyone else, of anything other than his necessities, I would run him through with my sword. On my life, I shall not fail to observe very punctiliously your commands."

Ten days later St. Mars writes again to assure the Minister that his orders are being carried out, and "nothing is truer than that I have never spoken of this prisoner to any one and as proof of this, many people here think he is a Marshal of France." So the great legend began. Because of the tremendous secrecy and security arrangements with which this prisoner was cloaked people came to think that he must be somebody of great importance.

Before Louvois could have received this letter he had written to St. Mars instructing him as to how his new prisoner was to be treated:

"You can give a prayer book to your new prisoner, and if he asks you for any other, give it him also. You can let him hear on Sundays and feast days the Mass that is said for M. Fouquet without however being at the same place, and you will see that he is so well guarded during that time, that he cannot escape or speak to anyone; you can even let him have confession three or four times a year, if he so wishes, and no more unless he should contract some dangerous illness."

These letters establish that in the summer of 1669, thirty-four years before the death of the masked prisoner in the Bastille, a prisoner named Eustache Dauger was committed to prison without trial or sentence. No hint is given of the reason for his imprisonment but it is significant that he was brought right across France from one frontier to the other to be guarded by the King's principal gaoler. If he spoke to anyone of anything other than his necessities he was to be instantly killed, yet he was only a valet, a person apparently of no importance. He had been arrested at the town of Dunkirk on the Channel coast.

St. Mars appears to have been lax in his efforts of security, for eight months after the arrival of the prisoner Louvois writes to him to say that his vigilance has proved ineffective and that the prisoner had been spoken to by one of Monsieur Fouquet's valets. No real harm had been done, however, because the prisoner had refused to say anthing and asked only that he should be left in peace. Somehow the valet had gained access to this mysterious prisoner, and Louvois must have heard of it from one of his spies. He instructed St. Mars to examine carefully the inside and the outside of the place where the man is incarcerated and to put it in such a state that the prisoner could neither see or be seen by anyone nor speak to anyone at all, nor hear those who might want to say something to him. St. Mars, feeling himself in disgrace, replied that everyone was inquisitive about the prisoner and asking information about him, so much so that he had been obliged to tell fairy tales to make fun of them.

St. Mars' troubles were only just beginning: in November, 1671 another prisoner, no less a person than the famous Comte de Lauzun, was sent to him. This Royal favourite had incurred the King's displeasure. Soehow, but we do not know how, Lauzun is linked with Dauger. It may not be without significance that Lauzun was Captain of the King's Guard in July, 1669, when Dauger was sent to Pignerol. There is no doubt that Lauzun knew Eustache Dauger, and, despite St. Mars' precautions, it is certain that Lauzun and Dauger met while they were both at Pignerol.

St. Mars made great efforts to keep his mysterious prisoners apart. In his care at the Keep at Pignerol were now Fouquet, Lauzun, and the mysterious Dauger. Each was lodged in a secure prison, the windows of which were protected by iron bars and a basketwork grille to prevent its occupant being seen. Iron bars were also placed in the chimneys to prevent the prisoners communicating. "Never will any of the prisoners know that they had companions," St. Mars assured Louvois. But Lauzun fooled him. Lauzun was determined either to break out of his prison or to communicate with the others he suspected were there. At his first attempt in 1672 he succeeded in burning a beam in the floor of his room but his escape route was found and plugged. His attempt to get in touch with accomplices outside the prison was scotched. In July of that year St. Mars writes to Louvois: "I used to think that M. Fouquet was one of the most wicked prisoners a man could have, but now de Lauzun had arrived I see that by comparison he is indeed a lamb."

While Lauzun and Fouquet were causing the governor so much annoyance the other prisoner, Dauger, remained apparently contented in his cell. It is of interest to note that while St. Mars was ordered to try to make his various prisoners speak, this did not apply to Dauger and in fact as far as he was concerned he was not allowed to speak to him at all, to find out who he was or from whence he came.

Early in 1676 Lauzun made another escape attempt. After three years' work he scratched a hole through the floor of his room and got into the vault below where he removed bars to a window and climbed into the courtyard where he came face to face with a sentry. The fury of Louvois knew no bounds and St. Mars was asked how he had permitted walls and windows to be torn down without realizing that something was taking place. Shamed and humiliated he replied that it would never happen again.

Meanwhile Dauger apparently had been the most tranquil of St. Mars' prisoners. We know only that he had been ill; in the correspondence he was referred to only as "the prisoner who was sent to me". Now a startling change occurred in Dauger's imprisonment. St. Mars wrote to Louvois in 1672 saying that he was finding great difficulty in securing a good servant for M. Fouquet and suggesting that the man Dauger would make him a very good valet. Of him St. Mars wrote: "as to the prisoner in the Tower, who was sent to me by the Captain of Dunkirk, he says nothing, he lives contentedly like a man completely resigned to the will of God and the King". Very grudgingly, in 1675, Louvois acceded to St. Mars' request and informed him that the man who had been sent to him in 1669 could act as a valet to M. Fouquet but on no account was he to be allowed to see or be seen by Lauzun.

It is significant that Dauger was allowed to meet Fouquet but on no account could he be seen by Lauzun. This suggests that Lauzun might have recognized him as someone he knew in July, 1669, and it indicates further that the mysterious prisoner from Dunkirk, or at least his secret, must have been known to Fouquet, who before his imprisonment in 1665 must have been familiar with all the secrets of France. Either Fouquet knew all about Dauger, or it was considered not to matter if he found out.

On 23 December, 1678, Louvois wrote directly to Fouquet, whom Dauger had now been serving as an additional valet for three years. This letter was brought to Fouquet with its seals unbroken and he was ordered to reply in secret, without the letter being read by St. Mars. Fouquet's answer has not survived but in his letter Louvois said that he desired to be informed whether the man called Eustache had spoken before the other valet who was serving Fouquet of "that on which he was up to before being at Pignerol". Fouquet was instructed that the King commanded that, without taking thought for what the result might be, he was to send the truth regarding the matter, of what Eustache might have said about his past life. Thus it appears that it did not matter what Eustache might have told Fouquet, but it mattered very much if he had spoken about himself before the other valet, who was named La Riviere.

When, a few months later, Fouquet's imprisonment was alleviated, St. Mars was carefully instructed by Louvois to see that when Fouquet and Lauzun met, as they were now allowed to do, every precaution had to be made to withdraw the man called Eustache from Fouquet's room before Lauzun came to visit him. Despite St. Mars' precautions and completely without his knowledge, Lauzun had been visiting Fouquet in his room for years and presumably seeing Dauger there. After Fouquet's death, it was discovered that Lauzun had removed the bars in his chimney and made a passage into Fouquet's room. It seems likely therefore that Lauzun must have learned about him. Louvois did not know of this at the time, and we find him writing to St. Mars on 15 February, 1679, to the effect that he must see above all that the man called Eustache Dauger be not permitted to speak to anyone in private. Six months later the Minister wrote again asking the gaoler for news of Dauger's health.

When in 1680 Fouquet died, St. Mars was instructed to inform Lauzun that the man called Eustache Dauger had been released along with Fouquet's other valet, La Riviere. But they were not to be released. The two valets were to be shut up in a room together in the more secure of the two towers and they were not to be allowed to communicate with anyone and every effort was to be made to see that Lauzun did not perceive that they were still in the prison.

When Fouquet died, St. Mars found in his clothing a particular paper which he took care to send by courier to Louvois. We do not know if this referred to Eustache Dauger, but from this moment Dauger entirely loses his identity and is no longer referred to by name in the correspondence. He becomes "one of the gentlemen of the Lower Tower" and as time went on he was referred to only as "la Tour" and "the Ancient Prisoner". Lauzun was released in 1682. On his return to Paris he had a private interview with Louis XIVth who generously compensated him for his loss of offices and imprisonment. Never to our knowledge did Lauzun ever speak or write of the mysterious prisoner Dauger, whom everything suggests he knew perhaps intimately in 1669.

Leaving Dauger shut up in the Lower Tower with the other valet, La Riviere, we can notice the arrival of another distinguished prisoner at Pignerol.

In the year 1679 Ercole Mattioli, the Minister of the Duke of Mantua, was brought to Pignerol. He had been abducted and brought to French territory because he had double-crossed King Louis XIVth in a plot to seize an Italian fortress. Everyone in Europe knew of Mattioli's duplicity and that he had been kidnapped and imprisoned. His punishment would have been completely nullified by secrecy. None the less he was well treated at Pignerol, being allowed his own valet.

Since Mattioli has been put forward so seriously as the masked prisoner who died at the Bastille in 1703, both the records of his imprisonment and that of the mysterious Dauger must be carefully probed.

When St. Mars was promoted in 1681 to the Governorship of the Fortress of Exiles some thirty miles from Pignerol, he took with him two prisoners, leaving three at Pignerol. The security of these two prisoners was of paramount concern to the King and it is clear from the correspondence that they were Dauger and La Riviere. Mattioli was left behind at Pignerol, as is disclosed in a private letter written by St. Mars on 25 June, 1681, which did not come to light until 1869. For thirteen years, until the time when St. Mars received further promotion, the security of a prisoner other than Mattioli was preferred. There is a strong presumption that the other of the two prisoners taken by St. Mars to Exiles was the valet La Riviere because he is described as suffering from dropsy as it is known Fouquet's other valet did. It is certain, too, that La Riviere died at Exiles because the man suffering from dropsy is so described in the correspondence. Moreover, the fact that he was allowed to make a will suggests strongly that it was La Riviere rather than Dauger, by whom the making of a will would have nullified all the years of intense secrecy. La Riviere, as a valet, not a prisoner, should have been released on Fouquet's death, but he must have known Dauger's secret. The acquisition of this unfortunate secret accounts for his imprisonment until his death.

At Exiles, the two unfortunate "valets" were incarcerated under even greater provisions of security than they had been at Pignerol. Sentinels watched the room of their Tower by day and night and they were allowed as a confessor only a very old priest brought from some miles away. That they were not considered of great importance is suggested by a letter still extant from Louvois to St. Mars in 1681 which reads: "the clothes of fellows like those must last three or four years." Louvois directs that the King has ordered that they be strictly guarded and that St. Mars is to take such precautions that he can assure that they will speak to no one, not only from outside but even of the garrison at Exiles.

Of this security of his two prisoners St. Mars writes to Louvois on 11 March, 1682:

"I have received your letter . . . that it is important that my two prisoners should have no communication with anyone . . . I have guarded these two prisoners . . .as severely and exactly as I formerly did Messieurs Fouquet and Lauzun who could not boast that they had either sent or received any news, while they were in confinement. These prisoners can hear the people speak as they pass along the road which is at the bottom of the tower; but they, if they wish it, could not make themselves heard; they can see the persons on the hill which is before their windows, but they cannot themselves be seen on account of the bars which are placed across their room. There are two sentinels of my company always night and day on each side of the tower, at a reasonable distance, who can see the windows of the prisoners obliquely. They are ordered to take care that no one speaks to them, and that they do not cry out from their windows; and to make the passers-by walk on, if they wish to stop in the path, or on the side of the hill. My own room, being joined to the tower, and having no other look out except towards the path, I hear and see everything, even my two sentinels, who are by this means always kept alert.

"As for the inside of the tower, I have divided it in such a manner that the priest who says Mass to them cannot see them, on account of the curtain I have made, which covers their double doors. The servants who bring their food put whatever is necessary for the prisoners upon a table on the outside, and my lieutenant takes it and carries it in to them. No one speaks to them except myself, my officer, M. Vigneron (the confessor) and a physician from Prage-las, which is six leagues from hence, who only sees them in my presence. With regard to their linen and other nec-essaries I take the same precautions which I did with my former prisoners."

In passing we can note that there is no reference so far to the prisoner being masked. The mask to prevent him be-ing recognized does not appear until he reached his third prison in the Bay of Cannes.

In January, 1687, St. Mars informed Louvois of the death of the prisoner who had been ill; from his description this was La Riviere. At the same time Louvois informed St. Mars that the King had raised him to the command of the prison on the island of St. Marguerite, in the Bay of Cannes, and he was instructed to convey his prisoner, who can only have been Dauger, there under great secrecy. St. Mars replied that all intercourse with the prisoner had been forbidden and had been punctiliously obeyed. He proposed to convey him to the island in a sedan chair covered with waxed cloth so that no one could see him.

On 3 May, 1687, St. Mars informed Louvois that the transfer of the prisoner had been effected. The journey had taken twelve days and the security surrounding the prisoner had caused people to ask and to try to guess who he was. On the island, he informed Louvois, he had placed "my prisoner who is sickly as usual" in a new cell specially built for him, one of the greatest possible security.

In 1691 the Marquis de Louvois, the Minister of War, died, and he was succeeded by his son, the Marquis de Barbezieux, who must therefore have been another person who knew the secret of the Masked Man's identity. It was de Barbezieux's mistress who in later years was to hint that the masked prisoner had been an illegitimate son of the Royal House, imprisoned because of his likeness to Louis XIVth. Soon after his appointment Barbezieux wrote to St. Mars asking him to tell him something about the prisoner "who has been in your custody for twenty years". This reference can refer only to Dauger, imprisoned in 1669.

In 1694, the prisoners whom St. Mars had left behind him at Pignerol in 1680 were transferred to the island of St. Marguerite. Though Mattioli is not referred to by name in the correspondence it is clear that he was one of these five prisoners because one of them is described as having a valet, which we know he had at Pignerol. None of the other prisoners transferred from Pignerol were of a condition to have rated a valet.

Shortly after the transfer, the man who must have been Mattioli died at St. Marguerite. Great confusion, however, is caused by the fact that this man's valet, who died at the island of St. Marguerite in 1701, is referred to in the legends as the "Mask's Servant". It seems possible that on Mattioli's death his valet may have been put in with Dauger. While Mattioli's death at St. Marguerite is apparently well established there is no reference to Dauger or his death there, and unless he was the man who died as the masked prisoner in 1703, is not otherwise accounted for. On 17 November, 1697, Barbezieux wrote to St. Mars, saying: "You have no other duty to observe with regard to those who are entrusted to your custody than to see to their safety without explaining to anyone what your Ancient Prisoner has done." Dauger had now been in St. Mars' safe keeping for twenty-eight years, the reason for his imprisonment still being the same, to prevent that upon which he had been occupied, or up to, before he was brought to Pignerol, from becoming known. The accentuation on his imprisonment was secrecy about his activities in or before 1669.

Suddenly a new element enters upon his security.

On 1 March, 1698, St. Mars was informed that he had been promoted to the governorship of the Bastille in Paris. He was ordered to be ready to leave at once and "to take with you in all security your ancient prisoner". In July he was instructed:

"The King approves of your leaving the island of Sainte-Marguerite to come to the Bastille, with your ancient prisoner, *taking all precautions to prevent his being seen or recognized by anyone.* You can write in advance to the King's Lieutenant at the Bastille to hold a room ready for putting the prisoner in on arrival."

It is at this stage that the mask first makes its appearance. It is possible, however, that the Ancient Prisoner was masked at St. Marguerite, as an alleviation of his imprisonment, when he was allowed to take walks on the island. The significant fact is this: after thirty years of imprisonment it was vitally necessary that Dauger should not be recognized. Recognized as whom, or by whom, we may ask.

On his journey to Paris with his masked prisoner, St. Mars made a stop at his own Chateau of Palteau, near Villeneuve. A century later the tradition was still extant that when they stopped the night there his prisoner was always masked and that when they dined St. Mars sat opposite him with two pistols by his plate. The peasants noticed that the man was tall and had white hair. As du Jonca recorded St. Mars arrived at the Bastille with his mysterious masked prisoner on 18 September, 1698.

There can be no doubt that the masked prisoner brought to the Bastille, and who died there in 1703, was Eustache Dauger, first imprisoned at Pignerol in July, 1669. All the other prisoners of state lodged in the care of St. Mars are accounted for. He was buried under a false name, and about him was a great secret, one which changed during the period of his imprisonment from care that it should never be known what he had been up to in 1669 to the instruction that he should be masked so that he should not be recognized thirty years later. As a final trick to obscure his identity for ever the name under which he was buried was made to suggest that he might well have been the famous Mattioli. But if Mattioli had been the Masked Man buried in 1703 why should all the years of security been brought to nought at the last moment by the registration of his name as Marchioly?

Had it not been for the chance discovery of a private letter written by St. Mars in 1681, which discloses that the security of another prisoner was preferred to that of Mattioli, it might well be that even today Mattioli would be looked upon as the man of the mask. It was clearly intended by Louis XIVth and his ministers that if enquiry should ever blossom about the mysterious masked man it should be concluded that he was Mattioli. Other factors rule out Mattioli's identification as the man of the mask. There was nothing secret about his imprisonment. It seems clear that he died in 1694. Barbezieux's reference to St. Mars' prisoner of "twenty years" in 1691 could not possibly have applied to Mattioli who had been captive for only twelve years. In that year Dauger had been a prisoner for twenty-two years. Six years later St. Mars is warned never to state what his Ancient Prisoner had done. Everyone in Europe knew what Mattioli had done.

Who was Eustache Dauger? Before making further enquiry into his identity it will be as well to summarize what we now know about him. He was secretly arrested at Dunkirk in 1669 and sent right across France to the guardianship of the gaoler who looked after the security of France's most important prisoners of state. Yet he was described as only a valet, possibly a false clue further to disguise his identity. He was to be killed at once if he spoke of what he had been up to. It did not matter if Fouquet learned the secret of Dauger's imprisonment but on no account was Lauzun to be allowed to see him. For thirty years the King and his ministers were continuously concerned in Dauger's security and well being. He appears to have accepted his imprisonment without question and without complaint. When he died in 1703 he was described as being about sixty years of age, tall and well built. He was clearly an educated man, a Catholic, and a Frenchman, a man named Eustache Dauger who disappeared from life in 1669.

From 1891, when Dauger was first picked upon by French investigators into the mystery of the man in the mask, diligent enquiries have been made to trace a man of that name living in seventeenth-century France. Forty years went by before he was identified.

Let us recount some theories which have been proved erroneous. The fact that the prisoner's face had to be masked so that he should not be recognized after thiry years' imprisonment suggested to many enquirers that he must have been somebody of importance. No one of any importance could be shown to have disappeared in 1669. It was suggested that the name "Dauger" might have been a blind, to conceal someone else's identiy.

In 1903 Andrew Lang, the nineteenth-century mystic,

advanced the theory that Dauger was a man named James de la Cloche, whose claim to have been the eldest natural son of King Charles II of England had previously been put forward by Lord Acton. While Lord Acton subsequently withdrew this identification, Lang went further, suggesting that this James de la Cloche, a master hoaxer, had, under the name of Pregnani, incurred the wrath of the King of France, and had been incarcerated as the man of the mask. The death of this de la Cloche in Naples is satisfactorily accounted for, and letters still extant show that Pregnani died in Rome before July, 1669.

Meanwhile a number of French scholars were industriously examining the old French records in their search for a man named Eustache Dauger who must have been about thirty years of age in 1669. He must consequently have been born in the late 1630s. While the surname of "Dauger" was not uncommon, the christian name of "Eustache" was unusual. Thus a person named Eustache Dauger born about 1638, if he existed, would surely be the wanted man. A number of men named Danger, Daugier, Auger, and Angers, different spellings of the same name, were traced in seventeenth-century France, but none of them fitted the description or answered to the Christian name of Eustache.

In 1930 M. Maurice Duvivier, searching through the files of the National Library in Paris, came across the name of a small land-owning family in Picardy known as de Cavoye, whose surname was variously spelled, Oger, Dauger. Amongst them he found a Eustache d'Auger, or Dauger, born in 1637, one of the six sons and three daughters of Francois de Cavoye, Captain of Cardinal Richelieu's Musketeers, and his wife Marie. There was no record of Eustache's death, and his younger brother, who lived until 1715, had been Grand Marechal of Louis XIVth's court. Four of Eustache's brothers had died in the King's service before 1667. In 1669 Eustache would have been thirty-two years old and in 1703 sixty-six. The identification seemed certain. But while Eustache appears to have been the black sheep of the family, an officer who was disgraced and dismissed from the army, nothing has been found to account for the reason why he might have been imprisoned for thirty-four years, even less why he should have been masked so that he would not be recognized.

Eustache's father and mother were close friends with Louis XIIIth, and Eustache and his brothers were brought up in the intimate circle of the young Prince who subsequently became Louis XIVth, and the gaoler of the man of the mask.

We can only surmise why Eustache Dauger might have been imprisoned for thirty-four years and masked so that he should not be recognized. Prior to the death of Fouquet it seemed to matter only that he should not speak of that on which he had been up to before 1669. One clue provides grounds for a theory which can perhaps account for the mask itself. Eustache's younger brother, the Grand Marshal of the Court, was reputed to resemble Louis XIVth closely. May not Eustache have done so, too?

Though Eustache was undoubtedly a rogue, there is little we know from his activities which would account for his sudden imprisonment in 1669.

In 1654 Eustache became the eldest surviving son, upon whom would fall, in the natural order of events, the lordship of Cavoye. The year 1659 seems to have been a turning point of his career. Although only twenty-one years of age, he was already the veteran of a number of campaigns, in which three of his brothers had been killed. One unsavoury incident occurred in which Eustache appears to have taken part. He figured in the celebration of a Black Mass on Good Friday, at which a pig was christened and eaten. But, while a number of celebrated people were involved, Eustache appears to have escaped scot-free. That his freedom may have been secured by influence is suggested by a letter which was written by the Chief Minister, Mazarin, to Eustache's mother. The letter, and others from the same source, suggest that the Cavoyes were well esteemed. However, in 1665 Eustache was forced to sell his commission and on the death of his mother he was disinherited. Eustache and another man killed a drunken page on the staircase of the Royal Palace, when the King was present, which made the crime that of lèse-majésté. From that moment Eustache ceases to use the title of a Guards Officer, and his mother, taking advantage of a clause of her marriage contract, made her son Louis the chief legatee and the Sieur de Cavoye. Eustache was left only a small annuity. In her will Madame de Cavoye stated "the said legacy being so made for good cause and considerations known to me."

In 1668 Eustache and Louis were living together. A few months later Louis was committed to the Bastille, where he remained until 1672, as a punishment for becoming involved in a duel with the husband of a Court lady. By the time he had been released, Eustache himself, we believe, had been sent to Pignerol. The last known reference to

Eustache occurs in 1688.

Eustache may have been a rogue and a charlatan. It has been suggested that he got himself involved with the infamous Marquise de Blainvilliers. She was a well-known poisoner and she was mixed up with a group of individuals who indulged in sacrilegious practices. Amongst these people was a surgeon named d'Auger, but there is no evidence that he was our Eustache. A point which may be of significance is that Eustache was arrested in July, 1669, at Dunkirk, then a port for England. It is possible that he might have been trying to escape from France. The King's instruction to the Captain of that port indicates that Dauger was expected to be found in that place. This gives some support to the suggestion that he was a fugitive from justice.

The famous masked prisoner became the symbol of unrivalled Bourbon despotism, the unfortunate victim of the ancient regime. But the imprisonment of Eustache can hardly have been due to the casual working of an arbitrary system. He did not languish, ignored and forgotten, for thirty-four years. The King and his Ministers were continually concerned with his well-being and security. Towards the end of his long imprisonment it became of vital importance that he should not be recognized. When he died in 1703 a false clue was laid to hide his identity. His gaolers never imagined that any rumour about him would ever spread out of the prisons he had been in; they thought their secret safe. But did they, just to make doubly sure, spread a rumour about the masked prisoner which, by its very audacity, served to hide the real truth? Minister Barbezieux's mistress, pressed for information, stated that the Masked Man had been an illegitimate son of the Royal House. Was she told this story purposely? It seems wildly improbable the the wife of King Louis XIIIth and the English Duke of Buckingham could have had an illegitimate son without the affair becoming known at the French Court.

Somehow, but we do not know how, the death of Fouquet served to deepen the mystery about Eustache. The ex-Minister of Finance must have known the secret connected with Dauger. Fouquet's other valet, Le Riviere, may have learned it too; after all, there must have been a reason why he was kept in prison for the rest of his life. The families of Fouquet and Dauger were distantly related; letters show that Marie de Cavoye, Eustache's mother, certainly corresponded with Fouquet. A strange twist to the matter comes from the fact that Lauzun, although it had been learned that he and Fouquet had met and talked to each other, was released. Did he know the secret about Eustache too? That he was the Captain of the King's Bodyguard in 1669, and undoubtedly knew Eustache from his youth, strongly suggests that he did. But though Lauzun lived to a great age he never mentioned the secret.

As to the suggestion that Eustache may have resembled Louis XIVth, he may have been, as the legends suggest, his illegitimate half-brother. While Eustache's mother, Marie de Cavoye, was noted for her fidelity, it is established that she was on friendly terms with Louis XIIIth. In fact, she was one of the few women with whom Louis XIIIth, a noted hater of the female sex, could put up. It is not impossible that Eustache and his brother Louis, both born at this time, were illegitimate sons of the Royal House. That Eustache closely resembled King Louis XIVth, either by birth or by chance, seems the only possible solution to his long imprisonment and the accentuation that he should not be recognized. By whom, or as whom, might he have been recognized after over thirty years of close confinement? One of the most extraordinary aspects of the mystery of the Man of the Mask appears to be his extraordinary resignment to his fate. He never seems to have complained of his life-long imprisonment, and he lived contented, subservient to the King's will.

This theory is an inviting one, especially because the later legends at least hinted at it. But Eustache may, of course, have resembled the King only by coincidence. He may have been employed as the King's double on some nefarious mission, and then silenced by perpetual imprisonment. Or he may have impersonated the King, perhaps on some amatory adventure, and so incurred his wrath. All this is surmise, but at the least it fits in with the myths and legends that grew and spread in eighteenth-century France. Some spark must have given them birth. Behind the long and close imprisonment of the masked prisoner must lie some dark secret. Everything we have learned about Eustache Dauger serves to identify him as the man who died in the Bastille in 1703, to which the records of his imprisonment so strongly point.

The intriguing fact is that Louis XIVth and his advisers determined that we should never solve the mystery. How nearly they succeeded. As it stands the mystery of the Man in the Mask is surely the most intriguing of all mysteries. Modern detective methods have at least succeeded in revealing the face behind the mask of black velvet. If we knew why Dauger was imprisoned and masked, the mystery would cease to be of interest. Those whose secret it was have preserved the final mystery.

LOST EXPLORER

COLONEL P. H. FAWCETT, the veteran South American explorer, his son Jack and the photographer Raleigh Rimell, disappeared in the jungles of Brazil in 1925 and no definite clue to their fate has ever been found. For forty years the civilized world has been intrigued by the Fawcett mystery. Time and time again it has been "solved" only for the evidence to dissolve into dust.

Fawcett was an explorer with an obsession; he believed implicitly that somewhere in the uncharted wilds of the Amazon Basin there existed a lost and dead civilization, founded perhaps by the survivors of Atlantis.

In 1920 and again in 1925 he set out to find the fabled lost city, a lonely oasis confined within ramparts of stone, surrounded by impenetrable jungle and swamps and inhabited by savage tribes. It had been seen and described in great detail by a Portuguese adventurer in 1754. A copy of his report was still extant, entitled: *Historic Account of a Large, Hidden City of Great Age, without Inhabitants, which was discovered in the year 1753*. This anonymous account was attributed usually to a man named Joao da Silva Guimaraes, who spent twenty years in the interior of Brazil and who claimed to have discovered the lost mines of Muribeca. His story is as follows:

The party was progressing through swamp and bush country when mountain tops were seen ahead. As the party approached them the mountainsides lit up in flame, for the setting sun was reflected back from innumerable crystals. To the explorers the slopes seemed studded with gems. Reaching the foothills at night the explorers observed next morning a steep range of black mountains. In front of them were sheer, unscaleable precipices and they spent all day trying to find a way to climb them. They camped for the night and some of the party went to search for wood to make a fire. One of them returned crying that he had found a way up. Following a deer track they found a deep cleft in the face of the precipice and saw that it led to the summit. Breaking camp they set off at once.

Three hours later they emerged breathless on a high ledge which led them to the ridge above. With amazement they stared at the view below them. At their feet, about four miles away, lay a huge city. Fearful of being observed by its inhabitants they threw themselves down. But they could see no sign of life. No smoke rose and no sound broke the silence. Cautiously they made their way down into the valley and pitched camp for the night. Next morning an Indian sent out to scout came back with the information that the city was uninhabited. Slowly and carefully the explorers approached it.

They came to a huge arched entrance and high above the central arch characters of some sort were graven deeply into the weathered stone. An impression of vast age brooded over everything. Some of the colossal uprights had been twisted slightly on their bases but otherwise everything seemed in a good state of preservation.

Passing through the arch they came to a broad street littered with broken pillars and blocks of masonry, on either side were two-storied houses built of great blocks fitting together with mortarless joints of almost incredible accuracy, the porticoes, narrow above and wide below, were decorated with elaborate carvings representing what seemed to be demons. Many of the buildings were still roofed with large stone slabs. Walking down the street the explorers came to a vast square in the centre of which was a huge column of black stone and upon it an effigy, in perfect preservation, of a man with one hand on his hip and the other pointing to the north. At each corner of the square stood carved obelisks of the same black stone and along the length of one side was a building of magnificent design and so decorated that they concluded it must have been a palace. A broad flight of ruined stone steps led into a wide hall, where traces of colour still clung to the frescoes and carvings. Over the doorway was a figure of a youth, portraying a beardless figure, naked from the waist up, with a shield in his hand and a band across one shoulder. Below were inscribed characters like those of ancient Greece, and the Portuguese explorer, the author of the story, copied them into his narrative. On the opposite side of the square was another huge building, evidently a temple.

Progressing farther they found that the city itself was in ruin, many houses and buildings were buried under mounds of earth on which not a blade of grass or any other vegetation grew. Here and there were gaping chasms, so deep that when the explorers dropped stones not a sound came to indicate depth. Clearly the city had been devastated by an earthquake. In some places whole buildings had collapsed into the chasms. In a few moments of time a city which must have taken the painstaking labour of many years to build had been destroyed. On the far side of the city ran a deep river and on its farther bank stood another great building. Surrounding it lay rich fields, which still provided food for the explorers, and everywhere was a profusion of game, other wild animals, snakes and birds.

Following the river the Portuguese explorers came to a cliff in which were signs of mine workings. At the mouths of these caves and caverns were scattered a quantity of silver ore. Other apertures were sealed with great stone slabs, and engraved with strange characters. They assumed these to be the graves of departed chieftains.

The party had little idea where they were but by following the river they eventually reached the San Francisco River. Then they journeyed to the coast of Bahia. From there the Portuguese explorer sent his story to the Viceroy of Brazil. By some official this strange document was pigeonholed and for a century or so it lay in the State Archives unobserved until Colonel Fawcett discovered it. Confirmation that such a lost city existed somewhere in the wilds of the interior came from the tales of travellers and the vague talk of Indians.

In 1920 there was apparently much to support the theory of a lost civilization somewhere in northern South America. The civilized world was beginning to learn something about the pre-Inca civilization of Peru and that of the Mayas of Yucatan. In the mountains of Peru and Bolivia and in the jungles of Central America vast stone cities revealing a high state of culture and knowledge and rivalling the great empires of the ancient world had been discovered. To archaeologists the great mystery of these American cultures appeared to be that they had sprung up ready made, and there was no evidence of any long evolutionary period. From where came these highly developed cultures?

Search of the Spanish records of the conquests disclosed widespread stories of the arrival of bearded white men from the east who had brought to the American Indians the blessing of civilization. From where could these men have come? In 1920, therefore, it was not a too-far-fetched hypothesis to believe rumours of an ancient and long dead Brazilian civilization, which might answer the riddle of the American cultures in Peru and Yucatan. "I know that the cities exist," declared Colonel Fawcett, and he set out in 1925 in quest of what might well be the greatest archaeological discovery of all time.

There is a vast area of unexplored country in Brazil, chiefly swamp and isolated mountain plateaux, one of which had given Conan Doyle his idea for his famous story of the *Lost World*, a plateau on which explorers found pre-historic animals still in existence. This area of "great forest", the *Matto Grosso*, was difficult of access. It was infested by poisonous snakes and disease-carrying insects, guarded by savage Indians determined to keep out the white man. There was lack of food and difficulty of transportation.

We know now that Colonel Fawcett set out in 1925 on a wild goose chase. Aerial photographs show that the supposed Amazonian cities of the dead, "the ruined bastions built by Titians", are no more than peculiar rock formations which, seen from a distance, look like ancient ruined temples and forts. These were undoubtedly seen by the Portuguese explorers of 1753: the details came from his vivid imagination. That many people still believe these stories is shown by an article printed in a Brazilian newspaper in 1955 which speaks of a subterranean city called Matatu-Araracuanga somewhere in the *Matto Grosso*, where, it is claimed, dwell the great spiritual avatars who rule the world's events and send out flying saucers in reconnaissance flights.

In May, 1925, Fawcett, his son, and Rimell, reached Dead Horse Camp, where Colonel Fawcett had been in 1920. They proposed to turn eastwards across the Kuluene River and explore the area between that river and the San Francisco River, where they believed the lost city to lie.

The fervency of Colonel Fawcett's belief in the existence of this city is shown by a letter to his other son. He had heard, he said, from the Indians about "collections of stone houses" and clothed Indians who worshipped the sun and guarded the approaches to their cities with savage determination. Records of missions and governments mentioned clothed white Indians occasionally sighted but never contacted; lost cities in the Brazilian forest on a scale greater than those of the Inca empire. Colonel Fawcett declared his belief that two at least of these ancient cities were inhabited by remnants of the race which built them, now degenerated into a state of savagery owing to their complete isolation, but still having traces of their original high culture. He expected these ruins to be more ancient than the oldest found in Egypt. He believed the writings of these people to be allied to some of the ancient European and Asiatic scripts.

Fawcett's declared main object was to reach a valley

surrounded by lofty mountains, in which stood a city approached by a roadway of stone. In the centre stood a pyramid temple. Two other half-buried and completely ruined cities stood nearby. The survivors of these ancient civilizations, to protect themselves, had surrounded their region with ferocious tribes over whom they exercised control in order to keep out all strangers, and that was why so little was known about these lost cities. He believed that they had some connexion with lost Atlantis.

Before the party left Dead Horse Camp, Fawcett wrote to his wife:

"We go on with eight animals, three saddle mules, four cargo mules, and a leading animal which keeps the others together. Jack is fit and well, getting stronger every day even though he suffers a bit from the insects. Raleigh I am anxious about. He still has one leg in a bandage but won't go back. I cannot hope to stand up to this journey better than Jack or Raleigh, but I had to do it. Years tell, in spite of the spirit of enthusiasm. I calculate to contact the Indians in about a week or ten days and we should be able to reach the waterfall so much talked about. You need have no fear of any failure."

That was the last word of Colonel Fawcett and his party. For three years there was no particular alarm about their fate. Fawcett had said that if he found the city he was looking for he might stay there for two or three years before returning to civilization to bring back his report. So it was not until 1927 that there was alarm and newspapers asked what had become of Colonel Fawcett.

Rumours percolated from the *Matto Grosso* region. In 1927 a French engineer named Roger Courteville, who reached Peru having crossed South America from the Atlantic to the Pacific, reported seeing a man, a month before, who might be Fawcett. Courteville had heard nothing about Fawcett's disappearance and he reported a conversation with the man who he noted had mosquito-bitten legs, and a feverish appearance. This description might have applied to any of a number of men who might be living or travelling in that area. In 1928 the North American Newspaper Alliance, which had sponsored Fawcett's expedition, despatched a rescue expedition under the command of Commander George Dyott, an experienced explorer.

Dyott reached Fawcett's last camp at Dead Horse. He was told by the natives that Fawcett and his two companions had crossed the Kuluene River and they had seen his camp fires for four days. They were certain that he had then been killed by hostile Indians. They offered to take Dyott to the scene of the massacre, but it was never reached. Dyott came to the conclusion that these Indians themselves may have killed Fawcett. In their camp he found a metal uniform case which had belonged to Fawcett, but it might have been left by him there in 1920. Dyott thought it was suspicious that the chief of these Kalapalos Indians was wearing a pair of European-made trousers, which he thought might have belonged to Fawcett.

It was quite impossible to check the Indians' story; it was even dangerous to investigate it too deeply. In his report Commander Dyott stated: "It is with the greatest regret that I have to announce Colonel Fawcett's fate. Both he, his son Jack, and Raleigh Rimell, were killed by hostile Indians five days after crossing to the east of the Kuluene River, some time during the month of July, 1925. There is not the slightest doubt about this. The story of how it occurred was told us too often, and we heard it from too many sources to leave any room for argument. The only question arises is who killed them?" In 1930 a journalist named Albert de Winton reached the same place as Dyott. He never returned.

In 1932 a Swiss trapper, Stephan Rattin, returning from the *Matto Grosso*, reported that Fawcett was the prisoner of a savage tribe on the River Bomfin, a tributary of the San Manoel River. He claimed to have spoken with him and he stated that while he was talking with these Indians, who numbered some two hundred and fifty men and a large number of women and children, there suddenly appeared an old man clad in skins, with a long yellowish-white beard and long hair. Rattin observed at once that he was a white man. He looked very sad and could not take his eyes off him, but the Indians tried to keep them apart. While the Indians were asleep this man came to him and asked him if he was English. When Rattin said he understood English the man asked "are you a friend?" and he stated "I am an English Colonel. Go to the English Consulate and ask them to tell Major Paget who has a coffee farm in the State of San Paulo that I am captive here." When Rattin asked the old man if he was alone, he said something about his son sleeping and began to weep, but he did not ask anything else.

The man showed him a gold locket which he wore around his neck, inside which was a photograph of a lady wearing a large hat and two small children between six and eight years old. The man appeared to be about sixty-five, approximately five foot eleven inches tall, and powerfully built, with bright blue eyes and a small scar over his right eye. He seemed to be in good health but appeared very depressed.

Rattin's story was carefully examined by the Brazilian authorities and it appeared to have some semblance of truth. Colonel Fawcett had a great friend named Sir Ralph Paget, who at one time had been British Ambassador to Brazil. But there were also several inconsistencies in his story. Fawcett's beard was grey and it would have been remarkable if, as Rattin stated, he had long hair for he had been bald from an early age. Colonel Fawcett was well over six feet tall and his eyes were grey, not blue. He had no scar over either eye. Why did not he tell Rattin his name? Rattin undoubtedly did meet some white man, perhaps some hunter or naturalist who had been made prisoner by an Indian tribe, but it seems certain that this man was not Fawcett.

In 1933 the Royal Geographical Society in London was sent a compass found near a camp of Indians in the *Matto Grosso*. It was identified as having been supplied to Colonel Fawcett in 1913, but it seems likely that Fawcett may have left or dropped it on his first expedition in 1920. In the same year the Royal Geographical Society received a report of an expedition to the Kuluene River which had been visited by a man named Virginio Pessione. An Indian woman, who spoke a few words of Portuguese, told him that she knew of the existence, for several years, of white men in the midst of the Aruvudu tribe, with which her own tribe was friendly. She said that then her son was a baby at the breast; he was now nine or ten years old. Three white men had come by canoe to the village of her tribe. One was old, another was his son and the third was a white man of greater age. The older white man had become the chief of the Aruvudus tribe and his son was married to the daughter of a chief. She had a son with blue eyes. She stated that these white men were greatly esteemed by the tribe and well looked after. When asked why they did not escape, she replied that there were no more bullets for their guns and they lived in an area filled with fierce tribes. Even the friendly Indians would kill them if they attempted to escape and they were always watched and followed.

This report became the basis for an incident which occurred in 1937. Brian Fawcett, another son of Colonel Fawcett, who lived in Peru, was informed that a white boy had been identified amongst a native tribe as being Colonel

Fawcett's son. Only with the greatest difficulty did he prevent this boy being despatched to him in Peru by air liner. This report stated also that Raleigh Rimell had died from infected insect bites and that the others, after staying with various tribes for a year, had died of starvation. In 1952 it was learned that this Indian boy was an albino and his parenthood was established as being entirely Indian.

There the mystery remained until after the Second World War when occasionally further vague rumours percolated from Brazil, some of which gave rise to newspaper headings. "Fawcett may be alive". These rumours may have referred to any odd man in the jungle. Great was the excitement in April, 1951, when it was reported that Colonel Fawcett's bones had been found. A confession was obtained from the chief of the Kalapalos Indians, on his death bed, that he had clubbed Fawcett and his two companions to death because one of them had consorted with one of his wives and Colonel Fawcett himself had slapped the chief's face. Nothing could have been more improbable from what is known of Fawcett and his companions. The bones were brought to London, where Brian Fawcett found himself quite unable to identify them and they were examined at the Royal Anthropological Institute, where they were found to be the skeleton of a man much smaller than Colonel Fawcett.

In 1952, and again in 1955, Brian Fawcett, now retired from Peru, led aerial expeditions over the *Matto Grosso* in search, not so much of his father, who could hardly still be alive, but in case Jack or Rimell might have survived. Every place from which rumours had come was carefully checked, but nothing could be established. It was, however, confirmed that the last that had been seen of Fawcett and his party was in the summer of 1925 when they crossed the Kuluene River, and, according to the natives, his camp fires were seen for four days.

The great Fawcett mystery has intrigued many for nearly half a century. It seems probable that he and his companions were killed in 1925 somewhere near the Kuluene River. Who may have killed them remains unknown. All clues to their fate have disappeared and it is unlikely that we shall ever know exactly what happened. The important fact is that there is still a part of the world so inaccessible and so savage that a number of rescue expeditions have been unable to learn the truth. It seems a strange quirk of human nature that man is setting out to explore outer space before he has resolved all the secrets of his own planet.

WRIT ON ROCK

THE Atlantic voyages of the intrepid Norsemen to the coast of North America are established historical fact. Five hundred years before Columbus chanced upon the West Indies, the Norsemen, at a time when most of the peoples of Europe were preparing for the end of the world in the year 1000, landed on the coast of New England, which they called Vinland. According to their Sagas their visits were fleeting and no attempts at colonization or the exploration of the hinterland were made, or so it was thought until the beginning of the twentieth century.

The strange find in Minnesota of a stone carved in Runic lettering indicates that the Norsemen penetrated deep into the North American continent, and an old stone tower on Rhode Island suggests that they may have made attempts at permanent settlement on the coast. Neither the Kensington Stone nor the Newport Tower is fully accepted as a Norse relic, so both remain enigmas which may either be authentic or perhaps, in the case of the Kensington Stone, a hoax. While some scholars accept that the tower at Newport is a Norse building dating from the fourteenth century, others believe it to be a stone windmill erected in the sixteenth century by the early English colonists.

About the year A.D. 1000 the Norsemen, the Vikings of Scandinavia, land-hopped via Iceland and Greenland and sailed down the eastern coast of North America probably as far as Rhode Island. Six hundred and thirty nine years later the first English settlers came to Rhode Island, an area which had been previously visited by a number of French, English and Portuguese ships between 1524 and 1619. The ancient Norse sagas which were written in Iceland between 1320 and 1350, after centuries of verbal telling, recall the visit of Leif Erickson to Vinland and his subsequent voyages. Although these Norse voyages had been known of in medieval Europe they faded from memory and it is debatable whether Columbus heard of them before he set sail across the Atlantic in 1492. He may have done so, although such knowledge would not necessarily have been of great value to him for, as far as the Norsemen knew, Vinland might have been only an island on the far side of the North Atlantic. The Norsemen in the year 1000 were quite unaware that they were landing on the fringe of a vast continent.

Realization that the famed and apparently mythical trans-

Atlantic voyages of the Norsemen were authentic did not come until 1837. When the old sagas were re-examined it was found that their descriptions of the geography, flora, fauna and climate of Vinland conformed almost exactly with the southern shores of New England. Yet nothing was found along that coastline to substantiate the accounts of the Norse voyages.

Leif Erickson and his men appear to have reached Cape Cod and sailed into Nantucket Sound, circled the two islands now known as Nantucket Island and Martha's Vineyard and they may have reached farther north-westward to the coast of Rhode Island and even to that island itself, the principal town of which today is Newport.

Two of the principal sagas (family histories) dealing with the Norse voyages are the *Flatey Book* and the *Hauk's Book*. Both were written in the fourteenth century and they represent two different traditions, the former those of Greenland and the latter those of Iceland, where different communities of Norsemen lived. The Norse colony in Greenland, established before the year 1000, was a See of Rome until the colonists disappeared about the year 1500. Probably they were wiped out by the Eskimos. One of Greenland's bishops, Eric Upson, appears to have visited Vinland in the year 1121. The *Flatey Book*, as the version derived from Greenland and a book describing voyages of discovery, is of greater importance than the *Hauk's Book* which is the record of one family only, a member of which led a voyage to Vinland. Both sagas give the impression of being the descriptions of eye-witnesses.

Leif, the "Lucky", the son of Eric the Red the founder of the Greenland colony, sailed southward in the year 1003, coming upon three separate promontories which he named Helluland, meaning "flat rock land", Markland or "forest-land", and Vinland.

These have now been identified as Newfoundland, Nova Scotia and New England. He sailed southward with a north-east wind and eventually, steering westward, passed a cape and came in to the mouth of a river. There Leif landed and built large huts. The saga then goes on to say in its description of the land:

"Salmon, larger than they had seen before, were plentiful in the river and the lake. The land seemed to him so good that there would be no need of storing food for the cattle in winter; there came no frost in the winters and the grass withered but little. Day and night were there more nearly of equal length than is the case in Greenland or Iceland; on the shortest day the sun was up over the marks both at morning and afternoon meal times."

From this description a number of clues derive which enable us to link Leif's description with the coasts of Massachusetts, Rhode Island and Connecticut. The mild climate of that stretch of coast is probably due to the Gulf Stream, which touches there before turning eastward towards Europe. As the sage states there is little frost in winter and the grass hardly withers. Salmon are not found in the rivers south of Cape Cod nor do true grapes grow north of it. Moreover the statement about the time of sunset on the year's shortest day forms the strongest corroborative evidence of the Norse visit.

Accoring to Leif the sun had not set at the time of the afternoon meal, which we know in Norse custom took place at 4:30 p.m. On 21 December the sun sets at Boston, about seventy miles to the north of Newport, at 4:30 p.m. There is no doubt, therefore, that the Norsemen reached that coast and that the subsequent voyagers may even have sailed as far south as New York. Until the year 1900 no one suggested that the Norsemen had gone deeply inland on the American continent.

Although it was not publicly known until some eight or nine years later, in 1898 came a startling discovery. In that year a farmer at Kensington in Minnesota who was digging out the roots of trees in the process of clearing land for cultivation came upon a flat stone embedded in the roots of a tree which he had cut down. The farmer, Olof Ohman, noticing that the stone appeared to have on it markings or an inscription believed at first it marked the site of an Indian treasure cache. The speedy recognition of the inscription as being in Runic, the script of medieval Norway and Sweden, was not surprising in what was a predominantly Scandinavian community, but the very fact that the area round Kensington had been largely colonized by emigrants from Norway and Sweden immediately gave rise to considerable suspicion that the so-called ancient runic inscription might be a modern forgery. Nevertheless many elements seemed to rule out the suggestion of fraud.

First, the stone itself requires our attention.

The Kensington Rune Stone is formed of a piece of rock known as Greywacke and it is 31 inches long, 16 inches broad and 6 inches thick. On the face and along one edge appears an inscription containing 220 characters, which makes this the longest runic inscription known and the only one so far found on the North American continent. Submitted to expert examination in 1899 it was immediately rejected as a modern forgery. The chief reasons for its rejection later became some of the strongest factors in its support. The experts who examined it first rejected it because, in their view, it contained two impossibilities. The language of the inscription was declared not to be old Norse but a mixture of Swedish, Norwegian and English words which were unthinkable in an inscription dealing with the eleventh-century Norse voyages. The inscription, too, described a mixture of Swedes and Norwegians in one expedition which was quite contrary to all the accounts of the Norse voyages, in which only Norsemen from Norway were included.

Rejected out of hand the stone was used by farmer Ohman as a door-step to his barn, and there it lay for nine years until quite by chance a man named Hjalmar Holand, an American of Scandinavian origin who had made a considerable study of runic, chanced upon it. He realized that the inscription related not to the time of the original Norse voyages about the year 1000 but to a period of some three hundred years later. He was able to translate the unknown numerals on the inscription which gave its date. These, he claimed, showed that the inscription related to an expedition in 1362. His translation was as follows:

Front

1. (We are) 8 Goths (Swedes) and 22 Norwegians on
2. (an) exploration-journey from
3. Vinland through (or across) the west (i.e. round about the west) WE
4. had camp by (a lake with) 2 skerries one
5. days-journey north from this stone
6. We were (out) and fished one day After
7. we came home (we) found 10 (of our) men red
8. with blood and dead AV(e)M(aria)
9. Save (us) from evil

Edge

10. (We) have 10 of (our party) by the sea to look
11. after our ships (or ship) 14 days-journey
12. from this island (in the) year (of our Lord) 1362.

Holand's study of the inscription convinced him that,

whether it was true or false, it had been condemned largely on erroneous premises. He knew that the old Norse language had ceased to be used before 1362. Therefore, once it was understood that the inscription related to an expedition in the fourteenth century, the objection that the inscription should have been in old Norse no longer applied. Added to that it was entirely in keeping with the fourteenth century to find an expedition made up of both Swedes and Norwegians in one party. His discoveries led to a revival of interest in the stone and to the beginning of a long controversy which is not yet concluded and which will probably never be satisfactorily settled, for the main objections to the stone and its authenticity relate to questions of runology which are understandable only to a few experts in that obscure and dead language. Although such objections must carry great weight and may prevent us from finally deciding about the truth or otherwise of the Kensington stone many other factors seem to corroborate its authenticity.

The inscription on the stone appears to represent a message written by the survivors of a massacre and a number of Norse weapons and implements have been found in the area in which the Kensington stone was discovered.

If we are to believe Mr. Ohman the stone was found embedded in the roots of a tree. Unfortunately he did not preserve the tree trunk itself for that might have confirmed the age of the tree and the date at which the roots might have grown about the stone. Some suspicion attaches to the find of the stone because local rumour says that Ohman had a cousin or brother-in-law named Fogelblad who was a broken-down scholar from Upsala University in Sweden who was interested in runes. He died in 1895, three years before the discovery of the stone, at the age of seventy. If he was the perpetrator of a hoax it means that he must have sat out on the prairie, in full sight of the neighbours, cutting the runes on an old piece of stone. The size of the stone, which weighs 230 pounds, hardly suggests that it could have been cut elsewhere and transported there without the perpetrators of the hoax being seen. Besides, why should either Fogelblad or Ohman have bothered to waste their time perpetrating such a hoax from which they could derive nothing? Various attempts have been made to estimate the age of the tree in the roots of which it was found and it is believed that the stone must have been in position somewhere between 1828 and 1885 at the latest. Prior to 1850 that part of Minnesota was outside the American frontier and was the exclusive domain of the savage Sioux Indians who would have made it impossible for any single white man to have sat chiselling a stone undisturbed. When Ohman set up his farm in 1891 it was on virgin prairie.

One of the most interesting aspects of the inscription is its date, a stumbling block which prevented its early acceptance. When it was first examined the numerals were considered to be quite out of keeping with Norse knowledge.

In 1909 a Norwegian philologist showed that such numerals were not, as had been thought, a modern invention, but were in entire accord with the runic numerals employed in the Middle Ages. He discovered this from a book written in 1643 by a Danish scholar named Ole Worm. It was knowledge of this discovery which enabled Mr. Holand to make his deductions.

The system of numerals and of dating were as follows. To each upright stave one transverse line was added for each unit up to five thus $=1$ and $=2$. As there was not enough room to add transverse lines up to ten the first five were collectively represented by a circle, cross lines then being added for each additional unit up to ten, thus $P=6$. By this method the date numerals on the inscription were translated as 1362. On this system other numeral symbols in the inscription were assumed to represent the eight Goths and twenty-two Norwegians.

The chief objection to this system of translating the dates and numbers is that in those days the decimal system was unknown in Northern Europe where a date would have been written, not in numerals, but in words as "One thousand three hundred sixty and three years". Alternatively, in the fourteenth century the date would have been given as the year in the reign of a particular king. But the use of the Arab decimal system of mathematics in Norway has been shown in a Norse manuscript dated in 1320, as is quite likely because the Norsemen, as the chief seamen of the Middle Ages, would have been familiar with Mediterranean ideas.

Once the date of the inscription was substantiated as applying to the fourteenth century it was an easy step to appreciate that by that time the old Norse language had given way to a period of linguistic transition (following upon the union of Norway and Sweden in 1319) in which it would be conceivable to find the mixture of old words and new forms which is found in the inscription. Of course, a period in which two languages were in a process of amalgamation represents a most difficult period in which to place a literary forgery. The objection made by some scholars that the inscription is full of grammatical errors supports rather than denies its authenticity for, according to the inscription, it was made not by scholars but by sailors working in haste.

Mr. Holand sums up his appraisal of the inscription by saying:

> "All things considered, the Kensington inscription seems linguistically to be a logical fourteenth-century product of such personnel as the inscription mentions. Dialectically, the inscription seems to be predominantly Gothic, which probably means that the artisan who inscribed the stone was a Goth . . . mixed with his Gothic dialect there are a number of words of probably Norwegian usage which may be the echoes of the dictation of the commander of the expedition or some other Norwegian member."

He goes on to point out that this assumption is supported by the fact that the Goths, rather than the more numerous Norwegians, are first mentioned.

Mr. Holand, who is the chief supporter of the authenticity of the stone, also points out that the inscription demonstrates great technical excellence, the lines being straight and the characters uniform in height, which indicates considerable skill in execution. He declares that the inscription made as late as 1362 would show changes in runic form and the addition of letters from the Latin alphabet, which was then superseding runic in Scandinavia. This the Kensington inscription actually does. If a forger existed he must have been familiar with niceties of scholarship to a degree far beyond anyone living outside Scandinavia in the late 1890s.

Mr. Holand avers that the three symbols "A. V. M." in Latin letters followed by the prayer "Save us from evil" probably represent the word "Ave Virgo Maria", the supplication to the Virgin Mary which would have been quite in keeping with the fourteenth century. How would a modern forger, unless he was one of the great linguistic experts of the world, have known that? he asks. On the other hand runologists who claim that the runic symbols employed in the inscription represent a degenerate form of sixteenth-century usage have great weight on their side. They assert that the writer of the inscription invented certain symbols which were unknown in the fourteenth century and which did not come into use from the Latin until after the year 1500.

While these questions of runology are quite beyond the layman there appear to be a number of corroborative factors which suggest that the inscription is a genuine one dating from the fourteenth century. The stone itself, as hard as granite, is one which weathers very slowly and this piece had obviously split off a larger rock. Experts who have examined the stone declare that the inscription on it must have been carved hundreds of years ago.

The message the inscription tells states five main facts, all of which can be substantiated. The first is that the party was composed of eight Goths and twenty-two Norwegians. They were on an exploration journey from Vinland to the west, and ten of their number had been killed at a camp by a lake in which were two small islands one day's journey to the north. The place where the inscription was carved was an island, and it was fourteen days' journey from the sea where the Norsemen had left their ship.

The spot where the stone was found, on the top of a wooded knoll, could by no stretch of the imagination be called an island nor could it have been an island at the time when the first settlers reached Kensington, but a survey of the area showed that some five hundred years before the marshlands surrounding the knoll had been part of a string of lakes which stretched, and many of which still exist, right across central Minnesota. This has been discovered only recently and could not have been known to a forger working about 1895.

The inscription tells of a massacre and was written by survivors who relate how they came there, where the massacre happened and how far they were inland from where they left their ship. Clearly these men, if they were Norsemen, could not have come overland from Vinland, nor would Norsemen have attempted an overland journey. They always preferred a water route and there are at least two such routes by which they could have reached central Minnesota, from the north or from the south. Either would have involved a journey of approximately a thousand miles from the sea.

It is considered unlikely that the party could have progressed up the Mississippi from the Gulf of Mexico for there is no suggestion, or recollection in records of Norse voyages, of the Norsemen ever having reached so far south. Alternatively the Norse expedition could have come up the St.

Lawrence River and then progressed either via the Great Lakes or southward from Hudson via the Nelson River, Lake Winnipeg, and the Red River which leads right into the string of lakes in Minnesota. It seems unlikely that the party would have described leaving their ship in the sea if they had progressed along the Great Lakes and it seems far more probable that they left their ship in Hudson Bay and proceeded inland in the small boat usually towed by Norse ships. They could have reached the spot in Minnesota via the Red River and lakes with only one short portage from the river to the first lake.

Further corroborative evidence comes from the statement that they were fourteen days' journey from the sea, as Kensington is approximately a thousand miles from the mouth of the Nelson River, which flows into Hudson Bay. The term "a day's journey" to the Norsemen represented an average run on water of about seventy-five miles and this would account for the statement that it took fourteen days' journey to reach Kensington.

Another thing tending to corroborate the authenticity of the inscription is the belief that an expedition set sail from Greenland or perhaps from Norway itself probably in the year 1355. As such exploratory expeditions were infrequent and at that time were becoming fewer and fewer, it seems possible that this is the one referred to in the Keinsington stone inscription dating from 1362.

There is a hint, too, that some members of the expedition may have returned to Norway in 1364. A letter has been found written by Magnus Erikson, the first joint king of Norway and Sweden, instructing a man named Paul Knutson to lead an expedition in search of the lost colonists of the western settlement of Greenland, the news of whose disappearance had been brought to Norway in 1348. That the text of this letter was not printed until 1888 seems to make it improbable that a forger in America could have made use of it to substantiate his fraud. The letter reads:

"Magnus, by the Grace of God, King of Norway, Sweden and Skanne, sends to all men who see or hear this letter good health and happiness.

"We desire to make known to you that you are to take the men who shall go in the Knorr whether they be named or not named, from my bodyguard and also from among the retainers of other men whom you may wish to take on the voyage, and that Paul Knutson, who shall be commandant upon the Knorr, shall have full authority to select the men whether as officers or men. We ask that you accept this our command with a right good will for the cause, inasmuch as we do it for the honour of God and for the sake of our soul and for the sake of our predecessors, who in Greenland established Christianity and have maintained it to this time, and we will not now let it perish in our days. Know this for truth, that whoever defies this our command shall meet with our serious displeasure and thereupon receive full punishment.

"Executed in Bergen, Monday after Simon and Judah's day in the sixth and XXX year of our rule. By Orm Ostenson, our regent, sealed."

We thus have knowledge of an expedition in 1355, and an inscription found in Minnesota dated 1362. It surely would be a curious coincidence if there was not a link between the two. There seem a number of points of corroboration. Knutson was one of the principal men in Norway, a lawyer or a judge. The expedition planned in the autumn of 1354 could hardly have sailed before the spring of the following year. It was formed both from Goths and Norwegians and it used a Royal trading vessel, known as a *knorr*. The fate of the lost colonists in western Greenland is unknown but those at home in Norway may have thought that they had wandered away westward. Bishop Gisle Oddson of Iceland recorded in the year 1342 that the inhabitants of Greenland had fallen away from the true faith and Christian religion and had turned to the people of America near which it was said that Greenland lay. It seems not unlikely, therefore, that the relief expedition from Norway would have gone to the North American continent to look for the lost colonists. The long interval between the report of the disappearance of the colonists and the relief expedition could be accounted for by the prevalence of the Black Death in Europe at that time and a Norwegian invasion of Russia which was unsuccessful.

That some members of the expedition returned to Norway in 1364, two years after the date of the inscription, is assumed from the appointment in that year of a new bishop of Greenland, a successor to Bishop Arne who had died in 1349, the long interval between his death and the new appointment being due to the fact that no ship sailed to Norway from Greenland until 1364, immediately on the arrival of which the new bishop was appointed. Another small point is that there is no further mention of Knutson in Norwegian records after 1355 which, as he had been prominent until then, suggests that he may have left in that year.

One of the chief objections to the inscription is overcome by the knowledge gained from this letter that such a strange mixture of personnel was included in an expedition. Only at that time would such an expedition have included both Goths and Norwegians. King Magnus's personal retinue were Goths and it is noteworthy that he instructed Knutson to select men both from the king's retinue and from those of other men. Knutson himself was a Norwegian and a member of the king's bodyguard and it seems entirely likely, therefore, that his expedition might well have included "Eight Goths and twenty-two Norwegians" as the inscription on the Kensington stone states.

It seems possible therefore that the Knutson expedition, after years of fruitless search for the missing settlers along the coast of North America down probably as far as Vinland, ventured northward and reached Hudson Bay where they left their ship and proceeded inland in the after boat, traveling by the Nelson River into the Red River and into the string of lakes in Minnesota where one day in 1362 ten of their number were killed by Indians. The survivors after reaching a place of safety inscribed a stone recalling their incident, and providing an obituary notice for their slain companions.

Thirty-six of the seventy-two words of the inscription are devoted to the circumstances of the death of these ten men. Their massacre took place by a lake in which there were two small islands one day's journey to the north of where the survivors inscribed the stone. Seventy-five miles north of Kensington lies Cormorant Lake in which there are two small islands and on the shore nearby Mr. Holand found three stones which are apparently Norse mooring stones. The Norsemen appear to have progressed through the forest land without molestation from Indians and were attacked only in the area of Cormorant Lake when they were out of the forests through which they may have progressed without being observed. The mooring stones found together at the foot of a precipitous cliff contained holes such as were employed by the Norsemen for an iron spike with a ring to which their boat could be moored. These stones were observed in that position by the lake in 1870, nearly thirty years before the Kensington stone itself was found.

Since then a number of similar mooring stones have been found along the chain of lakes and small rivers which the party must have used if they followed that route, and these are taken as striking proof of the authenticity of the stone. One such mooring stone was found at the foot of the knoll on which the Kensington Stone was unearthed. It seems possible, too, that the boat used by the expedition was found in 1910; a farmer excavating a bank at Grant's Lake near the village of Holmes City came across the remains of a boat which seemed unlike either the punts of the early settlers or the canoes of the Indians. It had stout ribs, a heavy stern-post and a rounded bottom, but unfortunately its remains were not preserved, so that it is impossible to say whether it was the actual boat of the 1362 expedition. A number of Norwegian weapons and tools have been found in the area, of types such as might have been left by members of the expedition or might have been carried away by the Indians after the massacre.

The Kensington Rune Stone is indeed a mystery. As long as the runic experts refuse to accept the inscription as genuine it is impossible for us wholeheartedly to accept the stone as a relic of a Norse expedition which penetrated far into the North American continent.

If the stone is a modern forgery it creates almost as extraordinary a mystery; it is virtually impossible to credit that some time in the 1890s in the distant American state of Minnesota there should have been an expert in runology ready to undertake without any profit the considerable task of faking such a stone as the Kensington. He would have had to combine the qualifications of a geologist with a considerable local knowledge, of an historian familiar with details of fourteenth-century religious practice and of the Magnus letter, he must have been a skilled stone cutter and a philologist highly experienced in one of the most unusual periods of Norse writing. He must, too, have been a man of vivid imagination to have coined the apt expression "red with blood and dead".

For sixty years a vast controversy has raged about the authenticity of the stone. Quite rightly the experts throw the onus of proof of autheniticity on those who put forward the stone as an authentic Norse relic. Like many other archaeological finds proof is difficult. There are frequently cogent objections made to the full acceptance of such finds, but somewhere along the line we laymen, as against the experts, must make up our minds about such discoveries. Everything in the case of the Kensington Stone predisposes us to accept it as genuine; the story it tells is a romantic one, a description of an expedition of Norsemen penetrating thousands of miles into the wilderness, five thousand miles from their own home, at a time when the rest of Europe was sunk in the apathy of the Middle Ages and when, for example, our own English seamen were venturing no farther than across the Channel to France.

What happened, we may ask, to the survivors of the massacre? It seems unlikely that they were among those who returned to Norway in 1364 because Norwegian records contain no knowledge of extensive lands to the west of Greenland and Vinland. In all probability those who had been left with the ship in Hudson Bay, giving up their comrades in despair, sailed for home leaving the survivors perhaps themselves to be massacred by Indians in the American middle west. They may even have become integrated with some Indian tribe and there is some very slight support of such a suggestion. The Mandans, a small tribe of Indians who became extinct in 1841 and who in the fourteenth century inhabited central Minnesota, were found to have many apparently European characteristics and customs.

A celebrated traveller, George Catlin, who made a close study of the American Indians, and who lived with the Mandans in 1832, wrote: "I am convinced that they have sprung from some other origin than that of other North American tribes." They were not Indians, he said, and they were almost white.

In their traditions they described how they were visited by a man whose body was white who came from the west in a big canoe. For many years the representation of a big canoe held the place of honour in the Mandan village square, and each year the Mandans re-enacted the arrival of this mysterious white man with a feast at which he had instructed them in religious practices. On the other hand, as is particularly demonstrated in Mexico and Peru, the American Indians in general appear to have had vivid recollections of the visit of white strangers who came from the east.

So much for the strange mystery of the Kensington Stone.

The Newport Tower is connected with it because, if it is a Norse building, it may have been built by the same men who afterwards perished in far away Minnesota.

C. Rafn, who confirmed the historical nature of the Norse voyagers in his book *Antiquates Americanae* in 1837, named the old stone tower at Newport, Rhode Island, a Norse chapel, but he was unable to advance any proof of its Norse origin and the belief that the tower was a sixteenth-century windmill, first documented in 1677, continued until the whole matter was reopened in 1942.

Although the stone tower is not mentioned in Colonial Records until 1677 it may be a building referred to in a petition addressed to Charles I in 1632, in which an old tower is mentioned as standing somewhere along that stretch of coast. Further proof that it may have existed before the arrival of the English colonists in 1639 is an old chart, drawn up in 1634, which locates on the site of Newport a town which is called "Old" Plymouth, whereas "New" Plymouth was the earliest English settlement to the north. It seems significant, too, that the first Governor of Rhode Island attempted to discover what tradition the Indians had about the tower. This, too, suggests that it may have been in existence when the English colonists first arrived. Against that, however, is the fact that the earliest visitor to Rhode Island, Giovanni Verrazzano, who spent fifteen days there in 1624, did not remark upon the tower; but this is not conclusive as he may have sailed up the west passage passing the island rather than the east channel on which the tower stands.

Governor Benedict Arnold refers in his will, dated 24 December, 1677, to "my stone-built windmill". While he claims ownership of the building he says nothing of its origin and it may have been referred to as a windmill solely because, superficially, it resembled a windmill of the period. It appears, too, that there was another mill in Newport, a watermill by the river referred to in a Deed of 1642, which would seem to render it unlikely that a town of that size would have required an ordinary windmill as well. Particularly is this so because the construction, requiring six thousand cubic feet of stone weighing five hundred tons, would have been a major undertaking for the community, especially at a time when they were constantly threatened by Indian attacks.

Architecturally the tower looks more like a fortified medieval chapel or church than a colonial windmill. Its top is not a perfect circle and could not, therefore, have held the rotating part of a windmill which must overhang the upper storey. Another strange feature of the tower is a fireplace on the second storey, an unusual feature for a mill, but one which might have been required in a fortified church. The fireplace in the tower is of the type usually found in medieval European buildings with a tunnel through the wall. The so-called window on the south-west side of the tower is held more clearly to resemble the medieval sallyport of Europe; it is twelve feet above the ground from which it could have been reached only by a ladder and is so low that a person entering would have to bend down and lift his foot over a lintel; this was a normal security measure against attack.

The weakest point of the theory that the tower was a fortified church is that it has open arches under which hostile Indians could have lighted fires to smoke out the defenders, but it is possible that the tower was never completely finished and that it was intended to build a wall round the bottom in a manner similar to that of fortified churches built in England in those days. Another curious feature of the tower is a groove eighty-eight inches long and forty-two inches above floor level obviously constructed to carry a table but at least a foot above the usual height; it seems likely that it was made to carry an altar at which a priest could stand.

It appears clear that the tower must be either a Norse building or, as was held for so long, a sixteenth-century windmill. While a number of Portuguese navigators who were lost on that coast must have lived there for at least nine years there are no points of similarity between the tower and contemporary Portuguese architecture. If it is a Norse building, it could not have been built by the early Norse visitors, Leif Erickson and his immediate successors. Architecturally it belongs to the period of the Paul Knutson expedition between 1355 and 1364.

The theory has been advanced that Knutson and his followers, despairing of finding the lost Greenlanders, voyaged south to Vinland, the location of which had never been forgotten, and there built a tower as a base while they explored the coastline and perhaps penetrated inland.

Like the Kensington Rune Stone, the question of whether the tower at Newport is a Norse building dating from the fourteenth century will probably never be decided but both represent mysteries at the solution of which we can only guess. If the stories told about them are authentic it conjures up a romantic episode in human history, one about which we are inclined to believe rather than disbelieve.

THE EGYPTIAN MYSTERIES

THE BELIEF that Ancient Egypt was a land of mystery is due largely to ignorance. The laying bare of Egyptian history has shown that the people of the Nile were a practical race, singularly realistic in their outlook. Their beliefs were no more "mysterious" than those of the other more recent religions which adopted some of them as their own.

In modern superstition the Egyptians are credited with two extraordinary achievements: they built the Great Pyramid at Gizeh, not as a royal tomb as has been supposed, but as a prophecy in stone, and they possessed a "Curse" so effective that it could reach out from the grave three and a half thousand years later to kill those who defiled a royal tomb.

Le us examine the pyramid prophecy first.

According to a small group of fervent believers who were especially prominent between 1890 and 1935, the Great Pyramid demonstrates the Divine plan for the Adamic Race. When the unit of measurement employed in the construction of the pyramid is translated into years, months, and days, the lengths of the pyramid's corridors and chambers are supposed to foretell the future of the Race from 4000 B.C. to A.D. 2045¾, the date of the Final Tribulation.

This startling theory was advanced in two pamphlets, published in 1924 and 1934, *The Great Pyramid, Its Divine Message*, and *The Hidden Truth in Myth and Ritual and in The Common Culture Pattern of Ancient Metrology*, the latter described as "A Study showing that the Common Culture Patterns in Myth and Ritual emanated from Messianic Prophecies current over 5,000 years ago, and that the Structural Expression of these Prophecies is enshrined in the Divine Revelation in the Great Pyramid of Gizeh". Both were written by Mr. David Davidson of Leeds, England, and in his preface he says:

"Ten years ago I published a series of studies which combined to show that what is now universally recognized to be a 'common culture pattern' *in the myth and ritual* of all ancient religions emanated from certain early prophecies concerning the 'Coming World Saviour'; and that these prophecies were promulgated throughout the ancient world by the progenitors of the Hebrews, over five thousand years ago. It was shown that the prophecies predicted the time and circumstances of the Advent of our Lord Jesus Christ, proclaimed the purpose of His coming, and gave details concerning His death, and victory over death and the grave; that the prophecies were not only promulgated in literary form and in oral and visual forms of Sacred dramas and ceremonies, but were also allegorically perpetuated within the structural symbolism of the Great Pyramid of Gizeh, by native Egyptian workmen building under the Divinely-inspired intuitive supervision of proto-Hebrew master builders; and that, in the course of time, the ancient prophecies and ritual associated with the Sacred dramas and ceremonies became paganized by the substitution of Osiris and other pagan deities for the promised Messiah."

From this it will be seen that the Pyramid Prophecy is essentially a Christian revelation: further study shows that it was even more particular in its scope, the true inheritors of the Adamic Race are the British, or at least the Protestant islanders.

The theorists proclaim that the pyramid prophecies "The precise day, month and year of the Birth of the promised Messiah, and the precise day, month and year of His Passion: and that the dates thus proclaimed are respectively the dates of the Birth and Crucifixion of Our Lord Jesus Christ". It suggests that "The recognition of this fact should surely compel the most hardened sceptic to realize that there was indeed a 'deliberate Divine Purpose' in the successive outcroppings of the originally Divinely Revealed Truth from the myth and ritual of the ancient pagan religions". Mr. Davidson adds: "The later researches have proved that my conclusions are correct, apparently without the academic mind being either able to appreciate the fact, or willing to admit it."

Mr. Davidson declares that the Messianic prophecies were promulgated about five thousand years ago by the "progenitors" of the Hebrews and that the "end" will come when the "Gospel of the Kingdom" shall have been preached to all the world for a witness unto all nations. It will be sufficient, we note, that they shall hear it only, for it is not necessary for them to believe it. He states that the Great Pyramid's scientific revelation exposes the Egyptian claim that the promised Messiah had already come in the person of their own God, Osiris, who the Egyptians substituted for the true Messiah. We are told that the Adamic Race came from central Asia, the "cradle of civilization", and one of them was the great architect of the pyramid.

The sponsors of the pyramid prophecy theory have allotted names and designations to the various passages and chambers which are contained inside the Great Pyramid. There is no evidence that any of these names were known to the ancient Egyptians. For example, the horizontal passage leading to the Queen's Chamber is called the Access to the "Chamber of Second Birth, or New Birth"; the ante-chamber to the King's Chamber is referred to as the "Chamber of the Triple Veil" and is also called "Truce in Chaos". The period of "Final Tribulation" commences with the passage to the King's Chamber, which is also called "The Chamber of the Mystery of the Open Tomb" and "The Chamber of the Grand Orient" and "The Hall of the Judgement of the Nations". The subterranean chamber under the base of the Pyramid is referred to as "The Chamber of Chaos" or of "Upside-Downness", during "Spiritual descent". The first descending passage is supposed to symbolize the descent of the human race in spiritual degradation and idolatry. The first ascending passage equals the period from the Exodus, when the Children of Israel were taken out from amongst the nations to be witnesses of the purer religion, and the preparation for the ultimate redemption of man, and the grand gallery is thought to represent the period of Christian dispensation which replaced the Jewish.

The startling claim that the Great Pyramid is a prophecy in stone whereby a particular unit of measurement was used to represent time, is based on the belief that its architect used a special "pyramid" inch of 1.0011 British inches. He employed this inch secretly to show an allegory of structural error in relation to the metrological "year circuit" of 36,524.2 actual pyramid inches. The fact that no such unit of measurement was used by the ancient Egyptians is no stumbling block to the theory because this particular unit was used secretly. The pyramid theorists put forward the argument that the various systems of measure in the ancient world were all derived from one system invented to form a standard basis for international use because "surely, a widespread diffusion of customs and institutions necessarily implies widespread commercial intercourse; and does not the latter postulate the need for a standard system of measures as a common basis for exchange and barter?" We may remark here that we know that in our own time the human race still persists in employing different systems of measures. Why, therefore, should we conclude that the ancients were more enlightened?

The means by which this secret unit of measurement was translated into the pyramid's design and construction is of a highly complicated nature. Modern architects have learned that the Great Pyramid was the most accurately built structure of the ancient world, yet we are told that its building fell short of its intended measurements by a purposeful error. It was left incomplete at its top, without an apex, because the cap piece was found to be too big to fit the platform. Surely if the Pharoah Cheops, who built the pyramid for his own tomb, had found that his structure was incomplete he would have had another apex made? The true reason why the pyramid has no apex is almost certainly that it was removed by the Arabs who used the pyramid as a quarry for building materials.

The pyramid prophecy theory demands from us the initial acceptance of the belief that the Great Pyramid was built solely in order to hand down a mythical number system, from which the entire history of the human race could be deduced by using the dimensional relationships of its corridors and chambers. According to the theorists the Pyramid enshrines an accurate system of astronomical chronology revealing the controlling mind of the Grand Geometrician of Creation and the Purpose of the Great Architect of the Universe. The Great Pyramid is, we are told, a "Bible in stone", but it took the human race over three and a half thousand years to detect the prophecies enshrined in its numerical system.

The Egyptologists who have spent their lives studying the monuments and history of ancient Egypt declare that the unit of measurement employed in the building of the pyramid was known as the Royal Cubit, which equalled 20.62 British inches. "Most ancient measures have been derived," says Sir Flinders Petrie, "from one of two great systems. That of the cubit of 20.62 inches or the digit of 0.729 inches. Both these systems are found in the earliest remains." The cubit was derived, he tells us, from the length of the human forearm, and the digit from the thumb. While the protagonists of the prophecy theory agree that these measurements are correct, they maintain that the Egyptians also knew a secret cubit measure of approximately 25 inches.

Even if they were correct in believing in the existence of this secret unit of measure, their whole system is based on an arbitrary starting date. This date is derived from what is clearly a false conception of the base length of the pyramid, the original form of which is lost beneath the debris of the centuries. Within the structure itself, the starting point of the history of the so-called "Adamic Race" is fixed at a point far below the surface of the ground by the entirely imaginary elongation of a line downward from the point where the First Ascending Passage joins the entrance corridor. Thus, once a fixed point had been decided upon to indicate the year 4000 B.C. it was not difficult to work out the years by inches along various corridors and passages, to portray the next six thousand years of human history.

The theory largely depends on the supposed symbolical names of the passages and chambers contained within the pyramid, in connexion with such biblical references as the "times of the Gentiles" and the time when Jerusalem shall be "trodden down by Gentiles until the times of the Gentiles are fulfilled". These corridors and chambers are supposed to symbolize the spiritual history of man and the duration of the Jewish and Christian dispensation to the end of the world.

We note that two of the strongest of the protagonists of the theory, Mr. Davidson and Colonel Garnier, differ as to the year shown by the Great Pyramid for the date of the Crucifixion. This applies also to other dates indicated by the pyramid prophecy, and the divergence is probably owing to the fact that Colonel Garnier wrote his contribution to the theory long before Mr. Davidson and before some of these events were due to occur. According to Colonel Garnier, 18 August, 1882, was shown by the pyramid structure to indicate the Second Advent of Christ. After this momentous moment in the world's history had passed without anything unusual occurring he pushed back the commencement of the dates shown by the main gallery of the pyramid so that the date of the Second Advent became 1913 instead.

This enabled him to symbolize "the change of attitude" whereby "self complacency was substituted for faith and endeavour" by the great step of the main corridor. When this date was reached the "last times" would be ushered in when "false Christs and false Prophets shall arise" to usher in the great day of the Lord referred to by the Prophets. A final outburst of rebellion would then occur before the millenium, and a world-wide conflagration would take place as a preparation for the new heaven and the new earth in which the Jews would be restored to Palestine and the faiths of Canterbury and Rome would be reconciled by a reversal of the "errors and idolatries of Rome".

Mr. Davidson, on the other hand, finds that the first low passage in the pyramid leading from the great step into the Ante-Chamber of Truce in Chaos fits exactly, according to the secret measuring unit, the years 4 August, 1914, to 11 November, 1918, the exact period of the First World War.

The father wall of the Ante-Chamber then takes us to 29 May, 1928, the date of the beginning of the Final Tribulation, and the end of the second low passage carries us to 15 September, 1936. The length of the King's Chamber, "the Chamber of the Mystery of the Open Tomb", symbolizes the years from 1936 to 20 August, 1953, and the line which is drawn on the plan down the centre of the Chamber denotes the dates 3-4 March, 1945. (No, this is not 3-4 May, the date of Hitler's death and the end of the Second World War.)

Finally we come to the years A.D. 2001¾ and 2045¾ which are declared to be the days of Final Tribulation and end of the world. While it is not difficult to see in the troubles with which the world has been beset since 1914 various terrible events which might have been prophesied by the Master Architect of the Great Pyramid, we note that many of these dates have passed, apparently, without anything very special having happened in the world. On the other hand apparent insignificant matters, of which we are unable to assess the true significance, may have occurred and we do not yet know their true import.

It is clear that belief in the pyramid prophecies arises from the craving of humanity to find a Divine purpose in history, to show that the past has a meaning for the present. This peculiar Hebrew philosophy was inherited by the Christian religion when it took over Jewish beliefs and customs. But the most careful examination of human history has been unable to discern any pattern, Divine or otherwise. The belief that mankind has a purpose is very natural, wishful thinking, but history shows that it has no basis.

The believers in the pyramid prophecy have also been actuated by piety, misplaced, but none the less, perhaps, understandable. Like many other Christians, ancient and modern, Mr. Davidson and Colonel Garnier were disconcerted to find that many of the Christian beliefs were far more ancient than Christianity. They set out to explain this unhappy contradiction by the theory that a race had long existed which were the true forebears of those who later adopted the Chrsitian belief. These imaginary people, the Adamic Race, were credited with prophesying all that was to come, and especially the Christian Revelation.

The comparative study of religion has shown that these age-old ideas, many of which were incorporated into Christianity, were the birthright of most of the human race. There was no Adamic Race. The Hebrews, who claimed to be descendants of Adam, were Semites who inherited their religious ideas from the general Semite tradition. While the Semites may have come originally from Arabia, Mesopotamia was the land of their adoption until some 2000 B.C. and there is no evidence that they lived in Egypt before the date of the Exodus. Most of the religious ideas of the Jews were acquired some five hundred years later, after the Exodus, it not even being certain whether the "God of Abraham" was Jahveh, who they may have acquired as a tribal deity only after their flight from Egypt.

Egyptologists are in no doubt that the Great Pyramid was built by the Pharaoh Cheops as a tomb for his own body. He spent the twenty-two years of his reign constructing a mausoleum which might resist the depredations of the tomb robbers, who in ancient times desoiled nearly every royal tomb in ancient Egypt. To construct this great edifice, one of the great wonders of the world, four thousand skilled artisans were employed continuously shaping and constructing the giant stones. For three months every year some hundred thousand labourers dragged the stones into position and up earthen ramps as the pyramid itself was constructed. Its construction was what we would call today a great public works programme, designed to employ the labourers during the inundation period of the Nile when they could not work on their own lands and fields.

The corridors and chambers inside the pyramid were constructed during its building and it is now thought there was a considerable change of plan in respect of the pyramid's interior. The original intention was that the subterranean chamber was to be the Royal tomb: then a new chamber was made above it, but before this was completed there was a further change of plan and the King's Chamber itself was constructed to hold the Sarcophagus of the Pharaoh. Above the King's Chamber five small chambers were constructed as relieving compartments to take the weight of the edifice. Great efforts were made to defeat tomb robbers. The lower end of the First Ascending Passage, leading to the Royal tomb chamber, was plugged with a gigantic granite block which was an inch wider than the mouth of the passage itself and must, therefore, have been placed into position during the building operations. Even this did not protect the Royal remains, for tomb robbers merely chiselled through the soft sandstone round the granite block and gained access to the chamber from which they looted everything, including the body of the Pharaoh. When the Great Pyramid was first entered in modern times, in A.D. 820, by the Caliph Ali Mamoun, it took some time to find the entrance to the Royal burial chamber. Forcing an entrance through the passage from the doorway in the north face the Arabs did not know of the existence of the Ascending Passage or the Chambers above it for this was still completely blocked. While digging, the Arabs heard a heavy stone fall above them and by this accident they learned that access to the Ascending Passage could be made through a casing stone which revolved on a pivot.

The Great Pyramid prophecy is little heard of now. Before the Second World War its believers opened offices in many towns; numerous pamphlets were sent off and many meetings held. These activities have declined. Perhaps people are not as credulous as they used to be.

The ancient Pharaohs of Egypt went to tremendous lengths to safeguard their remains in vast stone structures, or in caves burrowed out deep in rock and approached by secret entrances. Their efforts were largely unavailing for it has been found that nearly every Royal tomb has been rifled and desecrated. Did the Pharaohs try to make doubly sure by putting a "curse" on those who tried to desecrate their tombs? The succession of remarkable deaths which followed the discovery and excavation of the tomb of the Pharaoh Tutankamen in 1922 seems, at first glance, to give substance to this belief.

The discovery of the tomb of the Pharaoh, almost intact and filled with wonderful and rich furniture and objects, has been described as the world's most exciting archaeological find. For the first time it brought the man in the street in direct contact with the past and excited his interest in the Pharaohs of ancient Egypt.

At the time of the discovery many Egyptologists believed that there was nothing more to be found in the fabled Valley of the Kings, but both Howard Carter and Lord Carnarvon were convinced that the tomb of Tutankamen, who reigned about 1350 B.C., must lie somewhere in the valley, probably under the piles of debris left by the previous excavators. They started work just before the First World War and recommenced in the 1919-20 season. The first hint that the tomb really did lie in the vicinity did not come until 1922 when the remains of workmen's huts, which had often before indicated the site of a Royal tomb, were exposed. When they cleared this debris, on 3 November, 1922, a stone step was exposed, and further digging disclosed a flight of sixteen steps; at the bottom was the entrance to a tomb which was sealed with the seal of the Royal Necropolis. Inside the door an impression of the seal of Tutankamen was found, but the condition of the door indicated that soon after burial the tomb had been entered by plunderers.

Another door was found at the end of a thirty-two foot passage. Howard Carter made a small hole in it and, as Lord Carnarvon, his daughter Lady Evelyn Herbert, and Professor Callender, waited anxiously, Carter peered in with the aid of a candle. After some moments of intense anxiety, Lord Carnarvon could bear the suspense no longer. "Can you see anything?" he asked. "Yes, wonderful things," whispered Howard Carter. Entry into the tomb chamber was delayed until 17 February, 1923, and twenty Egyptologists assembled for the supreme moment. As Howard Carter slowly opened the door, the beam of his electric torch disclosed a chamber, 21 ft. x 13 ft. x 11 ft., completely filled with funeral objects and their eyes were dazzled by gold. The Sarcophagus was intact. The tomb itself had not been despoiled and there was every reason to expect that the body of the boy Pharaoh, buried there over three thousand years before, remained intact.

Slowly and carefully the Sarcophagus was opened, and it was found to contain three coffins, each nesting within the other inside the triple shrine. On the outer coffin, bearing the effigy of the dead King, lay the most poignant object in the entire tomb, a little bunch of withered flowers, perhaps the last offering of the widowed Queen. When the body was finally drawn from its last resting place, it was found to be that of a young man with face and head well preserved.

Six weeks after the opening of the tomb, a shadow fell across the scene, one which was to lengthen and deepen as the years progressed. On 5 April Lord Carnarvon died, his death being attributed to a bite on the face from a mosquito. He was sixty-three years old. All over the world it was said that his death resulted from the desecration and the despoiling of the tomb of the ancient Pharaoh, a sacrilege which had called down upon his head the ancient Curse of the Pharaohs, the revenge of the spirit of the dead Pharaoh, his "Ka", who was not dead but still alive in his tomb.

As death followed death people began to ask if even from the tomb, the spirit of the dead Egyptian Kings could reach out into the prosaic twentieth century to revenge themselves upon those who had disturbed their rest? Lord Carnarvon, it was said, had put his finger inside a vase, found in the tomb, on which was inscribed "Death shall come on swift wings to him that toucheth the tomb of the Great Pharaoh", and that when he withdrew his hand there was a tiny drop of blood on his finger. The weird story was told that on the day that the tomb was entered the atmosphere was absolutely still, there not being a breath of wind, but as the party descended the stairs a miniature sandstorm swept across the desert and circled over the tomb. As the sudden gust of wind died away, a hawk, the emblem of ancient Eyptian Royalty, came from the east, hovered over the tomb, and flew away westward in the direction of the other world of Egyptian belief. Had the opening of the tomb, it was asked, released the spirit of the dead Pharaoh to pass to his last judgement?

The Curse of the Pharaohs was not satisfied by the death of Lord Carnarvon. Within five months his half-brother Aubrey Herbert, M.P., who had visited the tomb, died. In popular fancy his death was attributed to mysterious causes, but in actual fact it was the result of acute peritonitis. Six years later, in February, 1929, Lord Carnarvon's stepmother died, her death being attributed to an insect bite.

The deaths of a number of well-known people who had visited the tomb, or who had had something to do with its discovery and excavations, were attributed to the Curse. Woolf Joel, the South African millionaire who had been yachting on the Nile, fell downstairs and died from a stroke. George J. Gould, the American railroad King, died on 16 May, 1923, his death being attributed to pneumonia, following a cold caught in the tomb itself. Two Egyptians, Prince Ali Fahmy, who was shot dead in the Savoy Hotel, London, and his brother Hallah Bey who took his own life, both of whom claimed descent from the Pharaohs, died by unusual means. In 1924 the Sirdar of the Egyptian Army, Sir Lee Stack, was assassinated, and on 9 March, 1934, the American author Louis K. Siggins, who had written a play about these mysterious deaths, also died.

Others who had been even more directly concerned with the "violation of the tomb" died from supposedly mysterious causes. Professor Laffleur, of McGill University, Canada, died on 9 February, 1924, and a few months later a young English Egyptologist, H. E. Evelyn-White, committed suicide leaving a letter which contained the words "I knew there was a curse on me". His death was followed by that of a sign-writer at the British Museum who had handled many of the relics from the tomb. On 18 January, 1924, Sir Archibald Douglas-Reid, the radiologist who had been specially selected to X-ray the body of the dead Pharaoh, died in Switzerland at the age of fifty-three, and another photographer who came to Egypt to photograph the Sarcophagus, Frank Raleigh, went blind and died. Two years later, two French Egyptologists who were present at the entry to the Tomb, Dr. Georges Benedite and Dr. Pasanova, died suddenly.

The revenge of the Pharaohs was not yet complete. The Hon. Richard Bethel, who had acted as Howard Carter's assistant, died in London on 15 November, 1929. Some of the treasures from the tomb had been stored at his house and there had been a mysterious fire in the building. Within a few months his father, seventy-eight year old Lord Westbury, threw himself from the window of his London flat. In his bedroom was found the alabaster vase bearing the inscription already quoted, brought from the tomb by his son. Five days later a boy of eight, Joseph Greer of Battersea, was killed by the hearse bearing Lord Westbury's body to Golders Green. Within two years the Hon. Mrs. Richard Bethel was dead, too, and in the war Lady Westbury was bombed out of her Putney home.

Other strange deaths followed. After the sudden death of two well-known Egyptologists, Professor Albert Lythgoe and Professor A. C. Mace, Arthur Weigall, the Inspector of Egyptian Antiquities at the time of the opening of the tomb, died from what was stated to be "an unknown fever". Professor James Breasted, of the University of Chicago, who had taken an active part in the excavation of the tomb, died at the age of seventy, on 3 December, 1935. His death was attributed to "severe streptococcal infection", the name given to a variety of micro-organisms responsible for virulent inflammation. Professor Breasted had said: "I defy the Curse. If anyone was exposed to it, I was, I slept in the tomb for two weeks and even had my meals there. I never felt better in my life."

The supposed chief despoiler of the tomb, in the popular view, Howard Carter, lived for seventeen years after the opening of the tomb, dying on 2 March, 1939, aged sixty-seven. Three other famous Egyptologists, who had spent their lives digging up the remains of dead Pharaohs, lived to an advanced age. Sir Wallace Budge, who declared "I have dug up mummies in many lands and yet no curse has descended on me", died in 1934, aged seventy-seven, Sir

Flinders Petrie, in 1942, at the age of eighty-nine, and Professor Percy Edward Newberry, who had entered the tomb, lived until 1949, when he died at the age of eighty.

Did these people die from the "Curse of the Pharaohs"? According to one theory microbes carrying some terrible disease, which could still infect and kill after thousands of years, had remained alive in the tomb. But the interior of the tomb would have been too dry for them to survive, for bacteria require damp and mildew to live on. That they had been at work in the tomb originally was shown by the partial decay of the fabrics. But that these fabrics were only partly destroyed showed that the bacteria had died thousands of years ago, before completing their work. The theory that Lord Carnarvon died from the poison bite of a mosquito in the tomb also collapses when we learn that, because of the lack of water, no mosquito is found in the "Valley of the Kings". Actually, Lord Carnarvon was bitten by a mosquito at Luxor.

If there was a curse of the Pharaohs, why is it that those tomb robbers, who desecrated the Royal tombs of Egypt soon after they were sealed, apparently escaped the curse? If the ancient Egyptians knew of such a potent curse, why did not they employ it, at least to frighten off these tomb robbers? There are no records of the mysterious deaths of tomb robbers, and if such deaths had occurred surely the priests or the Pharaohs themselves would have broadcast them as an awful warning.

The deaths of a number of people who were in some way connected with the opening of Tutankamen's tomb was purely coincidental. Modern Egyptologists are protecting, not despoiling, the dead. If the mummies and treasures of the ancient tombs were not removed to places of safety, the descendants of the ancient tomb robbers would have no compunction in destroying them and stealing their treasures. The ancient kings of Egypt, too, were too practical to worry about curses. They had long reconciled themselves to the fact that no tomb could be absolutely safe, however strong, or however deep it was dug, from the depredations of the tomb robbers. Their concern was to be well thought of by their contemporaries. They hoped only to save their bodies intact, to facilitate the ultimate journey to the other world. The Pharaohs knew the futility of curses. Though such curses are found in some of the most ancient of Egyptian tombs, the custom was given up long before the time of Tutankamen. The curses uttered on behalf of the Pharaohs by the priests were designed not so much to prevent tomb robbery as to protect the endowments the Pharaohs had made for the upkeep of commemorative services for the repose of their souls. The priests themselves, the beneficiaries of these endowments, saw to it that these curses were uttered at the time of the Pharaoh's burial.

Only the very credulous still believe that the curse of the Pharaohs reached out from the grave to kill some twenty or thirty people. When carefully examined none of these deaths was particularly mysterious. All can be accounted for by natural causes.

DAUPHIN AND DUCHESS

THE FATE of the little Dauphin, Louis XVII, in the French Revolution is the most touching and certainly the most enigmatic of all famous historical mysteries. Did he die in the Temple Prison or was a deaf and dumb boy substituted for him? If he was smuggled out, was Naundorff he? Then there is another even deeper mystery. Was the Dauphin's sister, the Duchess of Angoûlème herself an imposter? Why, if she was genuine, did she avoid seeing Naundorff?

Officially, the wretched Dauphin, his health weakened by barbarous captivity and the indifference of his gaolers, died in the Temple on 8 June, 1795. Certainly a boy died there and was buried. After the defeat of Napoleon in 1815 the Bourbons were restored to the throne of France in the person of his uncle, Louis XVIII, and his sister, who had been exchanged for certain French prisoners of war in 1795, returned to France as the Duchess of Angoûlème, the wife of the heir to the throne.

Thirty Pretenders claimed to be the Dauphin whom rumour stated had escaped. They were all easily exposed as imposters. Eighteen years after the Bourbon Restoration, Karl Wilhelm Naundorff, a clock-maker from Prussia, came to Paris and was recognized as the missing Dauphin by many adherents of the ancient regime. However, the Duchess of Angoûlème steadfastly refused to see him and indeed went out of her way to avoid him. Thus, if Naundorff was genuine he was denied his one great chance of establishing his identity. After the Duchess's death in 1851 it was suggested that it was she who was the imposter.

The story of the Dauphin's captivity is a tortuous one in itself: the claims of Naundorff and the mystery about the

Duchess are even more confused. To unravel them we must start in 1778 when Marie Thérèse, Madame Royale was born to Louis XVI and his wife Marie Antoinette. Seven years later the Dauphin, Louis Charles, was born. Early in the Revolution they were imprisoned with their father and mother in the Tower of the Temple, originally the home of the Knights Templar. In 1793 the King was executed and the Dauphin, now declared to be Louis XVII by the exiled Royalists, was removed from his mother and sister to a separate room. Then Marie Antoinette was guillotined and Madame Royale and the Dauphin met again only when he was persuaded to sign, in complete ignorance of its meaning, a horrible declaration against his mother. Brother and sister were then confined in separate rooms, under the guardianship of a shoemaker named Simon and his wife, who were certainly not the tyrants they were represented by the Royalists.

In the period in which Simon was the Dauphin's gaoler there is no record that he received any ill-treatment, and the details of the food and amusements provided for him strongly suggest that he was treated with kindness. There can be little doubt that the Dauphin, now aged nine, became good friends with the somewhat uncouth Simon who stated: "I would give an arm for this child to belong to me, so lovable is he and so attached am I to him". While it is doubtful if Simon would have used exactly such words his statement was recorded from an eye-witness of the occasion in 1817.

The vital moment in any investigation is 19 January, 1794, when Simon and his wife departed from the Temple, giving up the Dauphin's guardianship. If the Dauphin was removed from the Temple and another child substituted it is probable that it happened when Simon and his wife moved their belongings from the Temple Prison. There is no direct evidence that such a substitution took place but circumstantial evidence is quite strong.

Up to the end of Simon's guardianship the history of the Dauphin's imprisonment is well documented; from that moment there is complete silence. His sister, who occupied a room upstairs, says in her reminiscences of this period that up to that time she had heard her brother singing and laughing, adding: "On 19 January we heard a great noise at my brother's, which made us conjecture that he was leaving the Temple, and we were already convinced of it when, looking through a hole in our sunblind, we saw many packages being taken away". Madame Royale, as she was then, certainly noticed the removal of the Simons.

Yet there remained a child imprisoned on the second floor of the Temple. There were some unusual happenings that night. According to the usual practice four Commissioners, deputed by the National Assembly to be at the Temple each day, arrived to relieve the previous ones, but two of those who now signed in the record book did not belong to the Commune. They were complete strangers who had not visited the Temple before in this capacity. According to tradition, from the night the Simons left the wretched Dauphin was confined in his room completely without communication from outside; for the next six months there is no news of him.

It is said that he was kept in complete isolation, this child of nine, quite incapable of looking after himself, even of undertaking such necessary duties as cleaning himself or his cell, or of lighting and clearing his fire. No sound was heard from his room and the visits of the previously attentive doctors ceased.

It seems certain that this report must be untrue. The Temple was filled with guards and four Commissioners arrived each day to replace the previous four. Moreover, for some weeks Simon and his wife paid calls there. The important point seems to be that a cloak of secrecy was thrown about the prisoner. Whereas for months his condition and future had frequently been discussed at the meetings of the General Council, now there was no reference to him at all.

Throughout France plots to procure the safety of the Dauphin were rife. With the death of his father he had become an important pawn in the game of international politics. He might one day be needed to secure peace for France against her many enemies.

In the spring of 1794 Robespierre became master of France. No one to this day has ever unravelled his intentions, but whatever they were the Dauphin figured with some importance. The authenticated report of a British spy to Lord Grenville, dated 25 April of that year, suggests that Robespierre planned to carry off the little Dauphin, recognized by many as King of France, and to make a treaty with the Powers. On 11 May, according to Madame Royale, Robespierre visited the Temple. We can conclude only that he saw the Dauphin, as well as his sister. The British spy informed Lord Grenville that on the night of 23-24 May Robespierre took the Dauphin out of the Temple to a country house at Meudon and brought him back to the Temple on the night of the 30th. It has been suggested that Robespierre returned him because upon examination he found the boy was not the Dauphin, but he thought it better to pretend he was and to conceal the substitution of which he knew nothing.

Then Barras triumphed. Robespierre fell and was guillotined. Now all Paris heard a rumour that the Dauphin had escaped from the Temple. Barras himself may even have been the organizer of the great deception, the substitution of another boy for the little King. But he, too, had to keep up the great pretence. In a record of a visit to the Temple he says:

"I was at the Temple and found the young Prince in a cradle-shaped bed in the middle of his room. He was in a sound sleep and woke with difficulty. He was wearing trousers and a grey cloth jacket. I asked him how he was and why he did not sleep in the big bed. He replied, 'My knees are swollen and pain me at times when I am standing. The little cradle suits me better'. I examined his knees and found them very swollen, as well as his ankles and hands. His face was puffed and pale. After asking him if he had what was necessary and having advised him to walk, I gave orders to the Commissioners and scolded them for the neglected state of the room. Order has not been troubled at the Temple but the Prince is dangerously ill. I ordered that he should be taken for a walk and summoned Monsieur Desault (a doctor). It is urgent, I told him, that you should consult other doctors and that they examine his condition and give him all the care his condition demands."

Barras appointed new guardians for the Dauphin. Christophe Laurent became gaoler both to the Dauphin and to his sister but, as far as we can ascertain from the records, nothing was done to change the boy's lot and no doctor was called in. The ex-gaoler Simon had been executed with Robespierre, and we know that Laurent, on his own authority, ordered that seals should be placed on Simon's papers. That suggests there was something to conceal. Though orders had been given for the brother and sister to be united nothing was done, though Laurent frequently visited Madame Royale, who learned that her brother was always alone, served by Laurent only, no one else being allowed in his room.

Another strange fact comes to light, one which seems to

suggest that a substitution had already taken place. The National Convention gave orders that the children should be moved, quite openly, to a more suitable residence, but the orders were not carried out. Was the order neglected, it has been asked, because Barras knew or found out that a substitution had taken place? That could not be made public because such an admission would have been a triumph for France's enemies. Here the mystery deepens, for it is suggested that somewhere about this time yet another substitution took place and a boy, more taciturn and silent than the first, was placed in the Dauphin's room.

In 1918 there was found a report of a secret meeting of the Directory, the rulers of France, which took place on 28 April, 1796, at which the five Directors, including Barras, talked openly amongst themselves of the abduction of the Dauphin as an accomplished fact, and as one approved by them all. It was admitted that the Dauphin had been removed from Paris to the house at Château de Vitry of the well-known banker and Royalist, Petitival, but again, it has been asked, was Barras the originator of the Dauphin's escape or was he, too, a dupe? Barras, amongst others in French government circles, had much to gain from securing the person of the Dauphin; at that time many were concerned to secure their own safety should things go wrong in the war against the Royalists and their allies.

Further important events occurred in October, 1794. The Committee of Public Safety sent two of its members to the Temple to see the Dauphin and to verify his presence there. At the same time a man named Gomin was sent to assist Laurent as guardian of the Royal children. Gomin has been described by the Princess as a very honest man who was distressed by the state in which he found the Dauphin.

The next we hear of the Dauphin is a description recorded in 1814 by Harmand, one of the three members of the National Assembly sent to visit him on 19 December, 1794. Harmand's description of the boy he and the others then saw supplied the basic clue to the theory that the boy who died there later was not the Dauphin. The reader is forced to conclude from Harmand's description that the boy he then saw was deaf and dumb. It is not without significance that Harmand, before he died, was befriended by the Bourbons on their restoration and he was known to be a Royalist sympathize in 1794. His record of the visit to the Dauphin reads:

"We came to the door behind the terrifying lock of which the sole innocent son of our King was confined, himself our King.

"The Prince sat beside a small four-cornered table on which were scattered a number of playing-cards; some of these were folded so as to make little boxes or pockets; others were built up in the form of a castle. He was busy with these cards when we came in and did not stop his game.

"He was wearing a sailor-suit made of a slate-coloured material; his head was bare; the room was clean and well-lighted. His bed consisted of a little framework of wood; the mattress and linen seemed quite good.

"I approached the Prince. Our movements seemed to make no impression on him. I told him that the Government had been too late informed of the sad state of his health as well as of his refusal to take any exercise or to answer either the questions which were put to him or the proposal that he should take certain medicines and be examined by a doctor; that we had now been sent to him to obtain confirmation of these facts, and to repeat these proposals to him in the Government's name; that we hoped that he would assent to him, but that we took the liberty of advising him, even of warning him against keeping silence longer and taking no exercise; that we were empowered to give him the opportunity of extending his walks and of offering him whatsoever he might wish to distract him and help him to regain his health; and that I begged him to give me his answer, if he so pleased.

"While I was in course of making this little speech to him he gazed blankly at me without changing position; he was openly listening to me with great attention, but he gave no answer.

"I therefore repeated my suggestions as though I thought he had not understood me aright, and explained them to him somewhat as follows: 'It may be that I have expressed myself badly, or that you, Sire, have not understood my meaning, but I have the honour to ask you whether you would maybe desire a horse or a dog, a bird, or a toy of any sort, or one or two companions of your own age, whom we would present to you before they took up their abode here. Would you care now to go down into the garden or up the tower? Would you like sweetmeats, cake, or anything of the sort?' I endeavoured in vain to suggest to him all the things which a boy of his age

81

might covet, but I got not a single word or answer from him, not so much as a sign or movement, although he had his head turned towards me and gazed at me with a most astonishing fixedness, which seemed to express complete indifference.

"I therefore allowed myself to take a more emphatic tone, and ventured to say to him: 'Sire, so much obstinacy at your age is an unpardonable fault; it is all the more astonishing since our visit, as you see, has the purpose of making your residence more agreeable and of providing care for the improvement of your health. If you continue to give no answer, and do not say what you desire, how can we attain our end? Is there any other means of making these suggestions to you? Be so good as to tell us and we will arrange ourselves accordingly.'

"Always the same fixed gaze and the same attentiveness, but not a single word.

"I began again: 'If, Sire, your refusal to speak only touched yourself, we would wait not without concern but with resignation until it pleased you to break silence, since we must draw the conclusion that your situation displeases you less than we supposed, as you do not wish to leave the Temple. But you have no right over yourself. All those who surround you are responsible for your person and condition. Do you wish to compromise them? Do you wish to compromise ourselves? For what answer can we give the Government, whose agents we are? Have the kindness to answer me, I beseech you, or we shall be compelled to order you.'

"Not a word. Always the same immobility. I was on the verge of desperation and my companions also; that look in particular had an extraordinary expression of resignation and indifference, as though it seemed to say: 'What does it matter? Leave your victim in peace'.

"I repeat, I could not go on; I was near to breaking out in tears of the bitterest sorrow; but I took one or two paces up and down the room, recovered my calm, and felt myself impelled to see what effect a command might have. I made the attempt, set myself quite close beside him on his right hand and said to him: 'Be so good, Sire, as to give me your hand'. He gave it me and I felt it up to the armpit. I found a kind of knotted swelling on the wrist and another at the elbow. These swellings apparently gave him no pain, since the Prince seemed to feel nothing. 'The other hand, Sire.' He gave me that, too, but there was nothing there, 'Allow me, Sire, to examine your legs and knees as well.' He got up. I found similar swellings on both knees and in the hollows behind the knees.

"In this condition, the Prince showed symptoms of rachitis and deformation. His thighs and legs were long and thin, and the arms also. The upper part of the body was very short, the breast-bone very high, the shoulders high and narrow; the head was very handsome in all its details, the hair long and fine, well kept and light-brown in colour.

" 'Now, Sire, have the goodness to walk a little.' He complied at once, walked to the door which lay between the two beds, came back again at once and sat down. 'Do you consider, Sire, that that is exercise? Do not you rather see that this apathy is the cause of your sickness, and of the ills which threaten you? Be good enough to believe in our experience and our zeal. You cannot hope to restore your health if you do not follow our wishes and advice. We shall send you a doctor, and we hope that you will answer his questions. Give us at least a sign to show that you consent.' Not a sign, not a word.

" 'Be so kind, Sire, as to walk about once again, and for a little longer.' Silence and immobility. He remained sitting on his chair with his elbows propped on the table; the expression on his face did not alter for an instant. There was not the slightest movement to be seen in him, not the slightest surprise in his eyes, just as if we had not been there and I had not spoken.

"My companions had kept silence; we were looking at one another in astonishment and were just about to exchange our opinions when his dinner was brought in. Another pitiful scene followed; one must have seen him to have an idea of it. We gave orders in the ante-room that the disgusting diet should be altered in the future, and that from that day some dainties, such as fruit, should be added to his meals. I wished that he should be given some grapes, as they were rare at that season. As soon as the order had been given we returned. The Prince had eaten up everything. I asked him whether he were pleased with his dinner? No reply. Whether he liked fruit? No reply. Did he like grapes? No reply. A moment later the grapes were brought and set on the table before him. He ate them without saying a word. 'Would you like some more?' Still not a word. 'Do you wish, Sire, that we should go away?' No answer. After this last question we went out."

After making this report Harmand disappears suddenly from the scene. Almost at once he was appointed Commissioner to the East Indies and left France at once, which may have been one way of telling him to be discreet. Harmand may have been conditioned by the atmosphere in 1814 when he wrote his report suggesting that the Dauphin was ill. His illness was sudden, yet the symptoms described imply a long-standing condition. Twelve months' previously, when under the care of the Simons, he had been in good health and was gay and happy.

On 31 March, 1795, the gaoler Laurent was succeeded by a man named Etienne Lasne. Gomin remained as his assistant. Lasne, writing in 1814, described the Prince when he first saw him as showing "extraordinary impassability: he uttered no complaint and never broke the silence". According to Gomin, who wrote in 1834, the Dauphin spoke to him daily at this time. One of the two gaolers was lying.

Meanwhile the Dauphin had become the stake of European peace, the first condition of the cessation of hostilities. At a meeting between the French Commissioners and the representatives of the Allied Governments fighting the French Revolution it was laid down as the first condition of peace that the Dauphin should be handed over. If this was done the Spanish Bourbons would recognize the French Republic. France could thus have gained a great diplomatic victory, but strangely rejected the opportunity. Was this because the French Government knew that it no longer had the Dauphin in its possession?

The evidence about the Dauphin's condition, or the condition of the boy in the Temple Prison at this time, is completely conflicting. Whereas Harmand reported him in bad health, and completely silent, the menus known to have been served to him, from the Temple archives, indicate that he was well fed and in good health and supplied with suitable clothes. Yet another Government Commissioner who saw him early in 1795 says: "He was the most pitiable human being I have ever seen". At this stage it is clear only that there was a boy in the Temple about whom different people wrote according to how it suited their particular views.

On 3 May, 1795, the boy in the Temple was reported to be ill and on the orders of the Committee of Public Safety, Doctor Desault, the leading medical practitioner in Paris, was sent to see him. He continued to visit the boy until 29 May when he himself died under what are claimed to be mysterious circumstances. He collapsed and died suddenly on his return home after dining with certain members of the National Assembly. For six days the boy was without medical attention but on 6 June Doctor Pelletan, a man of great reputation, was sent to visit him.

Pelletan called in another doctor named Dumagins. According to Doctor Pellatan's recollections, written after the Bourbon restoration, he realized at once that the case was hopeless and that the boy was dying, but from his contemporary prescriptions and the food he ordered to be given to the boy it can only be assumed that he did not think life was threatened. It is impossible that he could have given such orders if he thought the boy was dying.

During the night of 7 June Pelletan was hurriedly sent for, and from the Temple he wrote a note to the Committee of Public Safety that the boy's condition was very serious. He demanded that a nurse be sent at once. Though finally granted, this request seems to have been a matter of grave concern to the Commissioners, who may have hesitated to introduce a stranger to the room.

The still extant reports of the boy's death are conflicting. According to Lasne he was alone in the boy's room and was administering to him when he died suddenly, just before Doctor Pelletan arrived. Gomin makes out that it was he who was present as the Dauphin gave his dying breath. Great secrecy was enforced. Pelletan was not allowed to leave the Temple until permission had been received from the Committee of Public Safety and Lasne kept the news of the boy's death secret from everyone else in the Temple, including the guards. He even continued to carry up food and medicines to the boy's room, thus keeping up the pretence that though ill he was still alive. Next day, at the Convention, the Dauphin's death was drily announced without comment.

On 9 June, Doctor Pelletan, assisted by Dumagins and two other doctors, Lassus and Jeanroy, performed an autopsy on the boy's body. Pelletan opened the body, taking out the heart secretly, and he dissected the head. All four doctors signed the following report:

"We arrived, all four of us, at eleven in the forenoon, at the outer door of the Temple, where we were received by the Commissioners who led us into the Tower. In a room on the second floor, we were shown the dead body of a boy who appeared to us to be about ten years old and who, we were told by the Commissioners, was the son of the late Louis Capet. Two of us recognized the child as one to whom we had had to give attention during the previous days. The child's death must be ascribed to a scrofula of long standing."

No identification was made of the body. Later, some of the officers of the guard were shown the body, its head tied in bandages, and they said they recognized him as the Dauphin, but the one sure and certain method of identification was avoided. Madame Royale, the boy's sister, was only a few feet away upstairs and it seems in keeping with the substitution theory that she was not brought down to identify him with certainty. Nor were any of the servants who had been in the Temple since the start of the captivity of the Royal Family brought upstairs to view the body. Yet it was in the vital interests of the French Republic to establish the Dauphin's death. A report of the secret police dated 12 June, 1795, says:

"The population of the Temple quarter say quite openly that the arrangements for the funeral of the little Capet were only a blind and that he is not dead, but has been allowed to escape and is now far away in safety."

That night the boy's body was placed in a coffin and buried in the churchyard of Sainte-Margeurite. At nine o'clock at night, just as it was getting dusk, a military escort, followed by the coffin, a barrier of troops holding back the crowd, proceeded to the churchyard where, according to the official report, the body was consigned to a common grave. But it may not have been left there.

After the Bourbon restoration both the undertaker and the Chief of Police for that quarter of Paris maintained that the body had been buried in a specially dug grave in another part of the cemetery, but they gave different locations for its site. The really remarkable part of the matter seems to be this. In 1816 Louis XVIII gave orders to seek the bones of both Louis XVI and Marie Antoinette but no orders were given to find those of the little Dauphin. The homage of France was accorded to his father and mother but not to the boy king who had not reigned. Efforts to find his grave were discouraged.

Dussert, the Police Commissioner for the Temple district, indicated the site of the Dauphin's grave and disclosed there had been great secrecy at the burial and strange movements had taken place at night. When the site he indicated was excavated an empty coffin was found. On the other hand the widow of the gravedigger told researchers that the coffin had been withdrawn from the common grave and re-buried in a grave dug against the foundations of the church against the left transept. When this site was excavated in 1846 it was found to contain a coffin in which lay the skeleton of a boy whose head had been sawn in two, but the examination of the remains by doctors indicated that they belonged to a boy of about fifteen years. At a further exhumation in 1894 doctors concluded that this boy had died of rachitis, and they gave their opinion, which was supported by that of a dentist, that the remains were those of a boy aged between sixteen and eighteen.

Unless the impossible coincidence arose that two children, both of whom had had an autopsy performed on them died the same night, it can only be concluded that these remains were those of the boy who died in the Temple on 8 June, 1795. Significantly, despite extensive searches in the churchyard, no skeleton of a ten-year-old boy was found anywhere near the various sites indicated as being where the Dauphin's body had been buried.

Other strange facts may be noted. On 21 April, 1796, the banker Petitival and all his family and servants were savagely murdered in their home, though nothing was stolen. According to rumour the mysterious child who had previously been living at the house had disappeared some months before.

Copies of letters supposedly written by Laurent, the Dauphin's warder, dated 7 November, 1794, and 5 February and 3 March, 1795, refer to a deaf and dumb boy being substituted for the Dauphin who had been secretly moved upstairs to the attic and to the problem of the conspirators faced in getting him out of the building. These letters have been accepted as genuine by G. Lenotre, the French historian, the principal investigator of the fate of the Dauphin, who he believed was smuggled out as part of a plot by Royalist adherents in the National Assembly, probably instigated by Barras and perhaps encouraged by his friend and mistress Josephine Beauharnais who later became Napoleon's wife. The family of Napoleon always believed she had assisted in the Dauphin's escape and she herself is reputed to have declared her belief he was still alive.

It is remarkable that Barras, Tallien and Freron, all members of the Committee of Public Safety in 1795, who were believed to have tried to save the Dauphin, were rescued and well treated by the Royalists after the restoration, but Barras's papers were confiscated on his death in 1817.

A possible clue to the fate of the Dauphin was provided by the widow of Simon, the Dauphin's first gaoler. She was sent to the Hospital of the Incurables in Paris in 1796, and lived there until her death in 1815. She repeatedly told the nurses that on 19 January, 1794, the day of their removal from the Temple, the Dauphin had been carried out in a cart in a linen basket and another boy substituted for him. She declared that the Dauphin was still alive.

When her story became known outside the hospital she was visited by the secret police to whom she confirmed her belief. No suggestion was made that she was either crazy or simple-minded and she never deviated from the story she told.

When the Duchess of Angoulême visited the hospital in 1814 the Widow Simon was hidden away, but when the duchess visited the hospital again some days later in disguise and talked to the Widow Simon, she immediately recognized her as the Princess she had last seen in the Temple in 1794.

From the Widow Simon's story was woven the tale by Raphael Sabbatini, the historical novelist, which related how the Dauphin was smuggled out of the Temple in a linen basket, and which purports to tell of his adventures and how he presented himself in Paris in 1814 to substantiate his claim.

While there is no definite proof that the Dauphin was smuggled out of the Temple and another boy substituted for him, or as to who may have been the organizers of the conspiracy, papers discovered in 1905 show that a Royalist plot to contrive his escape certainly existed in 1794. Its chief organizer, an Englishwoman named Mrs. Atkyns, who sacrificed her fortune in her endeavours to free the Royal Family of France, writes in a letter to Pitt the British Prime Minister on 5 February, 1795, in a tone which suggests that she believed the attempt to save the Dauphin had been successful. "It will be no news to Mr. Pitt," she says, "when I inform him that Louis XVII is no longer in the Temple and has not been there for some time." And she says she has the satisfaction of knowing that she assisted in the release of the boy and that the child now in the Temple was not the Dauphin.

In the previous December, General Frotte wrote to Mrs. Atkyns to say: "I give you my word of honour that the King and France are saved," and he urged her against further futile efforts to rescue the Dauphin. A year later he wrote to her: "I was much opposed to putting another child in the King's place." While there is no reason to doubt that Mrs. Atkyns and General Frotte and other conspirators did their best to save the Dauphin, it seems doubtful that, if he was saved from the Temple, he was taken out by them. It seems far more probable that the substitution, if it did take place, was by the design of someone in high government circles, someone with an axe to grind who was determined that he would get his hands on that important political pawn.

The most that can be said is that the Dauphin's death in the Temple in 1795 is not sufficiently established for us to be certain that he was the boy who died there. It seems doubtful that the Dauphin's condition could have deteriorated so badly from the time the Simons ceased to be his gaolers to his death. It seems impossible to believe that any boy of nine could have feigned or faked the condition of deafness and dumbness noted by Harmand in 1794. If he did escape from captivity it seems certain that two separate substitutions must have taken place. First, on 19 January, 1794, another boy was placed in his room while perhaps he himself was hidden upstairs. This boy was seen by various people who remarked that his health seemed bad but he still seems to have spoken. The boy seen by Harmand must have been one who was deaf and dumb, probably a second boy smuggled in to make the deceit more convincing.

If the Dauphin was smuggled out there are two possibilities to consider. Either he lived and died unknown, or the Pretender Naundorff was he. All the other claimants who arose both during Napoleonic times and after the Bourbon restoration were undoubtedly imposters. The identity of each was established.

Whether or not Naundorff was the Dauphin, as he claimed, he was a remarkable man who impressed everyone he met and who ended his life as the inventor of a new type of gun for which his descendants were paid a large sum by the Dutch Government.

Unfortunately we have little more than Naundorff's own word and his recognition by certain people who had known the Dauphin, to establish his claim. Perhaps the greatest indication of the validity of Naundorff's claim is that determined efforts were made to prevent him from establishing it.

There were attacks on his life before and after he was expelled from France.

The details given by Naundorff in his book published in London in 1836 are claimed by his supporters as facts which could have been known to him only if he were the Dauphin. Some of the incidents he relates were authenticated by Joly, Louis XVI's Minister of Justice, who declared they were typical incidents of small importance which might have impressed themselves on a child's mind. Naundorff invited the Duchess of Angoûlème to say whether the information he gave was true or not. He gives precise details of the Royal Family's flight to Varennes and he recalls that on the occasion when the Royal Family was taken to the National Assembly it was Joly who gave him something to eat. Many of the facts he relates are of quite trivial importance, just such facts as might have impressed themselves on the children.

According to Naundorff he was carried out of the Temple in a coffin after being given a dose of opium on 8 June, 1795 (the day of the reported death of the Dauphin), which fits in with the belief that a substitution had been effected and the Dauphin was secreted in the attic on the fourth floor. His story seems to be corroborated by the otherwise strange discovery of an empty coffin in the churchyard of Sainte-Margeurite. He says that he was taken by a Swiss lady to Italy where he posed as her son and they remained there until French troops invaded. He was then taken to England. Naundorff omitted many details of his life between 1795 and 1830, because he declared that he would reveal them only in court proceedings, which he was never allowed to do. As a result we learn only that he suffered various imprisonments during these years and he speaks of being shut up in a dungeon without a window. In the course of his flight from country to country he says he was rescued on more than one occasion by the intervention of Josephine, the future Empress.

He reached Frankfort-on-the-Maine, when aged twenty-four, in 1809, where his life was again saved by Josephine with the help of Barras. He then became caught up in the war which was raging and he was taken to Berlin, where he set himself up as a watchmaker. In the Prussian capital his story becomes more circumstantial for when Naundorff was asked for his passport he showed his papers to the Chief of Police, Lecoq, who, after consulting the King and Chancellor, advised it was too dangerous for all concerned for him to remain in Berlin and gave him identity papers in the name of Naundorff, a watchmaker, born in Weimar. He received a recommendation from Lecoq, which is still extant, to reside in Spandau.

The important clue here seems to be that the Prussian Chief of Police would not have given Naundorff false papers unless he had good reason to believe in his story of his identity.

In 1816 Naundorff wrote to his sister who had now been restored to France, but he received no reply. Two years later he married the daughter of a manufacturer and communicated with the Duc de Berry, who was murdered a few days later. Supporters of the Naundorff claim suggest that the Duc's murder had something to do with Naundorff.

In 1821, Naundorff who had moved to Brandenburg was arrested and sentenced for issuing counterfeit coinage. His guilt was never substantiated and it appears that the sentence of a few months' imprisonment imposed was not because of this offence but rather by reason of his declaration of his true origin at his trial. After his release he remained in Germany.

In 1830 the Bourbons were finally deposed from the throne of France. The way was now open to him to journey to France and present himself as the true Dauphin, but when he did so he made it clear that he was claiming not the crown but only his rightful position. Up to then both Louix XVI's uncle, Louis XVIII, and his sister, the Duchess of Angoûlème, had a vested interest in denying the claims of any Pretender. Their actions, and particularly those of the Duchess, suggest that both were aware of the possibility that the Dauphin had escaped from the Temple. In the case of one claimant, the Duchess had gone so far as to send him a questionnaire. This she would not do in the case of Naundorff. She and her uncle may well have known far more than we know today. Their apparent callousness in refusing even to consider the possibility that the Dauphin might still be alive, is put down to their desire to prevent the disruption of the Bourbon regime.

When in 1834 Naundorff journeyed to Dresden, where the Duchess of Angoûlème was visiting, she fled at once to Prague.

In Paris Naundorff was recognized as the Dauphin by Madame Rambaud, who had been the Dauphin's governess. She had no doubt of his identity because she found on him certain marks, a mole on the thigh in the form of a pigeon, triangular vaccination marks on his arm, a scar on his upper lip, which had been made by the bite of a rabbit, and his curiously shaped front teeth. She had been in daily charge of the Dauphin from his birth to 1792. When she wrote to the Duchess of Angoûlème stating that she recognized Naundorff as the Dauphin she received no reply. Both the ex-Minister of Justice Joly and Bremond, who had been secretary to Louis XVI, wrote to the Duchess asserting their belief in Naundorff. They declared that he had the words, the gestures, and the gait of Louis XVI, things which could not be imitated.

The Duchess did indeed make some attempt to inform herself about Naundorff, for she sent the Vicomte Larochefoucauld to interrogate him in November, 1833. He reported to his mistress:

"I at once betook myself to this person, who for some time past had been living quietly at some distance from Paris, and found myself in the presence of a man who undoubtedly bears a certain resemblance—taking his age into account—to the more careful portraits of Louis XVII, and possesses the general features of the Bourbon family. His behaviour was simple; he seemed in no way confused or self-conscious. I had given him notice of my visit.

" 'I do not know' I said when I met him 'with whom I have the honour to speak, and so far I can only regard you with the respect which I always feel for misfortune.' Then I spoke of the incident which had occurred earlier with Martin, and added: 'I have, Sir, devoted my whole life to the principles of legitimate succession, and I should have to reproach myself just as much if I lightheartedly accepted such an allegation as if I simply rejected it. As long as the truth of the circumstances which concern you is not proved to me as plainly as the existence of God, my loyalty and my political faith belong to Henri V (the Comte de Chambord) alone.

" 'I assume, Sir, that you are worthy of my entire respect, but I do not think that I should be worthy of yours if I were to adopt another manner of speech. It is of no importance to me what impression my words make on you. If I perform what I regard as my duty, it does not concern me whether I please or displease. I place myself at your disposal, Sir, not in the interests of Louis XVII, of whose (to me very doubtful) survival I know nothing. No, it is to give you the opportunity to prove your real identity with the person whom you profess to be.'

"Therewith I ended, and began to observe him, coolly and with grave attention. I repeat that his behaviour was deliberate and natural. His eyes were very penetrating; his features were calm and attentive, and showed neither self-consciousness nor over-eagerness. In the course of conversation he gradually became more animated; he understands French quite well, but often expresses himself somewhat clumsily.

"He shook my hand vigorously, and answered: 'What you say, Monsier le Vicomte, merits my entire respect. Something tells me,' he continued, laying his hand on his heart, 'that what I have been told is true, namely, that you are a man of honour. I offer you my entire confidence with the certainty that you will not abuse it, whatever may happen. I have been deceived in so unworthy a fashion that I have had to become more cautious; but with you I cannot be. The moment has come in which the decree of heaven will at last be fulfilled. I have been the victim of the most terrible persecution; I have much to complain of against my family. The Duc de Berry was the only one who attempted to contrive my recognition; he was murdered. My poor sister has been hatefully deceived; I will enlighten her; I wish even now to save the honour of my family.

" 'I will recognize Henri V. I protest against his attaining his majority at the age of thirteen, for I consider that this will be detrimental to the peace of France; I will merely claim the crown in order to set it one day on his head, and I desire that he shall be consecrated on the same day as I. Ah, it is hard today to wear a crown. I only demand it in order to obey the behest of heaven; for the moment I demand nothing more than a name and a family. But that I want at all costs.

" 'I am certain that my sister would recognize me after ten minutes talk; I propose that she should meet me; I demand it of her. Let her go to Dresden (from her place of exile in Prague) under some pretext or other. But if she is so unhappy as to refuse me, either of her own resolve or deceived by treacherous counsels—and may God protect me from this supposition—then my mind is made up. Woe to my family, woe to all those who have betrayed me. All their misdeeds will be revealed. My existence is known to all the sovereigns of Europe. (He became visibly excited.)

" 'I will place myself in the hands of the French Courts and demand a name which they will not be able to refuse me. Is that, Sir, the way a common felon would behave? Yes? Then let the court unmask him and let him spend the rest of his days in gaol. Yes, Monsieur le Vicomte,' he added with tears in his eyes, 'yes, I am indeed the son of the unfortunate Louis XVI, and the time is not far off when it will be proved. Take this book; it is the narrative of my unhappy life. I confide it to your sense of honour. It will tell you of terrible things. Excuse me, but I want my name, and it is time that justice were done. In three days I will see you again.'

"Madame will not find it easy to imagine the sort of dizziness which seized me nor to understand how I felt when I saw a man in this situation, speaking volubly about his family, which was none other than the Bourbons; about his sister the Duchess d'Angoûlème, and of the Duc de Berry, who had lost his life on his account; of Henri V, whom he was prepared to recognize and to have crowned and consecrated together with himself; of his protest against the circumstance of Henri's attaining his majority at the age of thirteen, etc., etc.

"My head and heart were in a maze, and yet, I must admit, there was nothing in his behaviour, in his tone, or in his manner of speech which suggested impudence or fraud, let alone roguery, and still less blackmail; it may be madness, monomania, an *idée fixe*, an obsession which has developed in his mind or been suggested to him . . . but he is so calm, so consequent, and so convinced, that one is almost convinced oneself.

"All this lasted about an hour and a half and I had to make an end. I took the book which he had offered me and said to him: 'I will read it attentively and doubtless with interest, Sir, but a statement is no proof, and you must allow me to say once again that proof is necsesary here, and proof of more than one kind.' 'It will not be wanting', he answered, 'I will furnish it whenever it is required; you can be sure of that.' So we parted. Since then I have seen him once again and have had the same impression."

Following his meeting with the Duchess's emissary, Naundorff sought a meeting with the Duchess herself in Prague but she refused to see him and left hurriedly before he arrived. Meanwhile the first attempt was made on Naundorff's life—he was stabbed by two men though not robbed. Why should an attempt have been made to assassinate an imposter, it has been asked?

Larochefoucauld wrote to the Duchess on 11 February, 1834, saying that he had again seen Naundorff and reporting "to be quite fair, I must add that the more one sees and observes the personage in question, the more one is tempted to see in him resemblances to the Royal Family and in more than one respect the mark of truth". And he declared that only Madame's own recollection and testimony could decide the man's identity. He warned her that the personage who claims to be Louis XVII proposes to hand himself over to the French Courts immediately and demand from them a name which could not be denied him if he possessed, as he claimed, indisputable proofs of his identity. But, the Vicomte pointed out, Naundorff was willing to refrain from this step if he had an answer from the Duchess.

The Duchess of Angoulême seems to have been in a quandary. When Madame Rambaud, the Dauphin's governess, went to Prague to see her in order to support Naundorff's claim, the Duchess of Angoulême procured an order to force her to quit the country. But thus refusing to listen to the one person who apart from herself could give infallible proof of Naundorff's identity, the Duchess of Angoulême at least shows that there was in her mind some great question about Naundorff. Everything indicates that she was afraid either to see Naundorff or to give him any chance to substantiate his claim. There seem to have been only two possible reasons for her behaviour, either she disbelieved he was the missing Dauphin, or she herself was an imposter, afraid of being unmasked. While she was in Dresden Naundorff's children, particularly his daughter who strongly resembled the female Bourbons, were pointed out to the Duchess but she refused to receive them.

Naundorff's first official move to substantiate his claim occurred in October, 1834, during the trial of the Baron Richemont, an imposter who claimed to be the Dauphin, who was being tried in Paris for fraud. Naundorff wrote to the Court asking for his claim to be tested. In after years Naundorff put forward the suggestion that Richemont and a number of others who claimed to be the Dauphin about this time were put up by his enemies to ridicule his claims by the very unlikelihood of theirs. Thus it was made to appear that a number of men, Naundorff included, were all trying to hoodwink the authorities.

On 13 June, 1836, Naundorff caused a summons to be delivered on Charles X, the ex-King of France, now that the Bourbon monarchy had been finally overthrown, and upon the Duchess of Angoûlème, demanding that they appear before a Civil Court in the Department of the Seine. Two days later Naundorff was arrested by the police and all his papers were confiscated. No reason was given for his arrest but his lawyer obtained a receipt for two hundred and two documents. By the decree of the Minister of the Interior he was expelled from France, and the documents he had collected to substantiate his claim were never returned to him, and have never come to light since. His arrest and expulsion were quite illegal and can only be construed as having been demanded from high quarters. Naundorff was deported and landed on the English coast.

In England, where he was known as the Duke of Normandy, one of the Dauphin's titles, Naundorff set to work to write the narrative of his life. When this was published in 1836 all the copies sent to France were confiscated at Calais and the French authorities in most European countries endeavoured to buy up copies and prevent their circulation. On 16 November, 1838, another attempt was made on Naundorff's life, when he was shot in the outdoor lavatory of his house at 21 Clarence Place. One bullet passed close to his heart but his life was saved. Later a Frenchman was arrested and charged with the attack. The next move of the French Government was to issue a totally unfounded statement that Naundorff was a Jew from Prussian Poland, a statement which the Prussian Government took the opportunity to deny categorically.

Living in England, Naundorff worked on the invention of a field gun and continued to try to get his cause brought before the French Courts. In May, 1841, another attempt was made on his life, his workshop being set on fire and he was badly burnt in an ensuing explosion. A year later another fire occurred and he barely had time to save his life. In November, 1841, Naundorff was arrested for debt and his furniture was sold and he was thrown into the debtors' prison. Released in 1845 he journeyed to Holland to try to sell his inventions to the Dutch Government. Before negotiations were complete he died there on 10 August, his death certificate describing him as Charles Louis de Bourbon, Duc de Normandie (Louis XVII), aged sixty, son of Louis XVI and Marie Antionette. At the autopsy the marks on his body, as remarked by Madame Rambaud, were recognized and noted.

The *affaire* Naundorff was by no means finished with in France. Naundorff's lawyer, Favre, continued the law-suit on behalf of his children, who it was claimed bore a remarkable likeness to the Bourbon family. Portraits show that his daughter was singularly like the Duchess of Angoûlème. In Holland his son was paid a large sum by the Dutch Government for his father's invention and he became an officer in the Dutch Army. By the Dutch Government the Naundorff family was officially accorded the name of Bourbon.

Julius Favre, afterwards a Cabinet Minister, continued as the advocate of the Naundorff family in France for over forty years and he has said in his reminiscences that he was quite convinced of the genuiness of Naundorff's claim. As Favre had access to government archives, to which of course he could not refer in Court proceedings as he learned them in his official capacity, his support is taken as another important step in the theory that Naundorff was the lost Dauphin. Portraits of Naundorff himself, and especially one drawn on his deathbed, show close resemblance to the Bourbons, and particularly to his presumed father and grandfather.

According to General de Larochejacuelin, documented in 1855, the Duchess of Angoûlème on her death bed in 1851 declared "my brother did not die: that has been the nightmare of my whole life" and she implored him to seek out the Dauphin and restore him to the throne of his fathers.

Because Naundorff was denied the opportunity of testing his claim before the Courts, we have no means of telling how strong it was. He certainly fulfilled many of the conditions required. He carried on his body marks known to have been on that of the Dauphin.

The great difficulty in any attempt to substantiate his claim lies in the vagueness of his story of the years between 1795 and his appearance in Berlin nearly twenty years later. While nothing of this period can be substantiated, his story of the vague wanderings from place to place, and imprisonments in dungeons without windows, is quite in keeping with the period of turmoil in Europe when armies were marching and counter-marching.

It may well be, as Naundorff maintained, that the Bourbon family were determined to resist his claim and set out to do everything in their power to prevent him making himself known. Louis XVIII and the Dauphin's sister were firmly secured on the throne and they may well have decided it was better both for themselves and France that the throne should remain in their hands and not be handed over to an inexperienced Louis XVII, however valid were his claims by inheritance. Naundorff's failure to establish his identity demonstrates the appalling difficulties that any claimant faces. It is virtually impossible, as history has so often shown, for any Pretender to substantiate his claim, especially when it is of Royal significance. It is virtually impossible to present convincing proofs, as has been shown by the recent claims of the woman in Germany who states that she is Anastasia, a daughter of the Czar of Russia, who is supposed to have escaped from the massacre at Ekaterinburg in July, 1918. It is far simpler to identify a dead body than a living one, as has been shown in a number of cases which have passed through the English Courts whereby pathologists have been able to identify a person perhaps from a few bones only.

We now pass to the third part of the great mystery, the identity of the Duchess of Angoûlème herself. This is even a more turgid tangle than what has gone before. In her lifetime no one suggested that the Duchess was anyone else but the daughter of Louis XVI, but almost immediately after her death the theory was put forward that she was a changeling and that the true Madame Royale had lived and died in secrecy in a castle in Germany.

The story starts in 1803 when a mysterious couple came to live at the little German town of Ingelfingen in Wurtemburg. The man was of striking appearance and the girl, although her face was thickly veiled, appeared to be beautiful. They were accompanied by a very superior manservant and arrived in a beautiful travelling carriage. They disappeared as suddenly and as mysteriously as they had arrived on the day that Napoleon's troops crossed the German frontier and seized the Duc d'Engien, who subsequently was executed. The mysterious couple received an express letter that morning. Their flight is believed to have been caused by fear of arrest.

We hear of them next in 1807 when the same couple and the same servant arrived in the Duchy of Hildburghausen, where the ducal Commissioner had booked a suite at the hotel for them and had given orders that when they arrived at midnight the rooms were to be brightly lit but no one was to be allowed to see them enter. While at the hotel the man received letters addressed to Vavel de Versay. Each afternoon he took the lady, who was always heavily veiled, out driving. After they had been at the hotel for some months the Duchess Charlotte intervened to procure them a house when the landlady was doubtful about letting it because of the very special demands that the couple made as regards secrecy.

In 1810 the couple moved five miles to the castle of Eishausen and there they lived in secrecy until the lady died in 1837 and the man in 1845. When the weather was fine the lady went into the garden, watched by the man at a window with a pistol. The procedure was always the same. The cook would open the garden door and stand behind it so that she could not see the lady and she took up that position again when the lady signalled with a handkerchief that she wished to return.

It was learned that the Count, as he was known locally, received large sums of money from Holland via a bank at Cassell and he made considerable gifts to local charities. Everyone wanted to know who they were but nothing could be learned. In 1812 an extraordinary friendship grew up between the Count and the local Pastor, Kuhner, who lived a hundred and fifty yeards from the castle. The friendship was to last for fifteen years. Yet they never met. Each day they communicated in a series of notes from one to the other. All the Pastor would say to inquirers was that the Count was a man of wide culture and great learning.

In 1826 a crisis developed when the Duchy of Hildburghausen was merged with the Duchy of Meiningen. The change of government made it necessary for the Count to produce "papers" to the police. He adamantly refused to do so and the demand was suddenly withdrawn on the intervention of the Duke. Throughout the sojourn of the couple at the castle it was clear that they enjoyed the special protection of the Duke who on one occasion declared that he had extended it to them from the very moment of their arrival in his dominions. It is believed that only the Duke and his Duchess knew their true identity. Inquiries from elsewhere were discouraged. In 1832 when the famous German criminologist Anselm Ritter von Feuerback came to the Duchy he was warned not to follow up his inquiries into the origin of the Count and the lady.

Year after year, the same routine was kept up at the castle, on fine days the couple were driven out in their carriage, the lady always heavily veiled. On one occasion a passer-by did see her without her veil and remarked on the strong resemblance of the lady to the Bourbon family. The cook at the castle, a woman named Weber, in the whole twenty-six years of her service, from 1809 to 1835, saw the lady only twice, on occasions when the Count was ill. When the lady died from a chill on 25 November, 1837, the Count told the doctor:

"My position now becomes more and more unbearable. This is not the separation of a married couple. It is more. It is the rending asunder of twins so closely bound to each other that one cannot live on without the other."

When he was asked to supply the name of the dead lady to the authorities he declared "no power on earth should ever make me disclose my secret. I shall take it with me to my grave." He said that the lady was not his wife, which if he had declared her to be, would have stopped all further inquiries. Finally pressed to supply her name he gave it as "Sophia Botta, spinster, bourgeoise, from Westphalia aged fifty-eight". While it is concluded that this was a false name, the age of the mysterious lady at her death, fifty-eight years, is believed to supply a possible clue to her identity.

The Count told the doctor that he had held a post in an Embassy in Paris and knew the Bourbons well, and he clearly sympathized with them. He declared that in 1803 he and the lady had journeyed to Vienna, where he had met the Czar of Russia, but he had been forced to keep the lady's presence secret.

Before he died on 8 April, 1845, the Count was seen to be hurriedly burning papers for days. After his death nothing was found bearing on the lady's identity. A passport and papers indicated that he was named Leonardus Cornelius van der Valck, that he was of Dutch nationality and that he had served in the French Army. In 1799 he had become secretary to the Dutch Legation in Paris and had left on a journey to Germany on 1 June. The discovery of a packet of letters, obviously from a dear friend, signed Agnes Barthelemy (wife of a French General from whom she lived apart), led to the belief that this was the lady's true name. This clue, howevern was found to be a false one when the death of Agnes Barthelemy on 28 February, 1827, was authenticated. Inquiries in Amsterdam proved that van der Valck came from that city and was a man of considerable wealth.

The death of the Count released throughout Germany a

wave of inquiry about the origin of the couple who had excited so much interest. A number of newspaper articles and novels were published suggesting a variety of identities. But all the people who were suggested as being the mysterious couple were accounted for by documentary evidence as having lived somewhere else and having died at quite different dates.

Bit by bit, however, small pieces of information did come to light. It was learned that der Valck had joined the French Army as a lieutenant in 1793 and had been a prisoner of war in England until 1797. He inherited great wealth in 1799. At the castle various small clues were found. Sacks of underclothing which clearly had belonged to the lady were found to be marked with what were apparently the Lilies of France. Amongst her possessions was a French prayer book printed in Vienna in 1756, a year after the birth of Marie Antoinette in that city. Was this the actual prayer book given to Madame Royale by her mother, on her birth in 1778, it was asked? It did not escape inquirers that if Madame Royale, the Duchess of Angoûlème, had died in 1837, she would have been fifty-eight years old, the age given for the mysterious Countess.

From this meagre information the theory was put forward that the mysterious lady was the true daughter of Louis XVI, a substitution having taken place in 1795, when Madame Royale was sent from France to Austria. Fascinating as the theory seems, there is not an iota of proof, and a very great deal to suggest that it is nothing more than a fantastic solution to what was without question a mystery about which no one, apart perhaps from the Duke and Duchess of Hildburghausen, knew anything at all. The chief support of the theory is the undoubted fact that the Duchess of Angoûlème was a person of quite different character from what is known of the young princess who left the Temple Prison at the age of seventeen. The strongest argument against the substitution theory is the utter failure of those who believe it took place to point to any moment on the Princess's journey to Austria when it could have happened. Added to that no one has ever been able to advance any reason why it might have been done.

None the less there are some strange facts to consider.

When the French Government agreed to exchange the Princess for French prisoners of war in 1795, Madame Royale was despatched in a carriage to Switzerland where the exchange would take place. Every stage of the journey is duly accounted for, and on 26 December she was formally handed over to the Austrian Ambassador, by whom she was conveyed to Vienna. The attendants who accompanied the Princess from Paris to Vienna knew her well. While they may have been in the plot it is strange that none of them in after life remarked or hinted at a substitution having taken place.

Substitution, if it did occur, could have happened only during a brief period when the Princess was driven up in a closed carriage to the house of a merchant outside Basle. She walked up the long drive, and as far as the records show she was immediately introduced to the Austrian Ambassador. One strange point upon which inquirers have picked is that the Princess refused to take with her the trousseau supplied to her in Paris and demanded that a Swiss costumier be sent to her to supply a fresh lot of clothes. It is suggested that this demand was made because the Parisian clothes would not fit the new Princess.

Attention to two other points as possible proof that a change was made is drawn by the protagonists of the changeling theory. In January, 1796, Madame Royale's aunt, the Queen of Naples, stated in a letter her fear that French scoundrels might attempt to hand over to the Austrians a young girl who was not the daughter of her sister. A few weeks later a story was printed in the *Gazette de France*, to the effect that after the Princess's arrival in Vienna "a young woman, an adventuress, or mad, declared that she was the French Princess, adding that the Princess who had recently arrived was a changeling". It was noted that the young woman had been arrested by the police, but nothing has ever been found in the Austrian archives to support this story.

Those who believe that the mysterious lady of the Castle of Eishausen was the Bourbon Princess, point to the great dissimilarity between the portraits painted of the Princess before her release from France, and those of the Duchess of Angoûlème after her return to France in 1814. The lady's nose in these pictures appears to be quite different. The Princess's nose is shown as being quite straight, while that of the Duchess was notably hooked.

After the Duchess's death in 1851, a number of hints were dropped by members of various Royal families in Germany that they knew well who the mysterious Countess was and that she might well have been a member of the Bourbon family.

Unquestionably some mystery surrounded the couple who lived so secretly at Eishausen. No one knew who the lady was. When a mystery cannot be solved the next step is to supply solutions which heighten it. The suggestion that she might have been Madame Royale seems a truly fantastic one, supported by no evidence. Still, there are some clues which appear to point to that identity. By the Count the lady was called "Sophie", the travelling name given to the Princess to cloak her identity in 1795, and the age of the lady at her death implied that she was born in the year 1778, the date of the birth of Madame Royale.

Did the poor little Dauphin escape from his prison in 1795? Was Naundorff he? Was the lady at Eishausen the true Madame Royale? Here are three great mysteries, the solutions to which we can only guess. They are fascinating subjects on which to ponder. The aggravating part is that we shall never know the truth with any certainty.

FORGOTTEN SCRIPTS AND SCROLLS

AT THE START of the nineteenth century our knowledge of the ancient world was largely confined to the Hebrew Books of the Old Testament which fortunately had been translated into Greek before the Christian era. From them information could be gained which indicated that great empires had waxed and waned on the banks of the Nile and the Tigris and Euphrates, which was strikingly corroborated by the vast pyramids and temples of Egypt and the mounds and ruins of Mesopotamia. Some of the writings of these ancient peoples could no longer be deciphered, little was known about them or about the antiquity of their civilizations. As a result Hebrew history gained a notoriety out of all proportion to its true significance.

Scholars guessed that the picture writing of the Egyptians and the wedge-shaped cuneiform of the peoples of Mesopotamia might enshrine long-forgotten secrets but no one could read them. How the keys to Egyptian hieroglyphs and the Semite, and even more ancient, cuneiform were found are romances of literary detection and they show the difficulties still to be overcome in the decipherment of several other dead languages. While the long-forgotten secrets of Egypt and Mesopotamia have been disclosed, those of the

Mayas, the Etruscans and the Easter Islanders still pose problems for which no solution is yet in sight.

No one knows when man first learned to write; his earliest attempts are still extant in the caves on the walls of which he painted pictures, his first attempt to perpetuate his thoughts. Paintings evolved into pictorial word signs and they grew eventually into phonetic alphabets in which each sign represented one or perhaps several sounds.

While it is possible to find the meaning of such sign sounds, if the language behind them is known, it is virtually impossible to do so if neither writing nor language is known, unless a bilingual key is found. That is what happened in the cases of the Egyptian hieroglyphics and the Mesopotamian cuneiform, but even then decipherment might not have been achieved, had we not known something of the history of these peoples and the names of many of their kings. These were the clues which gave a start to the decipherment of these forgotten tongues.

Even then it was largely a matter of trial and error. Each word sign had to be tested for probability, and the letters represented had to be considered for likely frequency on the known fact that certain letters recur far more than others. Then again there was the context of the text in as much as some inscriptions obviously referred to particular things. An inscription on a tomb, for example, would be likely to be laudatory and contain such phrases as "father of his people" and "king of kings", etc. If the inscription could be dated even approximately it might be possible to find the name of the actual king to which it referred. The signs for his name could therefore yield certain letters. Once these letters were established it was possible to build up an alphabet.

For half a century or more attempts were made to decipher the Egyptian hieroglyphs. This pictorial form of writing probably dated back to 3000 B.C. Almost all the examples of it found were carved in stone on temples and in tombs. It was a form of writing used by priests; the Egyptians possessed also two other methods of writing, the cursive script known as the hieratic, and the far more common demotic, both of which were found on papyri. Writing had developed in Egypt from pure pictographs to ordinary script, employing an alphabet system. But by the second century of the Christian era knowledge both of the hieroglyphs and of the more common cursive writing had been lost. When the Christians became all-powerful in the Roman world the

Egyptian temples were closed and the few remaining priests who understood the hieroglyphs disappeared. For nearly fifteen hundred years the story of ancient Egypt remained an impenetrable mystery.

When European scholars in the eighteenth century first attempted to decipher the inscriptions on tombs and temples it was noticed that certain words were contained in what is now called a cartouche, a circle which enclosed a word, suggesting that it was done to draw attention to a particular symbol as being of great importance, perhaps even a proper name. While this did not take the scholars very far it did at least pin-point certain words as proper names which, if the historical context could be found, might even yield the name itself. By trial and error it was found possible to translate certain of these names as those of kings of Egypt about which we knew something from Hebrew and Greek history.

Beyond that the scholars faced a complete impasse, until in 1798 a bilingual inscription was found in Egypt. During his invasion of Egypt Napoleon's engineers dug up a black basalt slab at a place called Rosetta in the Nile Delta. Three feet nine inches long by two feet four and a quarter inches wide and eleven inches thick, this slab carried three inscriptions, one of which was in Greek. When the British defeated Napoleon in Egypt, the stone was brought to England in 1802 and lodged in the British Museum where many attempts were made to translate the other two inscriptions and build up an alphabet.

The Greek inscription disclosed that the stone carried a proclamation in three languages made by Ptolemy V in 196 B.C. As the words in the Greek inscription could be read it did not seem an impossible task to translate the equivalent words in the other two inscriptions, one of which was in the hieroglyphs which the priests had used and the other in cursive demotic. But nearly twenty years went by before any great progress was made.

Dr. Thomas Young of Cambridge University, in 1819, pointed the way to the decipherment of the hieroglyphs, but their true meaning, and the building up of an alphabet from them, had to wait for the work of a Frenchman, Jean François Champollion. Champollion died in 1832, at the age of forty-two, but in his short life he was able to demonstrate that the hieroglyphs represented, not as had been thought merely things, but phonetic signs. He was able to recognize a number of proper names, such as Cleopatra and Alexander, and to build up the identity of over eighty hieroglyphic signs. He successfully demonstrated that other signs meant Rameses, the God Ra, and Tutmosis. This enabled him to establish the principle of the form of writing. From his work other scholars in France, Germany and Britain were able to identify all the other phonetic signs both in hieroglyphics and in the ordinary Egyptian script. As a result, by the end of the century it was possible to read all the great number of inscriptions found both written on rock and on Egyptian papyri.

Meanwhile other European scholars had been working for years on the decipherment of the Mesopotamian cuneiform. This is some ways was an even more difficult task than had been encountered with the Egyptian writing for, at that stage, there were far fewer inscriptions to work on. As time went on, and archaeologists worked on the banks of the Tigris and Euphrates, more and more hardened clay tablets, covered with wedge-shaped characters, came to light.

Two great names, both British, stand out in the story of the decipherment of cuneiform and the laying bare of the ancient history of Mesopotamia. While Henry Layard excavated the ancient sites of once famous and long forgotten cities, Henry Rawlinson made the first steps which led eventually to the decipherment of the cuneiform script. Between them they made known the history of one of the world's greatest civilizations, the original homeland of the Hebrews. At first it was thought that the city states of Nineveh and Babylon represented a purely Semitic civilization, but as great mounds of earth were excavated and as thousands upon thousands of cuneiform inscriptions were discovered, it was realized that the Semites, of which race the Hebrews were an off-shoot, were the successors of an even earlier Aryan people known to us now as the Sumerians. They flourished in the land of the two rivers some four thousand years B.C., and they gave way to the Semites who conquered them about the year 2000 B.C.

Eventually the Semitic Empires were conquered by Darius the Persian and in the fullness of time the great Persian Empire he established throughout the Middle East was conquered by Alexander the Great.

By the scholars who set out to decipher the cuneiform writing in the eighteenth century it was quickly realized that the cuneiform script had been used by many peoples and their inscriptions were in different languages, all using the same form of symbols or alphabet. Just as Latin characters had been employed by a number of different peoples, all in their own languages, throughout Europe, so cuneiform had for thousands of years been the form of writing in at least five different languages. None of these ancient languages was understood at that time but clues to their decipherment could be found in the modern languages of the peoples who still inhabited that area. The principle established that if the language was known the form of script could be deciphered was employed. If one of these ancient languages could be deciphered, it would lead eventually to the discovery of the meaning of the others, provided that somewhere inscriptions were found of a bilingual nature.

Since the sixteenth century European travellers had observed and noted a mass of inscriptions, with sculptured figures, high on a cliff at a place in Persia called Behistun, above the caravan road from Ecbatna to ancient Babylon. On a precipitous cliff three hundred feet above the road had been chiselled three separate inscriptions in old Persian, Elamite, and the even more ancient Accadian, together with a sculptured relief depicting a king overcoming what appeared to be rebels, in the presence of the Creator of the Universe, Ahura-Mazda. It was one thing to observe these inscriptions, quite a different matter to read them over or even to copy them. How Henry Rawlinson eventually climbed the cliff and spent years copying these inscriptions is one of the great stories of archaeology.

By the time Henry Rawlinson came on the scene in 1835, some cuneiform signs, those representing certain proper names, had been successfully interpreted by various European scholars. But without a known language, such as had been found on the Rosetta Stone, the task of interpretation was virtually impossible. Since the Behistun reliefs had become known in Europe in 1472 it was realized that in them might lie the key to cuneiform but it was considered that they were totally inaccessible, for those who had carved the inscription had taken care by cutting away the rock to make access to the narrow shelf above which the inscriptions lay virtually impossible. The travellers who had observed them for centuries from the road had put forward some startling theories as to what these sculptures represented, one theory suggesting that they showed the twelve Apostles.

Rawlinson, who was interested in ancient languages, joined the East India Company, and was sent to Persia in 1835. Like other scholars working on cuneiform inscription, he soon came to the conclusion that certain groups of signs represented proper names which could possibly be interpreted from what was known of the ancient history of the Aryans. By trial and error phonetic values were given to thirteen cuneiform characters. With this knowledge he journeyed to Behistun, and climbed the three hundred foot sheer rock precipice which brought him to a narrow ledge immediately below the inscriptions which covered an area one hundred and fifty feet long and a hundred feet high. The ledge was so narrow that it was barely possible to stand on it. He was able, however, to observe clearly that the sculptured figures represented a king, who wore a crown, his armed attendants and a number of captives whose necks were linked together.

The inscriptions he guessed represented three different forms of writing, probably the same message in each language. Before they could be deciphered they had to be copied. The first group of inscriptions, which he recognized as being in the old Persian tongue, were the most easily accessible and by the year 1836 he was able to make a copy of them and to identify certain of the characters, bringing up to eighteen the number known. One word, for example, which was easily identified, was the name of the city of Babylon, so familiar from the Old Testament.

Within two years Rawlinson, on a visit to England, was able to read a paper to the Royal Asiatic Society, in London, in which he gave a rough translation of the old Persian inscription which helped other scholars considerably in their efforts to decipher other cuneiform writing. Then for five years, from 1839 to 1844, Rawlinson was recalled to India while the Afghan War was fought. He was not able to visit Behistun again until 1847.

This time he came better prepared, bringing with him a ladder which he was able to support on the two-foot-wide narrow ledge and so to reach the upper portion of the inscription written, as he assumed, in the Elamite language. Crawling up the ladder day after day and perching at a precipitous angle he was able slowly but surely to make a copy in his notebook of the cuneiform signs of the inscription.

The third and final inscription represented a far more difficult and dangerous task; it necessitated the crossing both of an outcrop of rock and a chasm. To bridge the chasm he laid his long and wide ladder from one side to the other and crawled across. While he was dangling in space part of the ladder gave way and he was left with only the side from which the spokes stuck out on which to crawl over. Having reached the farther ledge he had to overcome a mass of overhanging rock before he could reach the final inscription. This was far beyond his own physical capabilities, but a young Kurdish boy succeeded in squeezing himself up a chimney in the face and driving in pegs at the top of the inscription from which was swung a cradle in which Rawlinson sat himself week after week while he took paper casts of the whole text, consisting of one hundred and twelve lines of cuneiform.

By 1850 Rawlinson had succeeded in copying the entire cuneiform inscription on the rock at Behistun and he made his work available to all the scholars in Europe who were working on cuneiform inscriptions. He himself, from knowledge of the old Persian tongue which he had gained from the native dialects of the area in which he was working, was able to ascertain the meaning of one hundred and fifty characters and the decipherment of some five hundred words in the inscription. Other cuneiform scholars made similar translations at the same time, and it was found that Rawlinson's translations were largely in agreement with theirs.

Meanwhile, Henry Layard had found the site of ancient Nineveh and better still a library of twenty thousand cuneiform books compiled by King Ashurbanipal. These included a number of dictionaries and phrase books which that king had collected to assist Semitic students of the even more ancient cuneiform languages. These books showed that the cuneiform writing had been invented by a people far more ancient than the Semites, the first clue coming from a tablet on which occurred the title of "King of Sumer and Accad".

Originally pictorial in origin, the cuneiform writing had been invented by a people known to us now as the Sumerians whose civilization and form of writing had been adopted by the Semites who conquered them. As more and more cuneiform inscriptions became deciphered it was learned that the Sumerians had been living in Mesopotamia from at least 4000 B.C., and they had founded a number of city states. About the year 2450 B.C. they had been conquered by a king whose name was Sargon of Accad and by the time of the great Semite King, Hammurabi, who lived about 2000 B.C., the ancient Sumerians had been absorbed into the new Semite civilization. At some period between three and two thousand years B.C. the original pictorial cuneiform had developed into wedge-shaped characters of phonetic meaning, being reduced from an original two thousand characters to less than six hundred.

When these cuneiform inscriptions were eventually translated, in all the languages used, they disclosed that the original Sumerians were people who possessed an advanced legal code, who had a system of weights and measures, who legislated for wage stabilization and price controls, undertook vast irrigation schemes, had a well-developed form of architecture and a deep understanding of both astronomy and mathematics. They knew that the day comprised twenty-four hours and the circle three hundred and sixty degrees. Their literature showed their beliefs in the original creation of order out of chaos, the original sinfulness of man, and the attempt of the gods to sweep man off the earth by prodigious floods. Their writings referred to commercial deals, marriages, contracts, historical events, myths, prayers and hymns, and gave a terrible human story of killings and conquests, battles and wars.

Most interesting of all, the decipherment of their writings disclosed that the stories that were well known from the Hebrew Books of the Old Testament originated thousands of years before the Hebrews adopted them as their own. When Abraham trekked with his flocks and herds from the City of Ur in Mesopotamia to Palestine he and his family brought with them epics and stories which had been current for two thousand years amongst both the original Sumerians and the Semite peoples of which the Hebrews were but a small tribe. The Garden of Eden, the land which lay between the Tigris and Euphrates, had been the common homeland of countless tribes and peoples who for centuries had been spreading over the area we now call the Middle East, and carrying with them the ancient legends and epics of a far older, and long forgotten people, the Sumerians. The word "Eden" was found to go back into the midst of antiquity, its meaning a "plain". The Book of Genesis was but a recapitulation of stories which had been told in Mesopotamia for two thousand years at least.

Thus, the decipherment of Egyptian hieroglyphics and Mesopotamian cuneiform had opened up knowledge of man's most ancient past, and they put into proper perspective the story of the Old Testament which up to then had been taken as representing the true history of man's origin.

Unsolved mysteries remain. Still undeciphered are the scripts of the Etruscans who lived in Italy before the Romans, the Linear A script of the Minoan civilization of Crete, the glyphs of the Mayas of Central America, and the odd pictorial signs of the Easter Islanders. To the Etruscan writing there is no clue, no bilingual inscription to unlock the secrets of the some ten thousand inscriptions known. Of the two cursive scripts used by the Minoans in Crete that of Linear B has been established to represent an archaic form of Greek, but the earlier script still eludes us. It is thought to have affinity with the oldest form of Egyptian hieroglyphic writing.

The secret of the Mayan glyphs was lost in the fifteenth century when the Christian Bishop of Yucatan, Diego de Landa, ordered the destruction of all the Mayan inscriptions. In his attempt to stamp out paganism he destroyed the history of one of the most curious and most fascinating of all ancient civilizations, one that flowered and matured during the first eight hundred years of the Christian era, without there being any knowledge of it in Europe.

There are now only three illustrated manuscripts of Mayan writing in existence but they show that the Mayas had achieved a knowledge of astronomy and of mathematics far superior to what was then known in Europe. There is still a possibility that these Mayan glyphs may be deciphered, for the Mayan language is still that of over a quarter of a million people living in Central America. If the glyphs represent a phonetic system they cannot long resist interpretation if the language in which they were written is known. On the other hand, if, as is possible, they represent an ideographic and not a phonetic system then the difficulties are insurmountable and we may never know the true meaning of the system.

The meaning of the Easter Island symbols, which represent men, fish and birds, became lost soon after the arrival of Europeans in the island. As there appears to be a strong affinity between these symbols and the early writing system found in China and India it is thought that the characters may have been brought to the island in the twelfth century when Polynesian voyagers reached that island in their slow progress across the Pacific. As the peoples of Peru, from where the original Easter Islanders probably came, possessed no written script, it seems unlikely that these symbols, if deciphered, would supply us with any greater information than is already known about the strange statues and their builders.

*　　*　　*

By the decipherment of these ancient scripts many problems have been solved, but no less intriguing mysteries remain. The true meaning, even the genuineness, of countless written documents is yet to be decided.

Of all modern manuscript finds the greatest problem surrounds the now famous Dead Sea Scrolls. The mystery surrounds the date of their composition. Why is it so important?

It is generally agreed that the ancient scrolls found in 1947 in caves at Qumran by the Dead Sea belonged to a Jewish monastic sect which had many similarities to the early Christians.

The sect's Founder was known as The Teacher of Righteousness, the Messiah of Israel, the Suffering Servant of Isiah, the "Son of God". He was fated to suffer and die for the atonement of humanity. He had been tortured and crucified by the "Wicked Priest" but he would rise from the dead, save the world, and sit in final judgment. He taught patience, humility, brotherly love, chastity, poverty, and the strict observance of the law. He founded a new faith, its rights, baptism, and a Messianic feast, in which he blessed bread and wine.

He might have been Jesus. The beliefs of his followers paralleled those of the Christians. Scriptural warrant was called in to prove him to be the Messiah and it was believed he would lead his people to victory in the final struggle of the last days to establish the Kingdom of Heaven.

But the Teacher of Righteousness lived a hundred and fifty years before Jesus. Of that vital fact the evidence seems irrefutable. If this is true, then the Christian Jesus was not unique; his teaching already had been declared by another. The rise of Christianity, which the Churches declared to be an act of Divine Inspiration, was no more than an episode in Jewish history.

While there is little doubt that this Teacher of Righteousness lived long before the Christian Messiah, how far he was to exact prototype of Jesus is a matter of violent scholarly argument. Much depends upon the interpretations of the scrolls which are often vague and uncertain in their meaning. The scholars who are studying them disagree widely. Only those who are deeply versed in Hebrew history, its metaphors and illusions, can understand them; the layman is perforce dependent upon their interpretations. Whom do we believe?

It is generally agreed that the scrolls represent the library of a sect who lived nearby in a monastery, the ruins of which have been found. Its sacred books were hurriedly hidden in caves when the Romans advanced down the Dead Sea in A.D. 68, in their operations to quell the great revolt of the Jews which culminated in the destruction of Jerusalem two years later. The monastery had been burned and Roman arrowheads have been found in its ruins. Coins establish the date. The scrolls found in 1947 were thus in existence in A.D. 68. Some books of the sect's library may have been found in the tenth century, for a Jewish writer of that period refers to the scrolls belonging to such a community which had existed in a cave near the Dead Sea.

Others survived in the dry atmosphere until 1947 when an Arab boy seeking his goats came upon them. The caves in which they were found have been thoroughly inspected by archaeologists who have established strong corroborative evidence in the form of countless fragments of pottery in which the scrolls were originally concealed. They have excavated the ruins of the monastery near which a cemetery containing a thousand graves has been found.

The ruined buildings must once have formed a structure a hundred and eighteen feet long and ninety-four feet wide, including a scriptorium, kitchens, and a bath for ritual ablutions. Coins and pottery found there in indicate that it was built between 103 and 76 B.C. and suffered an earthquake which ruined it. This must have been in the year 31 B.C. when an earthquake is known to have occurred in Palestine. Apart from the period of the earthquake, after which the monastery was untenanted for some thirty years, it was occupied by the community from at least 150 B.C. until A.D. 68. When the invading Romans reached the Dead Sea the Covenanters had barely time to dump their library in a cave before they were probably destroyed.

The scrolls consist of six books, the *Book of Isiah,* a *Commentary on Habbakkuk,* a *Manual of Discipline* (the rules of the Community), the *Apocalypse of Lamech,* and the *War of the Sons of Light with the Sons of Darkness.* These scrolls are now fully accepted as both ancient and genuine.

The great problem is the age of the scrolls, the date when they were written. This is deduced both by external and internal evidence. Scientific examination both of the material of the scrolls, which is parchment, and the linen in which they were wrapped, indicates that they were written somewhere between four hundred and fifty and fifty years before the Christian era. The examination of the language used and the texts and scripts employed suggest that they were written somewhere between 100 B.C. and A.D. 100. While these are wide margins, they indicate that the scrolls first came into being some time before the Christian era.

They are dated more accurately by what is said in the scrolls. The date of their initial composition is suggested by a number of references to outside events, or to people. These references are vague for obvious reasons. The sect appears to have been a persecuted community, needing to keep secrets from its enemies. Many passages in the scrolls suggest that the community at Qumran sequestered themselves away in a period of apostasy in order to keep their religious faith pure.

A further clue to the period in which the scrolls were written is found in a reference to foreign invaders of Palestine who are called the "Kittim", but whether these were Macedonians or Romans is still a matter of scholarly argument. The "Kittim" could be either Greeks of Alexander the Great or the various Roman invaders of Palestine.

How they are deduced to be the Romans is a fascinating exercise in literary detection. They are referred to in the scrolls as "swift and men of valour in battle" who "trample the earth with their horses and animals and from afar they come from the coasts of the sea, to devour all the people like a vulture without being satisfied". It is stated that they sacrificed to their standards and that their weapons of war are objects of worship.

We know from the works of the Jewish historian Josephus that the Romans set up their legions' standards in the Temple at Jerusalem after its capture in A.D. 70. On the other hand, it is pointed out that the reference to "animals" seems more likely to point to the elephants of the successors of Alexander but it is plain that as the Jews had a word for elephants they would have used it if elephants had been meant. It is thought also that the description of the invaders coming from afar applies more to the Romans who came from Italy than the Greeks who came from nearby. The Romans invaded Palestine three times, in 63 B.C. when Pompey took Jerusalem, in A.D. 6 when Judaea was made into a Roman province and again in A.D. 68 when the Romans reconquered Palestine. From these deductions it is concluded that the reference to the "Kittim" means the Roman invasion in 63 B.C.

The greatest argument about the dating of the scrolls surrounds the identification of the two figures, the Teacher of Righteousness and the Wicked Priest. Neither is actually named in the scrolls. While one theory finds in them the two Jewish leaders at the start of the great revolt against Rome in A.D. 66, Menahem and Eleazer, the far more likely theory places them in existence at least a century before. While the identity of the Teacher of Righteousness can never be established with any certainty, it seems likely that the Wicked Priest may have been the Jewish Priest—King Alexander Jannaeus. His period was one of internal revolt and religious controversy, and he introduced into Palestine the Gentile form of execution, that of crucifixion, the hanging of a man alive on a stake until he died of starvation or exhaustion. One of the books of the Qumran community credits Alexander with the introduction of this abhorrent foreign punishment.

The scrolls suggest that the community's own Master was put to death by the Wicked Priest as a rebel who had set himself up as the Messiah Priest in opposition to Alexander. Another scroll indicates that retribution for his persecution of the Teacher of Righteousness fell upon the Wicked Priest on the Day of Atonement. The only known catastrophe which occurred on that day is the capture of Jerusalem by Pompey in 63 B.C. If this interpretation is correct, it indicates that that particular scroll was written sometime after 63 B.C., probably about 41 B.C.

Josephus records the fate of the High Priest, Aristobulus II, who, after being arrested by Pompey, was poisoned in the year 46 B.C. His reign of three and a half years, between 67 and 63 B.C., was a period of bitter party strife. Another possible identification of the Wicked Priest is that he was Hyracanus II, the brother of Aristobulus, and he may well fit because the Jewish Talmud records that a man named Onias the Righteous, who may have been the Teacher of Righteousness, was stoned to death by his orders in 65 B.C.

These identifications are very vague and the reasons by which they are made are highly confused, requiring a deep knowledge of contemporary Jewish history, customs and controversies. The references, however, to the catastrophe which occurred the Day of Atonement and to the "Kittim" appear to establish that the scrolls were in existence and had been written sometime prior to 40 B.C. There seems little doubt that the Founder of the Community which took up its residence at Qumran was persecuted and martyred by the official priesthood of the Jews.

Attempts have been made to identify the community from what is known of contemporary Jewish sects. In the early days of the examination of the scrolls it was suggested that they might have been the Jewish Christians who survived the national disaster of A.D. 70 and who undoubtedly lingered on for some centuries in Palestine and Syria. The

115

chief objection to this theory, apart from the question of the date of the scrolls, seems to be that the community ceased to exist in A.D. 68. Added to that, the Christians were a missionary group, anxious to spread their doctrines, while the Dead Sea Covenanters were a monastic community who kept to themselves.

Another suggestion finds that the Qumran Covenanters were the Zealots, the extreme nationalists who fought against the Roman domination of Palestine. But the Zealots did not come into existence until A.D. 6. On the other hand, the Zealots were founded by two men, Judas of Galilee and a priest named Zadok, and it is known that the Covenanters sometimes referred to themselves as "The Sons of Zadok" by which, however, they probably meant the original Zadok, the founder of the priestly party in Israel many centuries earlier. The chief support for the Zealot theory is the discovery in the scrolls of an inscription of a dagger which almost exactly corresponds to the knife used by the extreme Zealots, and of trumpets which they are supposed to have blown at the start of the Jewish Revolt in A.D. 66. In this theory the Zealot leader Menahem is believed to have been the Teacher of Righteousness, the man who tried at the start of the Jewish Revolt to seize power from Eleazer, the priest who was in command in Jerusalem. Menahem was driven out and murdered.

The most likely theory of all identifies the community with the Essenes, a Jewish sect which flourished at that period and which is described by Josephus the historian, by the philosopher Philo of Alexandria and by the Roman historian Pliny. Undoubtedly they lived in much the same area as did the Covenanters.

Another theory is that they were a quite separate sect at a time when Jewish national and religious life gave rise to a number of different groups, amongst which we find the Zealots, the Essenes and the Jewish Christians. The first century B.C. and the first century A.D. were periods of considerable fragmentation in Jewish national life. There may have been many different sects, many small communities, which have been off-shoots from the Jewish national religion.

In the present state of knowledge and interpretation of the scrolls, all that can be definitely said is that they represent a community, a sect, which came into existence probably in the middle of the first century B.C. and were destroyed in the year A.D. 68. Their beliefs and practices were very similar to those of both the Essenes and the early Jewish

Christians. That is by no means strange, for the Jews at that time were beset by Messianic hopes, induced by their unhappiness at foreign domination. Many Jews believed the Last Days were at hand and searched their scriptures for support of their belief that in that final age the long expected Messiah would come to deliver them and exalt them to be the rulers of the world.

Whichever came first, the Founder of the Qumran Community, the Founder of the Essenes, or the Founder of Christianity, need not have drawn their ideas from each other, for these same ideas were current throughout Jewish life. That their beliefs and teachings were not dissimilar is not surprising for nearly all that the Teacher of Righteousness or Jesus announced, can be found in the sayings of the more enlightened Jewish Rabbis of that period. All were originally sects of Judaism.

As the matter stands mystery surrounds the Dead Sea Scrolls. Many years will go by before it is finally resolved and in the meantime controversy rages about their interpretation and their date. They represent a great challenge to Christianity, one of the greatest it has ever had to sustain. The idea that the Teacher of Righteousness preceded Christ, that there was a Teacher whose fire Jesus stole, is unpalatable to many. That possibility is the principal reason why controversy continues about the scrolls.

A GENTLEMAN OF SUSSEX

ALL THE civilized world now knows that the famous Piltdown skull is a fraud. That was established conclusively in 1953. When the discovery of the "Missing Link" was announced in 1912, a number of eminent scientists refused to accept "Dawn Man" as the Piltdown relics were claimed to be. From 1912 to 1949 their voices were submerged by vociferous acclamation for the find of the Sussex amateur archaeologist and solicitor, Charles Dawson.

To modern scientific knowledge it may seem incredible that the Piltdown "Ape-Man" was accepted in 1912 by people who should have seen at once that such an evolutionary freak was impossible; but at that time the evolutionists were expecting the discovery of just such an apparent link between man and ape. Charles Darwin had forecast in 1871 that the Missing Link would one day be found. The acceptance of

Piltdown man was largely wishful thinking in 1912. The scientists accepted him as genuine because they wished to believe. They were too credulous.

Some time about the year 1908, the date being strangely indefinite, Charles Dawson came into possession of parts of a human cranium found by workmen digging on the Barkham Manor Estate at Piltdown, Sussex. Dawson was the Steward of the Manor and on one of his visits he noticed workmen digging out what appeared to be ancient gravel near a road on the estate. Being a keen geologist, he asked them to look out for "fossils". Some weeks later the workmen excavated what they called a "coco-nut" which was broken up by their picks. They told Mr. Kenward, the owner of the Manor, who told Dawson, who rescued the pieces which he recognized as parts of an unusually thick human cranium, certainly very ancient because of the strata in which it had been found. Dawson's description of the find is as follows. He first explained that he had by chance lighted upon the existence of extremely ancient gravels left by the Sussex Ouse. He continued:

"I was walking along a farm-road close to Piltdown Common, Fletching (Sussex), when I noticed that the road had been mended with some peculiar brown flints not usual in the district. On inquiry I was astonished to learn that they were dug from a gravel-bed on the farm, and shortly afterwards I visited the place, where two labourers were at work digging the gravel for small repairs to the roads. As this excavation was situated about four miles north of the limit where the occurrence of flints overlying the Wealden strata is recorded, I was much interested, and made a close examination of the bed. I asked the workmen if they had found bones or other fossils there. As they did not appear to have noticed anything of the sort, I urged them to preserve anything that they might find.

"Upon one of my subsequent visits to the pit, one of the men handed to me a small portion of an unusually thick human parietal bone. I immediately made a search, but could find nothing more, nor had the men noticed anything else. The bed is full of tabular pieces of iron-stone closely resembling this piece of skull in colour and thickness; and, although I made many subsequent searches, I could not hear of any further find nor discover anything—in fact, the bed seemed to be quite unfossiliferous. It was not until some years later, in the autumn of 1911, on a visit to the spot, that I picked up, among the rain-washed spoil-heaps of the gravel-pit, another and larger piece. . . ."

Dawson appears to have shown these bones to a number of local people but it was not until early 1912 that he informed his friend, Doctor Arthur Smith Woodward, Keeper of the Department of Geology at the British Museum, a position he had held since 1901. He was regarded as the world's greatest authority on vertebrate palaeontology. Smith Woodward had known Dawson for a number of years in connection with various geological finds he had made in Sussex.

In the summer of 1912 Smith Woodward and another keen geologist, Father Teilhard de Chardin, a Jesuit priest who lived at Hastings, joined Dawson in his searches on the site. They were assisted by several other local amateur archaeologists. Almost at once a further startling discovery was made, part of a lower jaw or mandible, containing two molar teeth. Dawson describes the find:

"In a somewhat deeper depression of the undisturbed gravel I found the right half of a human mandible. So far as I could judge, guiding myself by the position of a tree three or four yards away, the spot was identical with that upon which the men were at work when the first portion of the cranium was found several years ago. Doctor Woodward also dug up a small portion of the occipital bone of the skull from within a yard of the point where the jaw was discovered and at precisely the same level."

Also in the gravel pit were found apparently strong corroboration of the great antiquity of the cranium and jaw, prehistoric animal bones and human tool artifacts, which dated the remains as some 500,000 years old. The cranium and jaw, which presumably belonged to the same individual, were fitted together, and from the reconstruction there emerged the skull of a single individual, a "man" whose brain case was human but whose jaw appeared to be that of an ape. The result was exactly the opposite of what scientists expected the Missing Link to be like: that a Missing Link would prove man's original ape-like affinities was an article of faith in the scientific world but it was expected that this Dawn Man would have a simian forehead and a man-like jaw. Piltdown man's combination of character-

119

istics was therefore the reverse of what was expected. This great palaeontological discovery left Piltdown man, if he was genuine, completely isolated in the broad stream of human evolution. He was a complete freak who destroyed scientific ideas of how man must have evolved.

None the less, on Doctor Smith Woodward's authority, Piltdown man was almost unanimously accepted as the long-sought-for Missing Link, as tangible and well-nigh incontrovertible proof of man's ape-like ancestry. He was a man who, while he had attained human intelligence, had not yet lost his ancestral ape-like jaw. From the strata of gravel in which he was found, supported by the bones of five prehistoric animals and the remains of human tools, he was assumed to have lived in Sussex some half a million years previously in the early Pleistocene Age. Charles Dawson's epoch-making discovery was announced to the Royal Geological Society on 18 December, 1912, and Dawson was accorded the high honour of having Piltdown man named after him as "Dawson's Dawn Man." Some scientists were sceptical: they declared that the finds at Piltdown represented an amazing coincidence, the discovery together of two individuals, the cranium of a fossil man and the jaw of a fossil ape. But no one doubted that the remains were ancient fossils.

The discoveries at Piltdown were not yet completed. On 30 August, 1913, Father Teilhard de Chardin found a human canine tooth in gravel which had been thrown out of the pit. This not only fitted into the mandible previously discovered but amazingly confirmed Smith Woodward's predictions of what Piltdown man's canine tooth would be like in shape, size, and in its amount of wear. X-rays confirmed that all the teeth, the two molars in the jaw and the canine tooth, were human. This was followed by the discovery in 1914 of a bone implement, the fossilized femur of an ancient elephant which had been shaped into a club head, the earliest known human tool. Then, in 1915, Dawson disclosed the discovery of yet another "Missing Link", the cranium bones of another Piltdown man, found two miles away in a field at Sheffield Park. This seemed devastating corroboration of the theory and many of the sceptics were convinced. The paradox of a Man-Ape was widely accepted and three hundred casts of Piltdown man were despatched to the Museums of the civilized world.

Dawson died, aged fifty-two, in 1916, and his great achievement was commemorated in 1938 by the erection and the official unveiling of a memorial stone by the pit at Barkham Manor, Sir Arthur Smith Woodward saying on that occasion it was erected "on the spot which the late Mr. Charles Dawson, F.S.A., found the fossil skull of Piltdown Man." Sir Arthur Smith Woodward died in 1944, and in 1948 his book *The Earliest Englishman* was published. Yet many world-famous scientists refused to be convinced, others remained sceptical, still others were puzzled. Many were unable to reconcile the paradox of a cranium of *homo sapiens* with a simian jaw.

The picture of man's evolution was by this time very different from what had been accepted in 1912. As well as the Piltdown skull, a number of other skulls had come to light. In 1857 Neanderthal man, in 1907 Heidelberg man, in 1891 and 1936 the skulls of the two Java men, and in 1938 Peking man. (Each find was named from the region in which it was discovered.)

Man and ape were now believed to have descended from a common stock, a common ancestor, which lived some 35,000,000 years ago. Millions of years elapsed before any creature existed to which the term "man" could be applied. The Proconsul skull found in Kenya is believed to represent the point of divergence between man and ape. About a million years ago there existed the *Hominidae,* a species which while it would eventually become man was not yet man. The skulls of a number of these pre-men have been found in South Africa and they show that their brain capacity was little more than that of a modern ape but, at the same time, they walked on two legs and had human teeth.

The first true men came into existence about half a million years ago, and they are represented by the Java and Peking skulls. They were brutish looking beasts who used tools and had knowledge of fire and they were probably an intermediate state between the more ape-like South African men and the *homo sapiens* who now began to develop in a primitive form.

Thus a mere 500,000 years ago was clearly far too late for a Missing Link, a Piltdown freak. However, it was thought that there had been isolated groups of men who developed differently, such as Neanderthal man with his strongly marked eyebrow ridges. Such a group separated from the common stock about 300,000 years ago, so that its later forms were less like modern man than the earlier. Some scientists believed that Piltdown man, with his curiously ape-like jaw was an extreme example of this difference in development, but others still clung to the belief that he was indeed the Missing Link.

The doubts which had beset scientists for forty years were to be cleared up by scientific tests which were not available in 1912. In 1948 the Keeper of Geology at the Natural History Museum, London, agreed that the Piltdown skull should be subjected to a number of tests. Doctor Oakley was to conduct a fluorine test which would disclose the relative age of the bones because it had been discovered that the amount of fluorine in fossils increased with geological age. His exhaustive tests were made and disclosed that the Piltdown cranium was that of a fossil man who had lived only some 50,000 years before at the period of the late Ice Age, when modern man was already fully developed, and that the jaw belonged to a modern ape. Both cranium and jaw had been deliberately faked to look like ancient fossils. Piltdown man was a fraud, a composite man created to deceive.

The faker, whoever he was, had planted prehistoric animal bones, which tests disclosed came from such widely separate parts of the world as Norfolk, Malta, and Tunisia, and a bone tool, which had clearly been shaped with a steel knife, as corroboration for Piltdown man's extreme age. The British Museum publication in 1953, which disclosed the findings of Doctor J. Weiner, Doctor K. P. Oakley, and Professor W. E. le Gros Clarke, says "it is now clear that the distinguished palaeontologists and archaeologists (who accepted the Piltdown skull in 1912) were victims of a most elaborate and carefully prepared hoax." They emphasized "the perpetration of the hoax appears to have been so entirely unscrupulous and inexplicable, as to find no parallel in the history of palaeontological discovery." As regards the staining of the bones they stated "The iron and chromate staining of the Piltdown jaw seems to us to be explicable only as a necessary part of the deliberate matching of the jaw of a modern ape with the mineralized cranial fragments."

Examination of the records of the Piltdown discoveries made by Dawson and by Dr. Smith Woodward disclosed a disconcerting vagueness both about sites and dates. It was difficult to discern just when and where the different pieces of the skull had been discovered and it was found impossible to determine the exact location of the discovery of the second Piltdown remains at Sheffield Park.

Who was the hoaxer? This has been fully discussed in two books both published in 1955, that of Dr. J. S. Weiner, entitled *The Piltdown Problem*, and that of Francis Vere which is called *The Piltdown Fantasy*. While he admits that final proof is lacking, Dr. Weiner suggests that the hoaxer was Charles Dawson. Francis Vere believed that Dawson himself was hoaxed and that the hoaxer intended that his fraud should be discovered early on. Dr. Weiner eliminates both Dr. Smith Woodward and Father Teilhard de Chardin from any question of duplicity, but it is clear that both men were far too easily convinced. Smith Woodward was too gullible and far too eager to believe in Dawson's Piltdown find.

Dr. Weiner says:

> The great success of the Piltdown hoax came from the clear conception on the part of the perpetrator that a man-ape of the right age appearing in the hitherto unknown gravel had a good chance of deceiving the palaeontological world. He planned and worked to admirable effect to provide a man-ape at Barkham Manor which would stand up to recurrent criticism, and so furnish him with an antique milieu as it would be stocked with the appropriate animal fauna and man-ape's tools. He was able to stage a second, if paler version at Sheffield Park."

Though the hoaxer was extremely resourceful and knowledgeable, he showed many weaknesses. In his staining of the bones to give a fossilized appearance he used bituminous Van Dyke brown rather than iron salt, a mistake fatal to the authenticity of his find. Then, to refute scepticism, he brought to light his too-convenient find of a second Missing Link two miles away from the first. The forger, thinks Dr. Weiner, was saved from immediate exposure partly by good luck but chiefly because of the eagerness of many scientists to accept the validity of his discoveries. By his finds of bones of prehistoric animals and the tools of ancient man he tried to add proof upon proof of Piltdown man's antiquity.

The three principals involved in the Piltdown discovery were all men of established reputations in the world of science. Dr. Smith Woodward and Teilhard de Chardin were both scientists of the utmost integrity. By Dr. Weiner both men are absolved from any complicity in the Piltdown fraud. Charles Dawson was an amateur antiquarian of high standing and a man of long and successful professional career, known to Smith Woodward since 1891. Dr. Weiner points out that the spot on Barkham Manor was easily accessible to a forger who could have placed his finds without being noticed and he suggests that there were a number of other men, keen local antiquarians, who might have had opportunities to deceive both Smith Woodward and Dawson.

The forger, points out Dr. Weiner, must have been a man of remarkable attainments and knowledge. He must have been closely acquainted with gravel formations, understanding of archaeological matters and with considerable palaeontological experience. He knew how to ante-date the tools he deposited before the supposed period of Piltdown man's existence and he placed in the pit animal bones appropriate to that period. He must have had the cranium fragments in his hands by 1908, and he could easily have obtained an ape's jaw from some taxidermist. He was clearly in close touch with the gravel pit and he was fully conversant with the necessity for additional corroboration of the discovery, to refute various points of scepticism as they arose. He knew that, given a gravel terrace believed to be older than that in which Heidelberg man had been found, the appearance of an ape-man in such a strata would be acceptable to the scientific world.

Dr. Weiner considers that the hoaxer was a man of extraordinary talents, an expert palaeontologist and geologist highly adept in chemistry, in human anatomy, and in dentistry. He knew the potential significance of an apparently Lower Pleistocene or Upper Pliocene gravel deposit and he knew with what kind of animal fauna to stock that deposit. He knew what type of tools an ape-man might have been expected to have used. Knowledge of the discovery of previous skulls would have been a guide to the probable features of a Missing Link but perhaps his most brilliant idea was that of abrading the teeth, an inspiration he might have derived from the jaw of Heidelberg man. It is significant to the fraud that the canine tooth turned up only when experts had decided what it would look like, and that the chin region of the jaw had been broken off and lost, to prevent recognition of its essential ape-like characteristics. The hoaxer was aware that fossil remains were often iron-stained, and he set out to give evidence of this condition.

The perpetrator of the hoax combined boldness and perseverance with his knowledge and he must have had a compelling motive for his fraud. The sequence of his finds were carefully timed. What may have been the hoaxer's motive, questions Dr. Weiner. Was he trying to score over his colleagues? Had he a mad desire to assist the theory of evolution by finding the Missing Link? Did he try to satisfy personal ambition by being the discoverer of that Missing Link? Or was he himself the victim of an associate, perhaps a blackmailer, an unhinged evolutionist, or a man of overwhelming ambition?

Dr. Weiner has found a number of circumstantial grounds to suggest that Dawson himself was the hoaxer. He was associated with all the discoveries, and he was conversant with every stage of discussion and enquiry. He would have known just what to find, when and where. He had complete access to Barkham Manor, and he was fully trusted by Dr. Smith Woodward. Above all, Dawson had the necessary knowledge and experience with which to perpetrate just such a fraud. It seems significant, too, that none of his discoveries was carefully documented and recorded at the time.

Visiting Sussex, Dr. Weiner found apparent corroboration for the belief that Dawson was the hoaxer. In the cabinet of fossils, which had belonged to a long dead local antiquarian named Harry Morris, was found a flint which Morris described on a card as "stained by C. Dawson with intent to defraud". Morris referred to Dawson as an impostor and had declared that the canine tooth which was found at Piltdown had been imported from France. "Watch C. Dawson," Morris had written. But Morris, a bitterly disappointed man because his own discoveries of ancient flints had been rejected by the recognized authorities, may have been actuated by spite, by jealousy of the success of his rival antiquarian.

Several other local antiquarians told Dr. Weiner that they believed at the time that the Piltdown discoveries were frauds. A Captain Guy St. Barbe said that in 1912 he had gone into Dawson's office and found him staining bones, his desk covered with crucibles. Both Captain Barbe and Major Marriott, Governor of Lewes Gaol in 1912, had believed that Dawson was "salting the mine". Another archaeologist, A. S. Kennard, declared that he had always known who the true perpetrator of the fraud was, but he was not Dawson.

Dawson had not been highly esteemed in local Sussex archaeological circles. Though buttressed by the weight of expert authority, his Piltdown discovery had not been widely accepted in Sussex, and in fact the local Sussex archaeological society had largely ignored Dawson's Piltdown finds. These doubts may have arisen from other causes. In Sussex archaeological circles Dawson was called "the Wizard of Sussex", by reason of his many spectacular discoveries in different archaeological fields. He was noted for his extravagant suggestions, such as his discovery of a new race of Eskimos from one bone, and his siting of a supposed sea-serpent in the Channel in 1906.

Two particular aspects of his career had come in for much local criticism. It was declared that Dawson's *History of Hastings Castle* had been largely drawn from an earlier work without due aknowledgement. He was believed to have double-crossed the Sussex Archaeological Society by his personal acquisition of a house which they were nego-tiating to buy as their headquarters. It was declared that Dawson had used his membership of the society to buy the property for himself. Clearly there was considerable local animosity and jealousy against Dawson in his lifetime, but that did not prove he was the perpetrator of the great Piltdown fraud.

If Dawson was the hoaxer, what exactly did he do? There seems little doubt that there was about 1908 a genuine find of a fossil skull, some 50,000 years old, in the gravel pit at Barkham Manor. The evidence of the owners of the Manor make this clear, and that Dawson was told about it and was given the cranium remains by the workmen. The alternative theory seems to be that, while he was given some such skull by the workmen, he switched it with some other skull which he had carefully stained to look ancient.

In his favour is the fact that undoubtedly he informed Smith Woodward of his staining of the bones, which in his belief would harden them for preservation. It is pointed out by Dr. Weiner that the gravels at that spot are not fossil-iferous and that a genuine neolithic skull would not there-fore have required staining. It cannot be proved that Dawson switched his own specially treated skull for the one the workmen probably found, which would incriminate Dawson without question, but it has been suggested that he had been given a locally-found skull, significantly lacking a jaw, in 1906. Dr. Weiner points out that the fraud took four years to develop, therefore the plot must have been hatched in 1908, long before either Smith Woodward or the Jesuit priest came on the scene.

Dr. Weiner declares that Dawson's actions coincide sur-prisingly with those of the perpetrator, especially in his reported use of bichromate for staining in the winter of 1911-12, that shows identity of practice with that necessary to further a fraud. If Dawson's activities were entirely in-nocent they were yet quite complementary to those of the culprit. Dr. Weiner points out "where Dawson had superadded the chromate, mistakenly for hardening (the cranium bones), the perpetrator had done this deliberately as part of the staining of fossils which needed no hardening".

If Dawson was completely deceived and was the victim of someone else there are many curious circumstances to be accounted for, such as the luck of the improbable find of Piltdown man II in the ploughed field two miles away from the first find, which added such tremendous corroboration for belief in the Missing Link. Doctor Weiner suggests that Dawson's activities at the sites seemed to have served the purposes and timing of the perpetrator uncannily well.

If, asks Dr. Weiner, Dawson believed the finds at site II to be genuine, why did not he give Smith Woodward precise details of their discovery? Dawson's omission and inaccuracies in the recording of his discoveries shroud the early history of his finds in complete obscurity, perhaps intentionally. If Dawson was the victim of another, perhaps an unwilling accessory to the fraud, why did he tell Smith Woodward about the discovery at all? If he knew he had been hoaxed, why did he go on with the hoax? As Dr. Weiner points, out, we find Dawson admittedly doing, apparently by sheer co-incidence, the same kind of things as the perpetrator, and therefore he helped the fraud inadvertently.

If Dawson was a victim, innocent or otherwise, this leaves an unknown figure in the background, the true hoaxer, whose name has never been disclosed. Of this unknown man Dr. Weiner says: "He has Dawson under the closest surveillance for very many years, the unsuspecting victim for no less, perhaps, than seven years, alternatively as his unwilling accessory for three years. In two features he is outstanding— his amazingly intimate and detailed knowledge of Dawson's interests and affairs and his complete grasp of geological, evolutionary, archaeological and faunistic potentialities of both the Piltdown sites." This shadowy figure came to share Dawson's appreciation of the possibilities of the local Piltdown gravel, as the graveyard of the prehistoric man. He was aware of Dawson's instructions to the workmen to look out for fossils and he had unrestricted access to the site and the ability to obtain the necessary specimens with which to salt it. He was absolutely certain that his victim, Dawson, would take the bait. Then he held back the discovery of the jaw until the interest of the British Museum was assured. He then made three further discoveries at just the right moment to substantiate the find and refute criticism; criticism about which he must have known intimately. Each stage of the

127

fraud, from beginning to end, places Dawson in flagrant possession of faked material. The extreme astuteness of the forger is disclosed by his knowledge and skill by which he set out to out-manoeuvre the scholarly doubts as they arose by further piling of proof upon proof of the authenticity of the original discovery.

Francis Vere considers that Dawson was the innocent victim of another's fraud, a hoax which it was intended would be disclosed early on. Mr. Vere believes that the hoaxer set out to take the apostles of evolution down a peg, and he thought that his trick would be eventually discovered. But his great joke on the scientists misfired because, to his amazement, it was completely accepted. The hoaxer wished to see his hoax disclosed, otherwise his great leg-pull of the scientists would bring him no amusement. He did not appreciate that Dr. Smith Woodward, by the secrecy with which he surrounded the Piltdown remains, would prevent their critical examination by specialized scientists.

The hoax failed to be disclosed because the other scientists were shown only the casts made of the Piltdown skull, not the original bones and jaw. The experts were too bewitched by the belief of a Missing Link, which they wanted to find, to examine the Piltdown finds critically and objectively.

The hoaxer, Mr. Vere thinks, decided to finish off the hoax with the discovery of the second Missing Link at Sheffield Park. This he thought was more than anyone could possibly stomach, the extraordinary coincidence of there being two Missing Links within two miles of each other. The scientists, he thought, would surely be struck with the impossible coincidence of a piece of bone and a molar in one place which fitted a cranium and a jaw in another place two miles away. There is no doubt now, Mr. Vere suggests, that the bones found at Sheffield Park belonged to the cranium found at Barkham Manor. But how stupid were the scientists not to notice it? The hoaxer was unmercifully pulling the legs of eminent scientists, but they refused to notice that their legs were being pulled.

Dawson, Mr. Vere suggests, made a genuine find of an ancient cranium in the gravel pit at Barkham Manor. He told his friends of his discovery and one of them decided to play a trick on him by planting corroboratory finds and by switching Dawson's cranium with another which he persuaded Dawson to harden by staining. Who this hoaxer may have been Mr. Vere does not say, except to stress that he must have been one of the local enthusiasts who assisted

Dawson, and later Smith Woodward, in the digging at the pit. He was a man who had access to collections of fossils, both human and animal, and tool remains. Dr. Smith Woodward, thinks Mr. Vere, was an enthusiast, who suspected nothing. If the hoax had been perpetrated by Smith Woodward it would have been far more skilled, and it is unlikely that it was perpetrated by the great scientist who would have known that after his death it must be exposed when the fragments came into the hands of other people who could examine them carefully.

Dawson, thinks Mr. Vere, would never have dared to have perpetrated such a fraud, the disclosure of which would have been fatal to his reputation both as an amateur archaeologist and as a solicitor. If he had been the perpetrator he would never have told Smith Woodward of the staining of the bones to harden them. He lacked the necessary skill in dentistry to fake the wear of the teeth. He could never have known that Smith Woodward would, inadvertently, support his fraud by his prevention of the critical examination of the specimen by other scientists. Mr. Vere points out that Dawson's many friends were shocked at the accusations made against him.

The attitude of the Sussex Archaeological Society told against him, and this led to the belief that he was himself the hoaxer. Mr. Vere presents some evidence to support his suggestion that Dawson was himself hoaxed. He discloses that a local schoolmaster and scientist, Robert Essex, was shown by a clerk in Dawson's office a jawbone which had been brought, the clerk said, in Dawson's absence by one of the diggers.

Mr. Essex declares that this jawbone had three molar teeth and was not the one subsequently put forward by Dawson as the one found in the pit. This Mr. X, who brought the jawbone to Dawson's office and took it away again when he found that Dawson was in court, was observed to be looking for something which he said he had lost at the Barkham Manor site, but he would not tell anybody what he was looking for. Mr. Vere considers that X was looking for the real jawbone which belonged to the genuine fossil cranium found by the workmen in the pit after he had substituted an ape's jawbone in its place in the gravel. He had put down the real jawbone and forgotten where he had laid it; it probably eventually was destroyed. Then having given the original fossil cranium the jawbone of a modern ape, which he had stained to look ancient, Mr. X added to his hoax by the addition of the faked articles and bones which he threw into the pit when no one was looking. Mr. Vere considers it significant that Mr. X had been in the Dordogne district of France where just such tools as an elephant's femur have been found. Mr. Vere adds substance to his theory by suggesting that if a genuine cranium was found in the pit, which seems completely certain, there must have been a genuine jaw bone belonging to it. Why wasn't it found?

The mystery of who was the Piltdown hoaxer is complete. It will probably never be proved if Charles Dawson was the faker, or whether, as Mr. Vere so strongly suggests, he was himself the victim of a hoaxer. If Dawson was the hoaxer he succeeded probably beyond his wildest dreams. If Dawson was himself deceived, then the hoaxer was a wildly disappointed man, denied his last laugh. Instead of making eminent scientists look ridiculous, his hoax made them into popular heroes. Mr. X, unless he lived until 1953, was denied his fun.

Piltdown man is now removed from the line of human evolution. The great freak has been destroyed, but he leaves with us one sobering thought. The astounding credulity of those who are determined to believe what they want to believe.

RUMOURS OF MONSTERS

EARLY IN the nineteenth century the celebrated French naturalist, Baron Georges Cuvier, stated categorically "there is little hope of discovering new species of quadrupeds."

In the last hundred years many hitherto unknown land animals have been discovered: the okapi, the pygmy hippo, the komodo dragon, the white rhinoceros, the zebra, the king cheetah, the giant panda, and dozens of smaller ones. The first platypus skin received in England from Australia was called a fake. The coelacanth, believed extinct for seventy million years, has been found very much alive in the Indian Ocean. Thousands of square miles of land remain unexplored and no one can foretell what the depths of the ocean may disclose. The fictional "Lost World" of Conan Doyle's story may yet prove to be fact.

The Yeti, the Abominable Snowman of the Himalayas, and the Loch Ness Monster may be survivals from the prehistoric past. It is not impossible that a giant ape man or man ape and a great reptile may have survived, though the existence of neither can yet be proved. Scepticism is as foolish as blind belief.

There are vast unexplored areas in Central Africa, the basin of the Amazon, the deserts of Australia, the forests and swamps of New Guinea and Sumatra, and in the mountainous Himalayas, where little pockets of ground may hide "living fossils" or "missing links" which may be eking out a precarious existence undisturbed by their natural enemies from which they fled perhaps hundreds of thousands of years ago. Animals believed to be extinct, or never even imagined by man, may in fact exist in such areas.

The natives tell stories of giant apes living in the jungles of New Guinea, an island as large as France and Italy combined. Before we dismiss such rumours as absurd, let us not forget that the gorilla, a legendary animal to the Greeks, was not proved to exist until 1870. The giant panda of China was heard of first by the outside world in 1870; none was captured until 1936. Scientists dismiss the Loch Ness Monster as a joke but its existence is well authenticated in local folk-lore. The Sherpas of Nepal have told stories of the Yeti for sixty years at least; its footprints have been seen and frequently photographed since 1951. Some Europeans have claimed to have seen it from a distance.

Zoologists declare that it is quite possible that some animals which became too specialized to survive amidst the hurly burly of "natural selection", the struggle for survival, may have taken refuge in deep forests, swamps and the mountainous areas of the earth. Having adapted themselves to such conditions they may have lived on, unknown to the scientific world. To authenticate the existence of unknown animals a particular pattern of events usually is followed. Stories of natives are at first dismissed as pure imagination; travellers' tales are scoffed at; bones and skins are declared to be fakes. Then finally an actual specimen refutes disbelief. The natives' stories are found to be based on fact.

The existence of a large biped, known as the "Snowman" and the "Yeti" of the Everest region of the Himalayas is well authenticated. But what is it, a langur monkey, a bear, or an unknown cousin of man, half ape, half man? It is a riddle of the twentieth century and the very fact that it may be a cousin of man, perhaps the long searched for Missing Link, increases the excitement of the chase.

The Yeti has been news since 1953 when, after the conquest of Everest, Sir John Hunt and his party brought back clear photographs of its tracks in the snow. He himself had seen similar tracks in 1937 and so had a number of other European mountaineers. Col. W. A. Waddell observed similar footprints in 1887 and he records Sherpa stories of the animal in his book, *Adventures in Himalaya*, published in that year. From the time of the first attempts on Everest in 1921, rumours of the Yeti percolated into Europe. Such famous mountaineers as Eric Shipton, Frank Smythe and H. W. Tilman, brought back pictures of the tracks in the snow and recorded Sherpa stories of the strange beast.

The only concrete evidence of the existence of the Yeti are its footprints. They are clearly made by a biped which walks or runs, placing one foot in front of the other. The prints disclose a foot between twelve and twenty inches long, a human, not an anthropoid foot, for it is not adapted for tree climbing. Its toes are close together like those of a man but it has a big toe which is "opposable" like a human or anthropoid thumb. The footprint is like that of the ancient prehistoric cave man. It is neither completely ape nor typically human. Man's feet show that members of the human race were never tree climbers, like the anthropoids. While the Yeti's foot suggests that its ancestors may have been tree climbers, it is far more human than anthropoid. One thing is clear. The footprint found in the Himalayas is not that of a langur monkey or of the Himalayan red bear. Photographs of these animals' footprints show striking dissimilarities to that of the Yeti.

According to the native peoples of the Himalayas, many of whom have seen Yetis quite close, it stands and walks upright on its hind legs, which no anthropoid ape or bear does for any length of time. It has a white face, a body covered with thick coarse hair, sometimes dark, sometimes reddish, thick bowed legs, arms which reach to the knees, and toes which turn inwards. It has a strikingly pointed head. The Yetis appear to be very strong and agile and they make a loud yelping cry.

The animal is believed to live in caves in most inaccessible parts of the Himalayas, and it is seen usually only at night. It is shy, elusive, but of great intelligence and is not aggressive to humans. It exists in the wild area on the borders of the snow line and has been seen as high as 19,000 feet and as low as 13,000 feet. It lives on lichens and small rodents, and comes near to human habitation only when driven by hunger. Significantly it disembowels animals before eating them, which amongst the animals only humans do. All the natives declare vehemently that the Yeti is neither a langur monkey nor a Himalayan red bear, both of which they know well. Langurs hibernate, the Yeti is seen frequently in winter. Bears are gregarious, the Yetis are usually seen alone.

One Sherpa story, recorded in 1949, is as follows:

"A squat, thick-set creature, of the size and proportions of a small man, covered with reddish and black hair. The hair was not very long and looked to be slanting upwards above the waist and downward below it: about the feet it was rather longer. The head was high and pointed, with a crest of hair on the top: the face was bare, except for some hair on the sides of the cheek, brown in colour, not so flat as a monkey, but flatter than a man, with a squashed-in nose. It had no tail. The Yeti stood slightly stooping, its arms hanging down by its side. Its hands looked to be larger and stronger than a man's."

Other Sherpa stories indicate that the Yeti is far larger than a man, and it is possible that there are either two species of Snowmen or observers have seen both adults and young.

Other Yeti stories are told by Europeans.

In 1941 five Polish prisoners escaped from a Soviet labour camp in Siberia. They crossed Mongolia, Sinkiang and Tibet, and in 1942 they crossed the Himalayas near the frontier of Sikkim and Bhutan. They saw some animals moving in the snow in the distance and when they came closer they observed two creatures only twelve feet below them.

One of these Poles, named Rawicz, who described his escape from Siberia to India in a book called *The Long Walk*, says:

"They were massive creatures nearly eight feet tall and standing erect. They were shuffling around on a snow-covered shelf. They looked at us and were quite indifferent. They certainly were not frightened."

The party watched the animals for over two hours at close range. One was slightly smaller than the other and they decided that they must be a male and a female. They described their faces and heads as being squarish, the shoulders sloped sharply to a powerful chest with long arms which reached to the knees. They held their heads erect. They were covered with long loose straight hair of the colour of rusty camel. They just stood together and moved around like people admiring the view.

The animals seen by the Poles were clearly not bears. No monkey would have held its head so straight as did these Yetis. This suggests that the Yeti is a biped of long standing, one which has been used to standing upright and walking on two legs for a hundred thousand years.

Another European encounter with Yetis in 1948 has been described by two Norwegian prospectors named Thornberg and Frostis. They report that while working in the Zemu Gap, they saw two apes with brown hairy backs and human shaped heads. They looked like medium-sized men and according to the Norwegians these Yetis had tails, which no other eye-witness has described. When a gun was fired they made off in great fear. It seems possible that the animals the two Norwegians saw were bears. The fact, too, that one of these animals attacked the Norwegians suggests that they could not have been Yetis, for there is no recorded instance of an attack by one on a human being.

In 1954 the London *Daily Mail* sent an expedition to the Himalayas to search for the Yeti. Its members saw and photographed a number of "Snowman" tracks but they never caught sight of a Yeti. Their most remarkable achievement was the discovery of several "Yeti" scalps preserved in certain Buddhist monasteries in Tibet.

The lamas told the scientific members of the expedition that records existed showing that the Yeti had been known for centuries. They had been seen by a number of monks on different occasions, frequently quite close. They were allowed to examine and photograph these scalps, which of course they were not allowed to take away. None of the scalps they were shown agreed in any way with scalps of either langur monkeys or bears. One such scalp was reputed to be about three hundred and fifty years old. Members of the party were allowed to remove several hairs and to send them to London for analysis. It was reported that the scientists were completely unable to identify them with any known animal. One scalp was 7½ inches high, 9¾ inches long and 6¾ inches wide. Its length from back to front over the crown was 17¼ inches and the circumference of its base 26¼ inches; all these measurements are far larger than those of an average man's scalp. The hairs which remained on the skin were extremely stiff and bristle-like; in colour they were a foxy red. The hair sloped backwards from the forehead and slightly downwards along the side as in the case of a man. The most extraordinary of all the features was the crest or "keel" which ran from the base of the forehead straight upwards over the crown and down the back. It was an inch wide and covered with bristle-like hairs which sloped inwards from each side so as to meet in the centre and form a crest.

This crest or "keel" has given rise to considerable scientific controversy. In fact, it seems a clear implication of the original nature of the Yeti. Nothing like it is known on any anthropoid ape or animal. It is possibly a unique feature of a giant biped, quite unknown to science.

The members of the *Daily Mail* expedition were told that mummified bodies of Yetis existed in inaccessible monasteries in Tibet. Unfortunately, Tibet is now a closed area to western scientists and it may be many years before these rumours can be checked. So far western observers have been able to carry out researches only on the southern slopes of the Himalayas, whereas the final solution to the mystery may lie far to the north in country quite inaccessible, both politically and on account of its mountainous nature. To track the Yetis to their lairs would take a vast expedition organized on a national scale which might have to spend months, perhaps years, in a huge area before they even saw a Yeti close to, far less being able to capture one.

What is the Yeti or Abominable Snowman as it has become named in popular thought? The natives' stories, collected together, suggest there are either two types of Snowman, one very large and standing eight or nine feet high and the other about five feet with reddish rather than black hair, or both adult males or very young specimens have been seen separately, giving rise to the belief that there are two distinct types. There seems little doubt that the Yeti is an animal unknown to science, a species on its own. The early belief that it was in reality either a langur or a bear has now been discarded. Its separate existence may be regarded as well authenticated.

The most probable theory is that the Yeti is a species of giant anthropoid ape, driven into a remote area, perhaps hundreds of thousands of years ago, in which it has survived by adapting itself to specialized conditions. Yet it is not a true anthropoid, because its foot indicates that its ancestors were never true tree climbers. Its foot is designed for walking, not for clinging to trees, but the toe indicates that it may have had some such experience, even only for a short time, not long enough for the foot to develop into that of a true anthropoid.

Unlike the other anthropoids, the Snowman walks and stands upright. Like man, this has enabled its brain to develop, and it is likely to have a far greater intelligence than the other anthropoids, perhaps even an intelligence bordering upon that of primitive man. It is thought that this ape man or man ape of the Himalayas may be some off-shoot of the tree of evolution, a separate peak. Apes and men are cousins, descended from a common ancestor. Man remained on the ground where he had to survive by the use of his intelligence. The apes withdrew to the security of the trees. If the Yeti, as it seems, is a biped of long standing, which has lived on the ground for perhaps over a hundred thousand years, it is possible that he approximates nearer to man than to the anthropoids.

There are possible clues to its origin. South-east Asia has produced two skulls, that of Java man and of Peking man, both of whom were possibly giant man apes which existed three to four hundred thousand years ago. Neither were true men or true apes. The Proconsul skull of South Africa, found in 1948, indicates a similar stage of development. Teeth found in Java and China in recent years indicate that some three or four hundred thousand years ago South-east Asia was inhabited by a species of giant man ape, the ancestors perhaps of the Snowman of the Himalayas, the last survivors of the giants who once inhabited the earth. These prehistoric giants were ill-adapted to life and failed to survive but the terror of their one-time existence has never been forgotten by the human race.

Many ancient records recall that giants once lived on the earth. Driven from the more habitable parts of the earth by the smaller but more intelligent humans, these giants may have retreated to out of the way corners, such as the mountains of Central Asia. There are rumours of the existence of similar man apes in New Guinea and Sumatra, and prints of unusually large feet with big toes have been found in the mud on these islands.

Everything about the Yeti is as yet speculation. We know only that a shy elusive animal inhabits a vast trackless area. It has never been seen by any observer trained and mentally equipped to give an authoritative opinion. We have only its footprints to go on. But the usual pattern by which unknown animals eventually become authenticated is set. There are countless native rumours of the existence of this strange beast. It is unlikely that the Sherpas of the Himalayas could have invented such an animal as they have so minutely described.

The numerous stories of the "all devouring demon",

which the word Yeti means, cannot be confirmed or denied until a specimen is brought to Europe for scientific study. Only time, and perhaps a very long time at that, will show whether these stories are baseless or true. The day may come when man learns that he has a cousin nearer to him than the apes. The elusive Missing Link, which has been searched for for over a century, may at last come to light in the form of the Snowman of the Himalayas. What shall we think of the Yeti when we finally track him down to his lair?

Perhaps it is even more pertinent to ask what will the Yeti think of us? Assuredly if one of these wretched creatures is taken on a tour of the world and allowed to see what humanity has done with its supremacy of the earth, it will wish to return as quickly as possible to the fastnesses of the Himalayas.

* * *

The story of the Loch Ness Monster of Scotland excites our incredulity far more than that of the Yeti. There is nothing to go on except vague eye-witness stories. The Monster of Loch Ness came first into the limelight in 1933 when a national newspaper reporter recorded the story of an A.A. patrol man in Inverness-shire who declared he had seen some very strange things in the Loch. He reported seeing a number of humps above the water line preceded by a long slender neck on the top of which was a small head. Its head was reptilian in shape and the neck sinuous and flat, the colour of its skin greyish black and it appeared to have an elephantine body of which the humps stuck out of the water. Since then the so called Monster has been observed by at least fifty local people or visitors to the Loch.

An extensive investigation carried out by Lieut. Commander R. T. Gould, who had written books about sea serpents and other natural oddities, disclosed that none of these sightings were the product of mass hallucinations. From his inquiry he came to the conclusion that the monster was a giant newt, perhaps some prehistoric monster which had become enclosed in the seven hundred and fifty foot deep Loch, twice the depth of the North Sea. The Loch is twenty-four miles long, and varies in width from one to three miles and its surface is fifty-five feet above sea level.

It soon became apparent that the sighting of the Monster in 1933 was merely a modern re-appearance of the "fearsome beast" observed in St. Columbia's day fifteen hundred years before. The existence of "a very odd looking beastie, something like a huge frog only it isn't a frog" was known to the local residents and the story had been passed down from generation to generation. The legend of the Monster was already ancient in 1810 when children were warned not to play on the banks of the Loch in case the Monster came ashore. A diver, Duncan McDonald, working on a submerged wreck in the lake in 1880, was surprised by a similar Monster swimming beneath the water.

Dismissed at first as a hoax, perpetrated by the local residents to attract tourists, the Monster has taken on a far more scientific guise since the Second World War. What was thought to be an old wives' tale has been refuted by the number of sightings of something strange at least in the Loch.

Few scientists will venture any statements or expressions of belief about the Monster, for they fear being made to appear ridiculous. Many popular beliefs, dismissed as fables, have been proved to be authentic folk-lore. The ancient belief that swifts roost in the heavens has been proved true by aeroplane pilots who have observed them flying high at night. Herodotus's tale that the Nile plovers enter the mouths of crocodiles to pick their teeth, laughed at for centuries, has been partly confirmed—they pick leeches off the crocodiles' tongues.

Photographs taken at Loch Ness show a number of humps sticking out of the water, indicating a creature of some thirty to fifty feet long. Many observers declare they have seen a long neck surmounted by a reptilian head arising from the water in front of the humps. One eye-witness, Alexander Campbell, forty years a Loch Ness bailiff, saw the Monster in June, 1934, for several minutes and again on 16 July, 1958, when it submerged quite near his boat, creating a minor tidal wave. On the first occasion he was fishing from a rowboat with two other men only from ten to twelve yards off shore when a dark, tough-looking hump arose between the boat and the shore and submerged slowly without a ripple. Another eye-witness, John Mackay, who runs an hotel at Drunnadrochit, saw the Monster when it broke surface on 22 May, 1933. He declared it to have an elephantine-like body and a peculiarly small head. The water frothed and foamed as it vanished.

A London man and his wife declare that they saw the Monster crossing a road two hundred yards in front of them by the lake on 22 July, 1933. They noticed its long undulating neck and a body five feet high. It was as wide as the road itself and it emerged from some undergrowth and moved in the direction of the loch where it disappeared. They say it moved in a series of jerks like a huge snail. This man, shown a drawing of a plesiosaurus reptile, declared that it had distinct similarity with the animal he had seen.

There are dozens of stories of Monster sightings in the lake. Clearly some strange water beast inhabits Loch Ness, and has done so for centuries. But what is it? The most attractive theory is that it is some extinct reptile possibly a plesiosaurus or some form of newt, which has survived for millions of years in this land-locked and particularly deep loch. Photographs suggest that it has a large body, a long neck and a tail. It swims just below the surface with its head slightly protruding from the water, it causes a great wash and a turbulence follows its humps. Is it a survivor from the age of reptiles, which ceased some seventy million years ago? At least one well-known scientist believes this theory to be possible. Dr. Maurice Burton, D.F.C., F.R.S.A., F.L.S., F.Z.S., stated this belief in August, 1959.

Another theory suggests that the Monster inhabits the loch only occasionally, coming from the sea by some underground water route. It retires to Loch Ness either at the breeding season, or to escape its natural enemies in the sea.

When in June 1958, the B.B.C. attempted a television programme about the Monster, a mysterious object was recorded under water on an echo-sounder. It moved some twelve feet down and submerged and disappeared at sixty feet. Two days later four men in a bus saw humps arise in the same spot, and there was a big wash as they submerged. In August, 1960 a party of university students visited the loch proposing to carry out a long and careful investigation about the Monster. They announced, wisely, that they would not disclose any of their findings until after they had left the loch Otherwise their investigations might have been hindered by crowds of sightseers which might frighten the Monster. It will be interesting to learn if this first scientific investigation into the Loch Ness Monster did produce any useful results.

As the matter stands it seems that there is something in the loch worth investigation. If a prehistoric reptile or giant fish does live in Loch Ness, the natives of the district are assured of a magnificent tourist industry for years to come.

THE PLATE OF BRASS

INTRICATE and and controversial problems arise when some apparently historical relic comes to light after perhaps centuries. Is it genuine, the real thing? Or is it a hoax, the work of a distorted mind bent upon hoodwinking the world while he laughs at our credulity? Think of the arguments there would be if someone produced Moses's Tablets of the Law or the original Battle Abbey Roll of the Conqueror's Knights. Columbus, history records, threw his log book overboard on his return to Spain in 1492; in 1892 it was "found" washed up on the coast of Wales, barnacle encrusted and written in English! No wonder the experts are cautious.

Experts do seem to be a little over-cautious about the Plate of Brass found in California in 1937 for everything suggests that it is the actual Plate set up by Sir Francis Drake during his famous voyage round the world in 1579.

Drake sailed from Plymouth on 30 December 1577. When he returned three years later he had circumnavigated the globe, the first commander to do so, in his own ship, since Magellan had died on the way. Entering the Pacific on 6 September, 1578, Drake sailed up the coast of South America looting the Spaniards who expected him in the Caribbean. Realizing that the Spaniards would try to cut off his retreat via the Straits of Magellan, Drake sought another way home, by sailing up the North American coast in search of the fabulous North-west Passage. First he decided to refit his ship. To do so he landed somewhere on the coast of California in the summer of 1579. On 17 June he came to a convenient harbour, anchoring there and remaining until 23 July. This harbour chosen by Drake was near and probably somewhere to the north of the present-day city of San Francisco, but it seems conclusive that Drake did not enter The Golden Gate, for surely he would have remarked on one of the most magnificent harbours in the whole world?

While the ship was being cleaned Drake set his men to build a fort on shore. Soon they were welcomed by a vast crowd of Indians who were perfectly friendly and, as was usual among primitive peoples, welcomed the strange white men as gods. On 26 June the Indian chief visited Drake attended by a bodyguard of a hundred tall and war-like men, one of whom bore the Sceptre or Royal Mace. Drake, according to the record of the voyage, accepted this ceremonial visit as the desire by the natives to have their land and country taken over by the visitors. *The World Encompassed* describes it as follows:

"These things being so freely offered our generall took the Scepter and dignity of the said countrie into his hand wherefore in the name and to the vse of her most excellent majesty and to her enjoyment of the riches and treasures thereof wherewith in the vpland countries it abounds."

Drake named the country of which he had taken possession on behalf of Queen Elizabeth of England as New Albion because of the white banks and cliffs which reminded him of England. All three accounts of the voyage describe the next stage of the proceedings. In *The World Encompassed* by Sir Francis Drake, the authorship of which is attributed to Francis Fletcher, a chaplain on Drake's ship, we find:

"Before we went from thence, our generall caused to be set vp, a monument of our being there; as also of her maiesties, and successors right and title to that kingdome, namely, a plate of brasse, fast nailed to a great and firme post; whereon is engrauen her graces name, and the day and yeare of our arriuall there, and of the free giuing vp, of the prouince and kingdome, both by the King and people, into her maiesties hands; together with her highnesse picture, and armes in a piece of sixpence currant English monie, shewing it selfe by a hole made of purpose through the plate; vnderneath was likewise engrauen the name of our generall."

The description of the setting up of the plate in the earlier account, known as *The Famous Voyage*, which was included in the 1589 edition of Richard Hakluyt's *The Principle Navigations, Voyages and Discoveries of the English Nation,* says:

"At our departure hence our generall set vp a monument of our being there, as also of her maiesties right and title to the same, namely a plate, nailed upon a faire great posts, whereupon was ingrauen her maiesties name, the day and yeare of our arriuall there, with the free giuing vp of the prouince and the people into her maiesties hands, together with her highness picture and armes, in a piece of sixpence of currant English money vnder the plate, where vnder was also written the name of our generall."

The Famous Voyage is generally considered to be an abridgment of Fletcher's full narrative taken from its original manuscript before it was printed in 1628.

A third short description of Drake's voyage known as *The Anonymous Narrative* says simply:

"in this place Drake set vp a greate poste and nailed thereon a vjd, which the contreye people woorshipped as if it had bin god also he nayled vppon this post a plate of lead and scratched therein the Queenes name."

Thus all three descriptions of the voyage note the setting up of the post upon which a plate asserting English sovereignty was affixed. The wording of the description is given with slight differences and in one account it is a plate of brass and in another a plate of lead.

When California became a State in the American Union in 1850 the question whether Drake's plate of brass would ever be found was freely discussed. It seemed not improbable that it might have survived for three centuries. Not unnaturally it was expected to lie somewhere near the bay on the coast above San Francisco known as Drake's Bay, the accepted place of Drake's landing because of the very noticeable white cliffs.

Interest in the discovery of the plate became so intense that Doctor Herbert Bolton, the Professor of History of the University of California, made a point of warning his students to keep their eye open when they travelled about the country in case this great historical relic should one day turn up. He himself was convinced that it would, so he was not surprised one day in February, 1937, when he received a telephone call from a man who gave his name as Beryle Shinn who told him that in the previous summer he had picked up a piece of discoloured metal in Marin Country on the northern shores of San Francisco Bay.

While Shinn's description of the piece of metal on which writing could be discerned sounded genuine the place of its discovery was strange for it seemed wildly unlikely that Drake either entered San Francisco Bay or set up the plate on its shores. Shinn told Dr. Bolton that he was driving in the district when one of his tires became punctured. In consequence he pulled to the side of the road and he and his companions decided to picnic before repairing the tire. Climbing a steep hill they found themselves above San Francisco Bay with the walls of St. Quentin Prison to their left. Shinn and his friends amused themselves by rolling stones down the cliffside and while picking up a stone he noticed the piece of metal lying on the ground partly covered by another stone. He put it in the car and took it home where some weeks later he partially cleaned it with soap and water, seeing on it a few words, one of which he deciphered as the name "Drake".

Dr. Bolton's mind leaped at once to conjecture. Could this at last be the famous plate of brass? One small point seemed convincing. Shinn on the telephone said that there was a jagged hole at the bottom of the plate, which to Bolton's mind immediately suggested the hole in which the silver sixpence had been placed, according to the narratives of the voyage.

When Shinn brought the plate to him, Dr. Bolton examined it carefully, "the authenticity of the tablet seeming to me to be beyond all reasonable doubt", he said. Its discovery was the most sensational in California's short history. Slowly and carefully Dr. Bolton cleaned and deciphered the tangled mass of threadlike engravings on the brass. When he finished the message which no white man had seen for three hundred and fifty-eight years lay before him. The wording of the plate read as follows:

BEE IT KNOWNE VNTO ALL MEN BY THESE PRESENTS
IVNE 17 1579
BY THE GRACE OF GOD AND IN THE NAME OF
HERR MAIESTY QVEEN ELIZABETH OF ENGLAND
AND HERR SVCCESSORS FOREVER I TAKE POSSESSION
OF THIS KINGDOME WHOSE KING AND PEOPLE FREELY
RESIGNE THEIR RIGHT AND TITLE IN THE WHOLE
LAND VNTO HERR MAIESTIES KEEPING NOW NAMED BY
ME AND TO BEE KNOWNE VNTO ALL MEN AS NOVA ALBION.
FRANCIS DRAKE
(Hole for silver sixpence.)

A few weeks later Dr. Bolton announced to the meeting of the California Historical Society: "Here it is. Recovered at last after a lapse of three hundred and fifty-seven years. Behold Drake's Plate—the plate of brass. California's choicest archaeological treasure."

The plate found by Shinn is of solid brass 5 inches long

by 8 inches wide and ⅛ inch thick. An Elizabethan sixpence exactly fits the jagged hole, and the wording almost exactly tallies with the account of the famous voyage of the setting up of the plate so that, as Dr. Bolton pointed out, "between the relic and the eye-witness record there is a spectacular and convincing harmony which no fraud would be likely to attain."

On the other hand, as sceptics were quick to point out, the similarities between the inscription and the accounts of the voyage were no proof of the genuineness of the plate, for anybody could have studied the accounts, composed an inscription and engraved it on an ancient piece of brass. No one doubted Shinn's integrity or questioned that he found the plate how and where he said he did. The very fact that he found the plate in a most unlikely spot miles away from Drake's Bay seemed to rule out the element of fraud as far as he was concerned. Added to that he refused to accept any money for his find.

Many excellent points have been advanced for and against the authenticity of the plate of brass. Both those who claim that the plate is authentic and those who reject it as spurious claim that the date 17 June in the inscription supports their contention. That was the date of the landing, whereas the formal recognition of sovereignty took place, according to the accounts of the voyage, on 26 June. Supporters of the genuineness of the plate asked would a hoaxer have chosen the date of landing rather than the more obvious 26 June? The date of 17 June which the plate bears surely supports its authenticity for both the principal narratives of the voyage state that the plate was engraved "the day and yeare of our arriual there".

The principal objections to the authenticity of the plate are in respect of the script employed and to the spelling of some of the words. The Roman lettering as is used in the inscription was not generally in use in England in the sixteenth century, it is claimed. It was employed solely by scholars, and such people as sailors would have been more likely to have used the ordinary Tudor black letter script in its round and ornamented form. As regards the spelling it is claimed that it is far too uniform for a period in which there were no dictionaries and as a result all spelling was widely different even of the same words in the same document. The spelling of certain words such as "King", "Queen", and "whole" for "hool" is said to be far too modern and such usage does not conform to Elizabethan forms of spelling.

The word which has come in for the strongest criticism is "Herr", a form of "Her" which was not supposed to be used in the sixteenth century. However, some support for its use in the plate is found in a document written as a prospectus for a formation of a corporation in England to exploit the land discovered by Drake. On the other hand, it is claimed that a modern forger would not have known of this corroborative example of this unusual spelling of the word. Against these objections it is possible that the writer of the plate employed a printed book as a model for his words and letters.

The crudity of the work is claimed, on the other hand, as perhaps the strongest point in favour of the plate, which is irregular in shape but is approximately rectangular. At top and bottom there are notches through which to drive spikes to fasten it to a post, just the sort of detail which a hoaxer might have forgotten to include in his forgery. The lettering appears to have been made with a sharp tool and the words are unevenly spaced and the lines are not straight. When the plate was found the letters were full of hardpacked dirt. The piece of brass closely resembled the type of brass work found on sixteenth-century ships when deck fittings and gun carriages were usually made of brass, and it is strongly suggested that, when the plate was suddenly needed, it was cut from a gun carriage, which would account for the slight curvature at its ends.

The University of California, which acquired the plate, subjected it to the most exhaustive tests by specialists. Experts from the division of Electro Chemistry at Columbia University of the Massachusetts Institute of Technology examined the plate for seven months. They reported that it exhibited poor workmanship and a hasty execution of the inscription. That the plate appeared to be part of a larger piece of hammered brass was a strong point in favour of its authenticity for the process of rolling brass had not been introduced in Drake's time. No indication of any artificial patination was found which also was strong support for the authenticity of the plate. These tests established without question that the piece of brass used was very ancient, dating probably from Elizabethan times. That did not make the plate genuine, for any hoaxer might have acquired a piece of ancient brass. The scientists, however, in their detailed report stated:

"It is our opinion that the brass plate examined by us is the genuine Drake Plate referred to in the book *The World*

Encompassed by Sir Francis Drake, published in 1628."

While these technical arguments were at their height a startling discovery was made. Beryle Shinn was not the first modern person to find the plate. As a result of newspaper publicity about the discovery of the plate, a Mr. William Caldeira came forward to say that he had found the same plate in 1933 near the beach at Drake's Bay, twenty-five miles from San Francisco Bay where Shinn had found the plate. In 1933, Caldeira, a chauffeur, had been waiting about while his employer, the vice-chairman of the Bank of America National Trust and Saving Association, was shooting quail. Kicking at stones to while away the time his foot struck a piece of metal which had a jagged hole in it. Washing it in a nearby stream, Caldeira noticed the name "Drake". The piece of brass held no significance to Caldeira and he put it in the pocket of the car and some weeks later threw it out near the spot where Shinn subsequently found it. This means that someone else must have intervened to pick it up and place it in the pile of stones where Shinn found it. No one in California doubted the probity of either Caldeira or Shinn. Neither was the type of person to perpetrate a hoax and neither man made any attempt to cash in on his discovery.

There the matter rests. No one can be absolutely certain that the plate is the actual plate of brass set up by Sir Francis Drake, but on balance of probabilities it seems more likely than not to be genuine. Caldeira's initial discovery of the plate half a mile from Drake's traditional landing place strongly supports its authenticity. This post may have been torn down by the Indians after the English ship had left and the plate might well have been carried half a mile inland.

Perhaps the strongest factor in support of the plate is the unlikelihood of the existence of a hoaxer who for no gain or reward would have executed such a remarkable fraud, for which, moreover, he would have gained no notoriety or benefit. Such a hoaxer would have needed to have studied the accounts of the voyages, composed an inscription, procured an old piece of brass and an Elizabethan sixpence, cut the brass and cut the inscription, faked it to look old by artificial means, and planted it somewhere near Drake's Bay. He must have been an expert in Elizabethan English, which would limit him to one of a few scholars.

Not more than ten people in the world could have executed such an inscription without obvious flaws.

While the exact question whether the plate can or cannot

be accepted as genuine can never be finally decided, the discovery of Drake's plate of brass poses a strange mystery, one which is perhaps made even stranger by a not dissimilar find in America of another example of Elizabethan inscriptions.

The fact that the Dare Stones are a hoax has unfortunately mitigated against the full acceptance of the Drake plate. These so-called Dare Stones, which purport to represent a diary of Raleigh's lost colonists, were found in Carolina and Georgia in the late 1930s.

In 1587 Sir Walter Raleigh's third Virginia Colony was established on Roanoke Island on the coast of what is now the State of North Carolina. When the relief ship arrived from England three years later the colonists were gone and no definite clue to their fate has ever come to light. The eighty-nine men, seventeen women and eleven children of the colony had disappeared completely. The fort had been dismantled and the only clue to the colonists' fate was the word "CROATOAN" carved on a post. This is thought to suggest that the colonists may have gone to a village of Croatoan Indians nearby. No attempt was made by the relief expedition to find them and it was accepted that the colonists had either died of starvation or had been massacred by Indians. One of these colonists was named Elizabeth Dare.

Between 1937 and 1939, forty-eight inscribed stones were found stretching from near the Island of Roanoke right across South Carolina into Georgia. On them were written in Elizabethan English messages which purported to show that the colonists had trekked inland, finally reaching a spot not far from the present-day city of Atlanta. The story told by these stone messages seemed to conform to what was known about the composition of the last lost colony and the names of the supposed survivors, at least forty-eight of which appeared on the official list. According to the stones, various colonists were killed by Indians as they progressed across the country, leaving finally seven, including Virginia Dare, Elizabeth's baby daughter, and her father Ananias Dare.

The first stone found carried the following inscription:

Front

Ananias Dare & Virginia went hence Vnto Heaven 1591
Anye Englishman Shew John White Govr Via

Back

Father soone After yov goe for Englande wee cam

hither
onlie misarie & Warre tow yeere
Above halfe DeaDe ere tow yeere more from
sickenes beine fovre & twentie
salvag with mesage of shipp vnto vs
smal space of time they affrite of revenge rann al
awaye
wee bleeve yt nott you
soone after ye salvages faine spirts angrie
suddiane mvrther al save seaven
mine childe-ananias to slaine with mvch misarie—
bvrie al neere fovre myles easte this river vppon
smal hil
names wirt al ther on rocke
pvtt this ther alsoe
salvage shew this vnto yov & hither wee promise
yov to give greate plentie presents
E W D

When this and the stones subsequently found were submitted to experts they could find little wrong with them.
They were apparently written in authentic Elizabethan English and the inscriptions appeared to have been cut with
such tools as might have been available at that time. When
more and more stones kept turning up the university to
which they were submitted for examination realized that
they were either being made the victims of a gigantic hoax
or they had stumbled on one of the greatest historical discoveries of American history.

There did not appear to be any evidence of fraud and the
weathering in the grooves in the inscriptions appeared to
accord with expectations. The wording of the message appeared to be just such as the lost colonists might have
written. In October, 1940, a committee of historians declared
their belief in the authenticity of the stones.

Then the stones were examined by a reporter of a world-
famous American magazine. He was not content to do as the
university professors and historians had done, examine the
stones alone for questions of authenticity. He went into the
question of the people who had found them, and he soon
discovered that they were people on whose bona fides very
considerable doubt could be thrown. Five different men had
been involved in the discovery of the stones over a distance
of four hundred and thirty miles. They all knew each other
well. One at least was a stone mason. Another made a busi-

ness of selling spurious Indian relics. Not one of them, however, was capable of the expert work involved in the inscriptions. Somewhere behind them was an unknown Mr. X, a man with the requisite knowledge to fake Elizabethan English.

Though this person has never been traced or definitely identified there is a suspicion that he may have been the perpetrator of the Drake plate. So there may have been a gigantic hoaxer, a man with expert knowledge of Elizabethan times, language and script who set out to hoax the American people with two discoveries, just the sort of relics which the American people, young in history, would be willing to accept.

BUILDERS IN STONE

THE GREAT stone circle at Stonehenge in Wiltshire is the most magnificent prehistoric building in northern Europe. Its conception and design and its construction at a time when Britain was barely emerging from barbarism represents a vast undertaking for a primitive people, so much so that antiquarians believe that the impetus required may have come from without, from far away Minoan Crete perhaps. Stonehenge may thus be evidence that the Greeks sailed out of the Mediterranean and voyaged northwards as far as Britain, to which so much else also points. Even with such romantic possibilities to consider, Stonehenge poses a number of mysteries. Who built it, when, and why?

Stonehenge stands on Salisbury Plain, eight miles north of Salisbury and two miles west of Amesbury. There were three distinct stages of development. Stonehenge 1 consisting of the enclosing bank and ditch, the "Hele Stone"and perhaps a wooden building in the centre constructed about 1850 B.C., as is disclosed by pottery finds and by the decay of radio-carbon in dead organic matter, a fairly exact method of dating which has come to be used by archaeologists.

A century or so later a wave of emigrant people spread from Europe across southern England as far as Wales and Ireland, progressing westward probably in search of iron. They built the first stone horseshoe, transporting giant blue stones from the Prescelly Hills in Pembrokeshire, one hundred and thirty-five miles from Stonehenge as the crow flies. A hundred or two hundred years later a fresh wave of emigrants brought in Sarsen stones from the Marlborough Downs, twenty-four miles away, some of them weighing as much as fifty tons; they reconstructed the monument into two stone horseshoes, one within the other. Stonehenge was thus completed a thousand years before the Druids, its builders in popular fancy, reached England.

Thus by perhaps 1400 B.C., about the time the Israelites were crossing the Red Sea, Stonehenge was in much its present form, suffering during the next two thousand years from the vicissitude of time and the depredation of vandals, it being doubtful if they were Romans or medieval Christians, who attempted to tear it down.

The modern visitor to Stonehenge finds huge masses of stone, some of them fallen, others in their original positions, arranged in concentric circles and enclosed by the original ditch and bank. Entrance is by a causeway. The original bank and ditch are typical neolithic earthworks; excavation has produced pickaxes made from the antlers of red deer and shovels from the shoulderblades of oxen. The ditch and bank are twenty feet wide and have a mean diameter of three hundred and twenty feet.

A mystery which has never been fully solved is represented by the fifty-six small circular pits dug around and inside the bank, some of them two feet deep and containing deposits of cremated human bones. Next comes the original stone, known as the Hele Stone, a large single block of Sarsen sixteen feet high and eight feet thick. Four feet of it is under ground. Its position indicates that it was so placed that an observer on Midsummer Day might see the sunrise over its top, but its position does not enable us accurately to determine the year of its erection, because only half the sun's disc can be observed sometime after sunrise which suggests that those who so placed it were doubtful of the exact point of sunrise. True sunrise will not be seen in that position until the year A.D. 3260.

Next we come to another Sarsen stone twenty feet long by seven feet wide and three inches thick which is known in popular fancy as the "Slaughter Stone", although there is no evidence whatsoever that it was ever used for sacrifice, human or otherwise. It seems to be the survivor of a pair of pillars forming a gateway. This brings us to the circle of Sarsen stones known as the Horseshoe of Trilithons, consisting of five huge stones. Two are intact, three had fallen inwards, but were re-erected in 1901, and the fourth and fifth are partially ruined. One of these is known to have been in position and fell on 3 January, 1797. All these stones at one time carried lintels, fixed to the top by a mortise and tenon joint made by an outcrop on one stone fitting into a hole in another. These Sarsen stones are found to have been derived from the Marlborough Downs and the most astonishing feature is that they were transported for twenty-four miles by sledge. How this was done is discussed later.

Inside the Sarsen circle comes the circle of upright blue stones which must have been brought from Pembrokeshire. Six of these are still upright, nine remain only as stumps, and two as fragments. Their setting is irregular suggesting erection after the Sarsen circle. These are in their natural state and have not been dressed or tooled as have been the later Sarsen stones. Within these two circles we find the stone, commonly known as the Altar Stone, sixteen feet long by three and a half feet wide and an inch and three-quarters deep, the largest of all the stones brought from outside. It is believed to have come from what are known as the Cosheston Beds near Milford Haven in Pembrokeshire.

How did the builders of Stonehenge II convey the blue stones one hundred and thirty-five miles from Pembrokeshire? These massive stones, some of which weigh from four to six tons, must have been carried either by land or sea by the most primitive methods of transportation, at a time when there were no such things as wheeled vehicles. Their great weight could not have been borne by pack animals. Everything points to the use of a water route. It would have been quite impossible to have carried these stones by sledge through the Welsh mountains across the River Severn and then by way of the Downs to Stonehenge.

It seems certain that, having been dragged down from the mountain to the shore at Milford Haven, they were carried by rafts up the Bristol Channel to the mouth of the Avon. There they were transferred to two dug-out canoes lashed together and carried up the river. Rafts large enough to have carried the stones by sea would have been too large to have navigated the shallow river. Two dug-out canoes, each thirty-five feet long and with a beam of four feet and a depth of two feet would have been capable of transporting the stones up the Avon as far as Frome. In 1954 tests both with log rafts and canoes confirmed that this operation would have been possible. From Frome to Warminster the stones would have required a portage by sledge and then a further journey by the River Wylye, leaving only two more miles by sledge to Stonehenge. All this would have been a vast undertaking involving years in time and the labour of hundreds of men.

The transportation of the later Sarsen stones, which make up Stonehenge III, from Marlborough Downs to Stonehenge, was an even more gigantic undertaking. These stones are far larger, some of them weighing fifty tons and although the distance was only twenty-four miles, it is calculated that the work of transportation must have taken a force of some fifteen hundred men working almost exclusively on the operation for ten years. The conveyance of each separate stone must have required at least nine weeks for each journey. Yet the work could not have been continuous for such a number of men could hardly have been withdrawn from the ordinary work of agriculture for so long a period. Added to that, time must be allowed for bad weather and for rest. The tremendous work involved shows how great must have been the compelling urge in the construction of the monument.

Attempts have been made to reconstruct the manner in which the transportation was done over the uneven ground between the Marlborough Downs and Stonehenge. Mounted on a sledge, and with the use of rollers each log of which must have been carried and placed in front of the sledge, would have required the work of at least twenty-five men to each stone. The average distance they could have hauled one stone in a day is thought to have been about half a mile. They faced at least one steep escarpment at Red Lion Hill which must have required perhaps the work of a thousand men hauling on each particular stone.

Before erection each stone had to be faced and dressed. Sarsen is one of the most difficult of all British rocks to work, and it is so hard that it would turn the edges of all but the most modern of steel alloys. The dressing of these stones could only have been done by the pounding of other stones. The work of polishing and grinding is believed to have taken the work of fifty masons labouring ten hours a day for seven days a week for nearly three years. There is no other example of such work in Britain and this suggests that the experience of such tooling and dressing of large blocks of stone must have come from some other part of the world where it was already a well established practice.

All this means that between ten and twenty years must have elapsed between the start of the operation and this point in our narrative. Once the stones had been tooled and dressed to the desired shape and design they had to be aligned and erected. How they were raised into position and sunk into the holes dug exactly in the desired position poses other problems. The apparently obvious suggestion that each was raised on an earthen ramp before being tipped into the desired hole suffers from strong objections. It would have meant that a separate ramp would have had to have been made for each stone, and it seems far more likely that a timber ramp which could have been moved from place to place was used. Once this timber ramp was in position each stone could have been pulled up to it and tipped into the hole dug.

Another probable theory is that each stone was raised on a wooden square until it reached the desired height, and this in all probability must have been the method whereby the lintels were raised to the tops of the stones once they were in position. Even so, the builders faced the problem of getting the lintels level, and it is thought that this may have been done by the use of a water trough raised on a wooden square and a plumb line. Like the modern spirit level, the level of the water would have ensured uniformity. The intelligence and experience shown by the builders of Stonehenge hardly suggests a primitive people. The work involved required a common effort on a vast scale and the direction of a chief, and of an architect, whose word must have been law to his subjects.

Of these men of the early Bronze Age we know a little from the evidence found in their tombs. They traded with Ireland and the eastern Mediterranean. Beads from Egypt have been found in their tombs and axes made in Ireland were sent in exchange. To the shores of southern England came Greek traders and amongst them craftsmen who were able to teach the Britons how to undertake such a vast stone structure. On the stones they helped to carve and erect they left an almost certain clue of their origin, the Mycean-type dagger, which only recently has been found carved on a number of the stones. This hilted dagger is found otherwise only in the eastern Mediterranean. As well as the daggers there is a carving of what appears to be a cult figure, perhaps a Mother Goddess. These hitherto unknown carvings were disclosed only recently by photographs taken at a time when the angle of the sun showed up the lights and shadows.

From Greece itself comes some corroboration for the belief that the great architect of Stonehenge may have derived his knowledge from the great classical civilization of the eastern Mediterranean. A passage in the *History of the Hyperboeans,* believed to have been written about 300 B.C., may represent knowledge of the existence of Stonehenge. Its author, Hecateus of Abdera, refers to an island in the ocean in the lands of the Celts, situated under the constellation of the Bear in which there is a sacred enclosure dedicated to Apollo, as well as a magnificent circular temple adorned with many rich offerings. The offerings referred to may mean the carvings on the stones at Stonehenge. It is a fascinating thought that the Greeks above all peoples of the Mediterranean were aware of Britain and of its great stone structure. The story of Odysseus and his ship the Argo clearly represent traditions and legends of Greek voyages outside the Mediterranean. It seems possible that the traditions of perhaps many voyagers brought together in this one story may represent even a voyage to ancient Britain, far away in the grey Atlantic.

Perhaps the most fascinating problem posed by Stonehenge is what it represented. Was it a shrine, a meeting place, or perhaps a market? It seems probable that it must have been a temple, for it is hardly conceivable that the impetus for its construction could have come from any cause other than religious. Nonetheless it may have been used for secular purposes as well, as the meeting place of the community as well as the *sanctum sanctorum* of its belief. The general alignment of Stonehenge suggests that those who built it were sun worshippers and its central motive may well have been the observance of the winter equinox on 21 December, at which time on a clear day the setting sun would have fallen straight on the axis on which Stonehenge was built.

At the true meaning of Stonehenge we can only guess and about its builders we can do little more than surmise. But one thing is clear. Stonehenge is a monument to man's preoccupation with the problem of time. Its successive builders laboured to construct a monument for eternity. They believed that human existence had a purpose. Why otherwise would they have laboured to construct a vast work which many of them at least could never expect to see finished?

Like our Stonehenge, the ruined city of Zimbabwe in Rhodesia poses problems which may never be solved satisfactorily.

The ruins of Zimbabwe consist of an eliptical temple, its walls eighty-three feet in circumference, thirty-four feet high, and ten feet wide at the top, a fortified hill half a mile away and in between a labyrinth of stone walls, built of dry masonry without cement, and composing one thousand tons of granite all of which had to be conveyed from a considerable distance.

Who built Zimbabwe—Phoenicians, Egyptians, Israelites or African Bantus? For over a century there has been argument as to whether it is an ancient or a medieval structure. A century of research has failed to show more than that Zimbabwe is an enigma, its history lost in the mists of time. No clue to the date of the city's origin can be derived from the stones themselves. Thus the two usual means of dating, architecture and construction, offer us no key to the solution of the mystery. Nor does any ancient folk-lore about its construction survive amongst the native peoples who today inhabit that part of Africa.

Significantly perhaps Zimbabwe is located in the part of Africa which is famous for its ancient gold mines. Seventy-five thousand ancient, pre-European, mine workings have been found in the area and it has been estimated that they must have produced some six hundred and fifty tons of gold to the present-day value of £150,000,000. This fact has, perhaps too obviously, given rise to the romantic theory that Zimbabwe was the Ophir of the ancients. The remarkable fact is that it is difficult to ascertain from where the ancient world could otherwise have obtained its gold. Prior to the Spanish conquest of South America in the sixteenth century all gold in use in Europe and Asia must have come either from alluvial washings in rivers or from some secret mines such as we find today in Rhodesia. The histories of the Egyptians and Israelites suggest that somewhere to the south of the Mediterranean, probably in Africa, prolific gold mining took place.

The Queen of Sheba was dazzled by Solomon's gold which he told her he obtained from the Land of Ophir. His navy brought him from Tharish once in every three years, a rich cargo of gold, silver, ivory, apes and peacocks, the typical products of South-east Africa. His ship sailed southward from Ezion-Geber in the Red Sea. Everything suggests that they traded with modern Rhodesia, the land lying between the Zambesi and Limpopo rivers. Long before Solomon's time the Israelites knew of a gold producing land named Harvilah in the direction of Ethiopia.

Pictures and inscriptions found in Egyptian temples show that in the time of Queen Hatshepsut, who may have lived about 1500 B.C., the Egyptians were despatching expeditions southward to the land of Punt.

Possible corroboration for Egyptian visits to Zimbabwe

and to the ancient gold workings of Rhodesia come from the pictures found on the walls of caves throughout the southern part of Africa. The people depicted in these drawings appear to be reminiscent of those of ancient Egypt, rather than of bushmen, pigmies, or other Negroid types. One picture is supposed to represent the Osiris legend and both men and women in other drawings are considered to be representations of red-haired peoples. A hieroglyphic of Thothmes III, the co-ruler of Egypt with Queen Hatshepsut, is supposed to have been found on the coast near Zanzibar, not so very far north of Rhodesia. Egyptian drawings, illustrating the voyages to Punt, represent the beehive huts of the Africans and it is pointed out that one South African tribe worships an eagle god, named Ra-Venda, possibly the "Ra" of Egyptian mythology.

Modern archaeologists and historians discredit the ancient origin of Zimbabwe. When the first Portuguese voyagers arrived on the coast of East Africa about the year A.D. 1500 they heard stories of strange ruins and gold mines in the interior but no one knew who had built or worked them. It seems equally unlikely that the native Africans, the Bantus, built Zimbabwe. They did not build in stone. Nor, as far as it is known, did they mine gold. They were a purely pastoral-agricultural people, and the knowledge that they have no ancestral memories of the building of Zimbabwe may come from the fact that they were a continually migrating people, with the result that those whose ancestors may have built the ruins may have progressed a thousand miles to the south.

Another theory, the medieval theory, suggests that the builders of Zimbabwe were Arabs, Indians or Chinese, and evidence for the visits of such people to that part of Africa is not lacking. Ancient Chinese coins have been found on the East African beaches, and it seems clear that both gold and ivory were brought to China fully a thousand years ago. It would have been quite practical for Indians or Chinese to have made voyages to and from Africa, being carried there and back by winds and currents.

Zimbabwe is an out of the way archaeological site. Very little research has been done on its ruins, but this will soon be rectified, for it has been indicated by no less an authority than Sir Mortimer Wheeler that archaeologists will concentrate on Zimbabwe in the not far distant future.

Africa has produced anthropological finds which suggest that it may have been the cradle of the human race. We may still learn, despite the present rejection of the theory, that Zimbabwe was an ancient Ophir, King Solomon's mines themselves. It is an intriguing thought that at least one great archaeological mystery does still exist.

BIBLICAL MYSTERIES

THE HEBREW scriptures leave us with two great mysteries; did the flood happen and was it universal, and how and when did the Israelites cross the Red Sea? The Hebrew deluge story, in which the Ark comes to rest on the summit of Ararat, a mountain 17,000 feet high, suggests that the entire earth must have been covered to that depth. Yet our geological knowledge of the lands surrounding Mount Ararat shows that they were not at any time submerged by a great flood. Such a deluge as is described in Genesis must have left its imprint upon deserts, rivers and hills.

Belief in the universal nature of the Great Flood led to a recent expedition to Mount Ararat itself in search of the remains of the Ark. A Russian aviator in the First World War reported he had seen the Ark while flying over Ararat. In 1948 an American expedition ascended the mountin, but nothing was found and it is now concluded that the flyer saw only a landslide which from the height at which he was flying gave indication of some ark-like shape. By a strange coincidence the American scientists were in the Caucasus, just at the time when the Russians were exploding their first atomic bomb in that area.

The truth of the deluge story, which is told in Genesis, Chapter VI, verse 5, to Chapter IX, verse 17, is, like the earlier Creation myth, a compound of two distinct legends, the earlier tradition, as will be corroborated later, was acquired by the Hebrews while they lived in Mesopotamia long before Abraham trekked from Ur of the Chaldees, around about the year 2150 B.C. Handed down for over a thousand years by word of mouth, it was written down about the ninth century B.C. Then some hundreds of years later, after many Jews had returned to Jerusalem from their captivity in Babylon, a further version of the legend was added, the two being merged together into one story.

In the earlier, simple story, the heroes' ship grounds on the slopes of a mountain, the summit of which was visible. To this quite feasible account, the later writer adds that the Ark grounded upon Ararat, thus turning a purely local flood into a universal one. This later writer also adds the dimensions of the Ark and he states that the flood lasted for three hundred and sixty-four days, as against the far more feasible sixty days of the earlier version. The fact that he chooses the duration of the solar year indicates that he wrote after the Jews had learned to correct the errors of the old lunar calendar by observations of the sun.

Even so this later priestly editor adds information omitted by the earlier collector. He tells us that the Ark was caulked with bitumen, incidentally the usual shipbuilding practice in Mesopotamia, and, by showing that Noah was a descendant of Adam, he indicates that the flood was believed to have occurred comparatively soon after the establishment of civilization. He adds, too, other details which we now know come from the earlier Mesopotamian flood legend, such as the placing of the bow in the sky as a promise that the flood will not recur.

The great difference between the later and the older Hebrew accounts of the flood lies in the appreciation of its religious significance. The story teller sets out to emphasize the ritualistic implications of the story and to reaffirm the contractural relations between God and His chosen people rather than to state the purely historical record.

There are other clues which corroborate that there were two quite separate versions of the flood legends. The priestly editor leaves out Noah's sacrifice after his rescue because in the eyes of a Jewish priest the offering of the sacrifice by a layman was an unheard-of impropriety and a dangerous encroachment on priestly rights; something not to be encouraged. The fact that the older author shows ignorance of the law of sanctuary which forbade the offering of sacrifice except in the temple at Jerusalem shows that he wrote long before this had become an established practice. The original Hebrew tradition, that which they brought with them from Mesopotamia, related that God decided to destroy the human race because of its wickedness. But Noah found grace in the eyes of God and he was instructed to save himself and his family by building an Ark. The story proceeds:

"And Jehovah said unto Noah, Come thou and all thy house into the ark; for thee have I seen righteous before me in this generation. Of every clean beast thou shalt take to thee seven and seven, the male and his female; and of the beasts that are not clean two, the male and his female; of the fowl of the air, seven and seven; to keep seed alive upon the face of all the earth. For yet seven days, and I will cause it to rain upon the earth forty days and forty nights; and every living thing that I have made will I destroy from the face of the ground. And Noah did according unto all that Jehovah commanded him.

"And Noah went in, and his sons, and his wife, and his sons' wives with him, into the Ark, because of the waters of the flood (and the animals too). And it came to pass after the seven days, that the waters of the flood were upon the earth. And the rain was upon the earth forty days and forty nights. And Jehovah shut him in, and the waters increased, and bore up the Ark, and it was lifted up above the earth. All in whose nostrils was the breath of the spirit of life, of all that was in the dry land, died. And every living thing was destroyed which was upon the face of the ground, both man, and cattle and creeping things, and fowl of the heaven; and they were destroyed from the earth; and Noah only was left, and they that were with him in the Ark, and the rain from heaven was restrained; and the waters returned from off the earth continually.

"And it came to pass at the end of forty days, that Noah opened the window of the Ark which he had made; and he sent forth a raven, and it went forth to and fro, until the waters were dried up from off the earth. And he sent forth a dove from him, to see if the waters were abated from off the face of the ground; but the dove found no rest for the sole of her foot, and she returned unto him to the Ark, for the waters were on the face of the whole earth; and he put forth his hand, and took her, and brought her in unto him into the Ark. And he stayed yet another seven days; and again he sent forth the dove out of the Ark; and the dove came in to him at eventide; and, lo, in her mouth an olive leaf pluckt off; so Noah knew that the waters were abated from off the earth. And he stayed yet another seven days; and he sent forth the dove; and she returned not again unto him any more.

"And Noah removed the covering from the Ark, and looked, and behold, the face of the ground was dried. And Noah builded an altar unto Jehovah; and took of every clean beast, and of every clean fowl, and offered burnt offerings on the altar. And Jehovah smelled the sweet savour; and Jehovah said in his heart, I will not again curse the ground any more for man's sake, for that the imagination of man's heart is evil from his youth; neither will I again smite any more every thing living, as I have done. While the earth remaineth, seedtime and harvest, and cold and heat, and summer and winter, and day and night shall not cease."

We are left thus with the story of a purely local inundation which lasted for some two months. The flood occurs in Mesopotamia, the original home of the Hebrews.

None the less, the Hebrews' story gave rise to considerable speculation and concern amongst early Christians. The dimensions given for the size of the Ark showed that it must have been a ship of approximately 17,000 tons burden. There was great discussion how Noah coped with the housing and the feeding of the animals, and many suggestions were put forward how he kept them apart and prevented them from fighting amongst themselves. Whether or not he had allowed the animal pairs to mate led to great argument until a worthy scholar pointed out "it was not a time for leisurely love making".

Until the middle of the nineteenth century the Christians were secure in the knowledge that the Hebrew flood legend was original. It was known, however, that a Babylonian priest named Berossus, who wrote about 300 B.C., related that Xisuthros, the tenth King of Babylon, had been warned of the coming of a great flood and had been ordered to build a ship and embark upon it with his family and friends and to take with him food, drink and a number of animals. The ship he built must have been as large as the *Queen Mary*. The story told was not dissimilar to the Hebrew one. After the flood had been on the earth for some time, it abated and he sent out a succession of birds, the last of which did not return. Then looking out upon the desolate scene he found that his ship had stranded on the side of some mountain and he left it and offered sacrifice and he and his friends learned that they were in Armenia, not far distant, we note, from Ararat. This story was thought to be a late re-rendering of the Hebrew scriptures.

About 1850 thousands of cuneiform tablets were found in the Royal Library of the Assyrian Kings at Nineveh, and they were deciphered. A far older story of the flood emerged. A draughtsman employed by the British Museum, George Smith, reconstructing a number of fragments, read the words "the ship rested on the mountains of Nisir" and there followed the description of the sending out of a dove. He realized at once that he had stumbled upon a version of the flood myth dating from at least 626 B.C., the year of the creation of the library. Within twenty years the fragments had been pieced together and classified as the twelve episodes in the life of a king who is now known to us as Gilgamesh. It soon became apparent that this Epic of Gilgamesh was derived from far older texts, which were written in the Sumerian cuneiform characters.

Since then a complete Sumerian version of the flood has been found carrying back the written record to over two thousand years B.C. This shows that, long before the Hebrews left Mesopotamia for the Promised Land, there existed a tradition in Mesopotamia of a terrible flood disaster which concerned the land between the two great rivers, Tigris and Euphrates, one of the birth places of civilization. Many Mesopotamian kings are stated to have reigned before or after this great flood.

The original flood story was told by a man named Uta-Napishtim. He lived perhaps two thousand years before his story became interwoven into the written Epic of Gilgamesh.

Uta-Napishtim describes how he was living at Shuruppak, an old city on the banks of the Euphrates, when the gods decided to send a great flood. He was warned (British Museum Publication, *The Babylonian Story of the Deluge and the Epic of Gilgamesh*):

"Throw down the house, build a ship.
 Forsake wealth, seek after life,
 Hate possessions, save thy life,
 Bring all seed of life into the ship,
 The ship which thou shalt build,
 The dimensions thereof shall be measured,
 The breadth and the length thereof shall be the same,
 Then launch it upon the ocean."

He asked what he shall tell the people of the town to account for his actions and he is told to disarm their suspicions by saying that he is leaving in order to escape the wrath of the god Bel who hates him, but on them Bel will rain riches. Uta-Napishtim builds his ship, and on the seventh day when it was finished he made a feast for his workpeople. On the ship, which was caulked with bitumen, a deck house of six storeys was constructed, and into it he loaded all he possessed, silver, gold, seed, cattle and handicraftsmen. For its navigation he appointed a sailor.

"The sender of (the flood) made a hail to fall at eventide,
I watched the aspect of the (approaching) storm,
Terror possessed me to look upon it,
I went into the ship and shut the door."

The storm is vividly described in symbolic terms:

"As soon as something of dawn shone in the sky
A black cloud from the foundations of heaven came up,
Inside it the god Adad thundered,
The gods Nabu and Sharru (i.e. Marduk) went before,
Marching as messengers over high land and plain,
Irragal (Nergal) tore out the post of the ship,
En-urta went on, he made the storm to descend.
The Anunnaki (the storm gods of the southern sky)
   brandished their torches,
With their glare they lighted up the land.
The whirlwind (or cyclone) of Adad swept up to heaven,
Every gleam of light was turned into darkness,
. . . the land . . . as if . . . had laid it waste.
A whole day long (the flood descended) . . .
Swiftly it mounted up . . . (the water) reached to the
   mountains.
(The water) attacked the people like a battle.
Brother saw not brother.
Men could not be known (or, recognized) in heaven,
The gods were terrified at the cyclone,
They shrank back and went up to the heaven of Anu,
The gods crouched like a dog and cowered by the wall."

Uta-Napishtim tells how the "gods bowed themselves and
sat weeping. Their lips were shut tight (in distress)" and
"for six days and nights . . . the wind, the storm raged, and
the cyclone overwhelmed the land".

The storm abates:

"When the seventh day came the cyclone ceased, the
   storm and battle
Which had fought like an army.
The sea became quiet, the grievous wind died down,
The cyclone ceased.
I looked on the day and voices were stilled,
And all mankind were turned into mud,
The land had been laid flat like a terrace."

162

He opened the air hole and "the light fell upon my cheek. I bowed myself, I sat down, I cried, my tears poured down over my cheeks." He looked everywhere, "at twelve points islands appeared and the ship grounded on the mountain of Nisir". After seven days, he sent out a dove, a swallow and a raven. The first two returned as they had no place to alight. The raven fed on the carrion on the waters and came not back. On the peak of the mountain, Uta-Napishtim made a sacrifice and "the gods smelt the sweet savour. The gods gathered together like flies over him that sacrificed." The gods argue about the sending of the flood, and as a sign that it will not be repeated, the great bow of Anu is placed in the sky, and Uta-Napishtim goes to dwell afar off at the mouth of the rivers.

Uta-Napishtim's story is the earliest known flood legend. He was clearly an eye-witness of a flood of unusual magnitude and as his story was told and re-told through generation after generation omissions of detail were made, and many other details were added.

That this story of a severe local flood in lower Mesopotamia was based on fact was confirmed in 1929 when successive layers of ancient civilization were excavated at Ur by Sir Leonard Woolley; at 150 feet below the surface, he came suddenly on a layer of solid, clean clay, eight feet thick, which ceased as suddenly as it had began and marked a complete break in the continuity of habitation. Both above it and below it were relics of a pure Sumerian civilization. No ordinary rising of the river could have left such a deep deposit and the flood that caused it must have been unparralleled in local history. Similar layers of mud at the same depth were found at other towns in the neighbourhood. The depth at which these sediments occurred clearly dated the great flood as having occurred about the year 4250 B.C. Deep as was the flood, it probably destroyed and inundated only mud villages, leaving the brick-built cities of the Sumerians set on high ground above the waters.

A probable explanation of Uta-Napishtim's story is that he, the headman of the village of Shuruppak, was warned by some other villager who may have realized that the river dams were too weak to withstand the annual spring flood which brought the melting snows down from the mountains to the north in that particular year. On the other hand, the fact that Uta-Napishtim was told not to warn his fellow townsmen, suggests that the Sumerian overlords may have intended purposely to destroy a particular village by the breaking of a dam. This theory is supported by Uta-Napish-tim's appeal to the gods after his rescue to employ other means in the future to destroy mankind, and he himself emigrates to the "mouths of the rivers" to seek safety in the future.

Modern knowledge suggests that the great Mesopotamian deluge, the story of which is told by a number of different peoples whose ancestors experienced it, may have been caused by a combination of unusual circumstances. As a result of heavy winter snowfall the usual spring flood may have been of unusual volume. Or a dam may have burst. A hurricane from the south, from where the storm is indi-cated to have come, accompanied by torrential rain, may have piled up the flood waters. The great deluge, of which the best-known account is that of the Hebrew scriptures, was clearly a local one, confined to the low-lying areas of Mesopotamia.

Those who still believe that the flood was a universal one point to the fact that flood legends are found all over the world. Clearly, Uta-Napishtim's story could not have reached the Pacific and American continents, where flood myths abound. Only in Europe and Africa are there no flood legends. Nor do the ancient Egyptians have any legend of a famous flood. Clearly the flood stories of India and China reflect purely local inundations of their own great rivers.

The Greeks had a flood hero named Deucalion and his story is not dissimilar to that of Uta-Napishtim. But the conquests of Alexander the Great brought the Greeks into contact with the peoples of Mesopotamia and they may well have learned there the earlier story.

Another theory suggests that the Greek flood myths reflect knowledge of the breaking out into the Mediterranean of the waters of the great Asiatic inland sea which caused a rise in the level of the Mediterranean, resulting in the submer-gence of land and the bursting of the barriers which divide the Black Sea from the Mediterranean. According to this theory, which was first advanced in 1923, there once existed a vast inland sea of which the Caspian and Arian Seas and Lake Baikal are the sole survivors. The Dardanelles was formed by the breaking out of the pent-up waters of the Black Sea. Geological surveys suggest, however, that the Dardanelles was formed by a slow process of erosion, not by a sudden rush of water.

The flood myths of the American Indians, which appear to be genuinely pre-Christian, contain stories of the sending out of birds, to learn if the waters were abating. This is taken as conclusive proof that all these universal myths related to one particular flood. But the idea of sending out birds to learn if the waters had abated was a remarkably sensible one which might have been adopted by many different flood heroes in widely separate parts of the world. Perhaps the best refutation of the theory that the flood was a universal one comes from an intelligent Emperor of China who told an Arab traveller "as to thy belief that the whole earth was covered with water, I remark that this would be so remarkable an event, that the terror would keep up its recollection, and all the nation would have handed it down to their posterity."

Apparently there were a number of Noahs and Uta-Napishtims in the world. There were many great floods and men behaved in much the same way to cope with them and attributed them to much the same reason, the anger of the gods.

The maps of the world appear to provide striking corroboration of the story that the Israelites crossed the Red Sea. The Red Sea exists at this day. Therefore the Israelites crossed it.

According to the Hebrew scriptures, a number of tribes migrated westward from Mesopotamia, where they had long formed part of the Semitic population, shortly before the year 2000 B.C. One group, led by the patriarch Abraham, reached the land of Canaan. About the same time, we learn from the history of the Near East, a Nomadic people known as the Hyksos, of Semitic race, moved from Asia Minor and invaded and conquered Egypt, where they ruled until 1580 B.C. About the year 1875 B.C. the clan of Jacob migrated from Canaan to Egypt to escape famine. There they found friendly Semitic rulers who gave them land in which they could continue with their pastoral life. One of these Israelites, Joseph, rose to the position of Grand Vizier to the Pharaoh and we learn that he and his tribe sojourned in the land of Goschen.

When the Hyksos rulers were expelled at the start of the Eighteenth Dynasty the Semitic Hebrews, kinsmen of the hated Hyksos, became out of favour with the Egyptians, a people who became enslaved by a Pharaoh who "knew not Joseph". The wretched Israelites were forced to labour in making bricks and in the building of two store cities of Pithom and Ramases. To prevent their increase, Pharaoh ordered the two Hebrew midwives to kill all male babies, but the women of Israel delivered their babies before the mid-wives could reach them. One of these children was hidden in an ark in the bulrushes where he was found by Pharaoh's daughter who adopted him and gave him the name of "Moses". Reaching manhood, he saw an Egyptian smiting an Israelite and killed him. Pharaoh sought to slay Moses who fled to the desert, returning on that particular Pharaoh's death to Egypt where the Israelites were complaining of their bondage.

When Moses and Aaron supplicated the new Pharaoh to allow the Israelites to leave Egypt he refused and ordered that their burdens should be increased. They were no longer to be given straw, but had to find it themselves, yet they still had to make the same number of bricks. To soften Pharaoh's heart, Moses and Aaron sent plagues on the Egyptians: the Nile was turned to blood; frogs covered the land; lice came from the dust; there were swarms of flies and a murrain came on all the beasts; plagues of boils and blains affected the humans; hail and fire smote their flax. The Egyptians were tormented by a plague of locusts. Thick darkness covered the land and the first born of Egyptian families died. After each plague Pharaoh hardened his heart until after the last disaster, in desperation, he cried to the Israelites "go forth."

Carrying the bones of Joseph, the Israelites left Egypt where they had lived for four hundred and thirty years. It is stated that they comprised six hundred thousand men. Before them by day went a pillar of cloud, by night a pillar of fire. They encamped by the sea. They learned that Pharaoh had changed his mind and was pursuing them. Held back by a strong east wind the waters were divided and the sea was made land so that the Israelites could cross, but as the Egyptians followed, the waters came back again and drowned them. After wandering in the desert for forty years the Israelites, now forty thousand strong, entered the Promised Land of Canaan.

Clearly, if the ancient legend is to be believed, and it seems unlikely that a people would have invented a tradition of their own serfdom, the Israelites succeeded in crossing some patch of water, but where was it?

While the Book of Exodus suggests that the Israelites in Egypt must have numbered about two million people, this number is brought down to a mere five thousand when the text is carefully examined. The land of Goschen could have supported no more than four thousand people, and there is the reference to the two midwives which hardly suggests that the Israelites were a numerous people. Then, forty years later, the Israelites who succeeded in reaching Canaan number only forty thousand. This disparity in numbers may have arisen from a mis-translation of the Hebrew word *elef*, which means either "families" or "thousands". On this basis, the tribe of Judah in the Old Testament can be numbered either at seventy-four thousand, six hundred people or seventy-four families comprising six hundred people.

The ten plagues by which the Egyptians were beset are clearly historical, for we know that just such natural disasters occur in that part of the world. Many modern travellers have observed that when the Nile rises to its greatest height in August, its waters turn a dull red and give forth an unpleasant smell, arising probably from the enormous quantities of minute organisms which are carried down at that time of the year. The diseases recorded could have arisen from the flies and frogs at this period of inundation. Swarms of locusts brought from the desert by the wind are no unusual phenomenon in Egypt, and the ninth plague, the darkness, is easy to identify. The annual hot wind, the khamsin, which blows for twenty-five days before and twenty-five days after the spring equinox, is an oppressive blast of sand and dust which blackens the sky.

The Israelites probably celebrated the ancient shepherd's meal of the first born lambs or goats just prior to their departure. The sprinkling of blood on the tent poles was an ancient custom to protect the human first born from evil spirits. The pillar of cloud by day and the fire by night, by which the Israelites were guided on their journey, were probably no more than the cloud of dust raised by the marching column, and by night the torches of the foreguard which preceded the march.

Considerable controversy has raged about the location of the "sea of passage" and the escape route of the Israelites from Egypt. While the places named in Exodus are possible clues, the snag arises that these places can no longer be identified with certainty. But it is possible to make some good guesses.

We know that the Israelites intended not only to escape from Egypt, but to try to reach Mount Sinai, which was probably a mountain situated at the head of the Gulf of Akaba. We know, too, roughly from where the Israelites set out. They would have found water only on established and recognized trade routes. That the column is described, after the sea crossing, to have been without water for three days, suggests a detour from the established route. The Egyptian frontier was situated some thirty or forty miles east of the land of Goschen, and it was guarded by a string of lakes and a line of forts. The Israelites knew that Pharaoh's grudging permission to leave might be rescinded at any moment. Haste was essential and it seems clear that they would have taken the shortest route to reach the frontier. When they reached that line, they were turned back by the guards and they turned southwards to "Pi-Hahiroth" where Pharaoh, who had changed his mind, caught up with them.

The land of Goschen, a marshy area triangular in shape, lay between the Nile and the eastern frontier. Most, but not all the Israelites lived there, for Exodus indicates that some of them lived in the various towns and cities of the neighbourhood, for there only could they have learned the Egyptian arts and crafts which we find them practising later. The mother of Moses, for example, must have lived in the vicinity of the royal palace, for Pharaoh's daughter found the child in the bulrushes of the river when she went to bathe. Moses and Aaron, too, must have lived not far from the royal palace because we read of their frequent audiences with Pharaoh. Probably the first stage of the Israelite's flight from Egypt was the collection of the city dwellers to join their compatriots in Goschen, from where the whole column could set out together.

The Israelites had four possible routes to the east. Exodus expressly states that they did not use the northerly route from Egypt to Palestine, "the way of the Phillistines", leading to the town of Rafa. This route, which has been called "the oldest road in the world", was their most likely route. As a variation to it, the Israelites could have gone north of Lake Serbonis, and skirted the actual shores of the Mediterranean. Even so, this would have been dangerously narrow for such a multitude with their flocks and herds, for in places it is only a yard or so wide.

Another "main road" by which the Israelites might have proceeded, was that taken by Abraham on his journey into Egypt, the Way of Sur, across the desert to Beersheba and Hebron. This, like the more northerly route, had the disadvantage of being a main road, one to be avoided by a fleeing multitude.

It seems more likely that the Israelites went by the way of Lake Timsah, which joins the ancient trade road to Arabia, and which later became the pilgrim's way to Mecca. This led directly to the head of the Gulf of Akaba. A minor variation to this route lay between the smaller of the two Bitter Lakes and the Gulf of Suez and continued on as the ancient road to the mines of the Sinai Peninsula. If they had adopted this fourth route, they could have crossed either the southern extremity of the Little Bitter Lake, or even the head of the Gulf of Suez, which is only two-thirds of a mile wide at that spot. Yet it seems unlikely that they adopted this route, for Exodus says that after crossing the waters they entered the wilderness of Sur which is much farther to the north. It is more probable that they used the direct route by way of Lake Timsah. When Pharaoh came in sight they turned south; being caught between two fires, their only chance lay in discovering some little-known road across the frontier. They probably found a ford across the southern extremity of the lake or across the marshy ground which in those days connected Lake Timsah and the Great Bitter Lake.

The Hebrew words used, which have resulted in our belief that they crossed the "Red Sea", mean really a "Sea of Reeds" or "reedy sea". To the Israelites the word "sea" meant a large expanse of land-locked water, not an ocean or large expanse of what we call sea. This description of a sea of reeds particularly applies to Lake Timsah which has been described by modern travellers as a mere pond of "brackish water full of reeds". It had no great depth and the waters may have been piled up at one end under the influence of a strong east wind. Such a phenomenon, by which the waters were piled up leaving a stretch of almost dry land, has been observed by modern travellers. After the wind abated the pursuing Egyptians were drowned, probably because they tried to make a short cut across another part of the lake. Having crossed the reedy sea, the Israelites reached the desert and struck across the ancient trade route to Akaba. A later editor of the ancient story probably added the "walls of water" which suggest that the Israelites progressed through a well defined channel of water, piled up on either side with the fishes looking out at them.

It seems clear that the "Red Sea" (or reed sea) which the Israelites undoubtedly crossed was the reedy Lake Timsah. The detail with which the journey is described, and its modern corroboration, suggest that the crossing of the waters actually took place. But when did the Israelites leave Egypt? Five separate dates have been put forward, but the most likely year seems to be 1445 B.C., and it is supported by the most convincing arguments. That there is no corroboration in

Egyptian history of the Exodus of the Israelites is probably not surprising, as to the Egyptians it was an event of quite minor importance. First let us examine the early and late theories.

Some scholars believe that the Israelites left Egypt with the Hyksos as early as 1580 B.C., but this seems most unlikely as the story of the Exodus indicates a distinct change of official attitude towards the Israelites which can only be accounted for if they were in Egypt after the Hyksos had left. This early date also presumes that the Israelites wandered in the desert for two hundred years, not the forty mentioned by Exodus. The late theory carries them out of Egypt in the year 1130 B.C., which bristles with chronological difficulties, being far too near the time of the commencement of the Hebrew monarchy. Another date which achieved temporary popularity, at the time of the discovery of Tutankamen's tomb, takes them out of Egypt between the years 1383-66 B.C. This made Tutankamen the Pharaoh of the Oppression. Those who have studied the question minutely narrow it down to a choice between the year 1445 B.C., during the reign of Thutmose III (1501-1447 B.C.) as the Oppressor, and that of his successor, Amenhotep II (1447-1420 B.C.) and 1225 B.C., which makes Ramses II (1301-1224 B.C.) the Oppressor and Meneptah (1233-1224 B.C.) the Pharaoh of the Exodus. Both Thutmose and Ramses were great conquerors and prodigious builders, which might have accounted for the labour of the Israelites.

The choice of these two Pharaohs really narrows down to the date when the Israelites first entered the Land of Canaan. Advocates of the later date, 1225 B.C., claim support from the statement in Exodus that the store cities of Pithom and Raamses, in the Delta of the Nile, were built by the Israelites. The latter city was built by the second Pharaoh of that name and therefore the Israelites were there in his reign. It is thought, however, that the editor of Exodus, writing many years later, may have named the cities as being built by the Israelites, yet they were not in existence at that time. There is some dispute whether the site of Raamses has been found and whether it is the modern town of Tanis. Both there and in the neighbouring town of Kantir objects have been found which date back to the year 1850 B.C.

The strongest argument which can be put forward in support of the later of these two dates is that, as Canaan remained under Egyptian domination until 1185 B.C., and as Hebrew history of the conquest of Canaan does not refer to the Egyptian occupation, the Israelites could not therefore have conquered Canaan until after that date. But the revolt of the Canaanite kings against their Egyptian overlords, and the Hebrew invasion and eventual conquest of the country took hundreds of years.

The Israelites slowly won control of Canaan from other Hebrew tribes. The famous Tel-el-Amarna tablets indicate that Hebrews may have entered Canaan as early as the year 1400 B.C. If they had wandered in the desert for exactly forty years, as Exodus states, they must have left Egypt about 1445 B.C. The Egyptians were certainly still in control of Canaan about 1400 B.C., but by 1366, the end of the reign of Akhenaton, the land had been over-run by tribesmen, some of whom may have been the Israelites. The end of Egyptian control may well have been the opportunity for which the desert peoples, including the Israelites, had been waiting to seize possession of the fertile land of Canaan. The Tel-el-Amarna letters indicate that a people named the Habriu, who may have been the Hebrews, were invading Canaan from the south in conjunction with other tribes from the east and north. These particular "Hebrews" may have been the Israelites who had escaped from Egypt into the deserts of Sinai and Seir some forty years previously.

It seems certain that the Israelites had left Egypt before the year 1228 B.C. for, in that year during the reign of Meneptah, the boast is made that "Israel is destroyed, its seed is not", a claim which could hardly be made if the Israelites were still sojourning in Egypt.

Other facts seem to corroborate the year 1445 B.C. as the date of the Exodus, as is already suggested by the Tel-el-Amarna letters. Excavations at Jericho show the city fell to the Egyptians about that time. Another possible clue comes from a picture found in the tomb of the Vizier of the Pharaoh Thutmose III, which depicts an overseer holding a whip over a gang of slaves who are making bricks, which has been taken to suggest that he was the Pharaoh of the Oppression. The identification of Thutmose III as the Pharaoh of the Oppression is peculiarly convenient because it makes possible the identification of the daughter of Pharaoh who rescued Moses from the bulrushes with Thutmose's co-ruler and sister, that remarkable woman Queen Hatsheput. If she rescued Moses from the river, her death in 1479 B.C. might account for his flight into the desert and his return after the death of her brother, who might not have been favourably disposed towards the child his sister had found in such a remarkable manner.

Hebrew history also supports the date of 1445 B.C. for the Exodus. If Abraham left Mesopotamia about 2090 B.C., and the Israelites arrived in Egypt two hundred and fifteen years later, their sojourn in Egypt at four hundred and thirty years would bring the date of their exodus to about the year 1450 B.C. Taken from the other end, the four hundred and eighty years which appear to elapse in Hebrew history from the Exodus to the building of Solomon's temple which took place about 966 B.C., calculated backwards, brings us to the year 1445 B.C. as the date at which the Israelites left Egypt.

While none of these dates can be certain it seems that the probability points to the year 1445 B.C. for the Exodus and the controversial crossing of the waters.

It is not unamusing to note some of the other theories which have been put forward to account for the famous Exodus. One of these, presented in 1951, suggests that the story referred, not to the Exodus from Egypt, but enshrines a far more ancient legend of the migration of the Hebrews from their original homeland in Central America over the ice of the Behring Straits and westwards across Asia to Canaan. In this somewhat startling theory the Hebrews take their rightful place, as the carriers of a common culture, like the survivors of fabled Atlantis. This theory seems to be nothing more than the reverse of an even earlier one which made the Indians who inhabited America originally Israelites, who reached the American continent from Asia by passing over the ice of the Behring Sea. They show to what lengths some people will go to explain the mysteries of human migration.

We can be satisfied that the Israelites crossed a reedy or marshy lake in a perfectly natural order of events, rather than progressed through a deep sea, the waves of which were parted by divine command.

DOUBTFUL IDENTITIES

SOME OF the most fascinating mysteries are connected with personal identity. Proof of identity can often be difficult, as this chapter shows. Before the days of fingerprints, dental charts and forensic medicine, it was well nigh impossible to prove who you were. Even now it is not easy to prove who someone is unless they are dead and can be laid out on a laboratory bench. Sometimes there are clues which may help us to decide several famous and mysterious cases of identity.

*   *   *

The American President, Abraham Lincoln, was shot at Ford's Theatre on the night of 14 April, 1865, at the moment of victory after four years of civil war, by the actor John Wilkes Booth, a member of the famous theatrical family. Officially, Booth himself was shot and killed by a party of secret service men on 26 April at Garretts Farm, Virginia. But almost immediately the legend grew that it was not Booth who was shot. It was said that he was allowed to escape. For many years a mummified body, declared to be Booth, had been exhibited at fairs in the United States and the publication of a number of books at the end of the century has given rise to the belief that Booth's escape was connived at by those who plotted Lincoln's death.

As the President sat in his box at the theatre with Mrs. Lincoln, Major Rathbone and Miss Harries, Booth entered by an unguarded door and shot Lincoln in the back of the head at point blank range. He leapt to the stage crying, *"Sic semper tyrannis,"* catching his foot in the flags draping the box and breaking a bone in his leg. He was able to escape to the stage entrance where his horse was waiting, but as a result of his injury his escape was impeded and it led, we believe, to his capture and death twelve days later. Booth was a sympathizer with the cause of the Southern States and he had been planning to kidnap the President for some time. It is thought that he was either a madman or the dupe of others. It has been suggested that a living and talking Booth was the last thing the conspirators wanted, and consequently secret orders were given to ensure that his mouth was shut for ever.

There does, however, appear to be considerable doubt about the identity of the body buried as Booth. Although many Americans appear to have believed at the time that Booth had been allowed to escape, the question did not come into prominence until some forty years later when a number of people, late in life, disclosed facts hitherto suspected but never confirmed.

The great "Booth" mystery started in 1910 when a man named F. L. Bates published a book called *The Escape and Suicide of John Wilkes Booth,* which claimed that the man who had ended his life by arsenic poisoning in the town of Enid, Oklahoma, in 1902, named David E. George, was really Booth. It was the body of this David George which has been exhibited throughout the United States as the body of the assassin of Lincoln.

Two other books increased interest in the mystery in 1937. Otto Eisenschiml, in his *Why was Lincoln Murdered?* discusses the inconsistencies in the official record of Booth's death and suggests that Booth may have been the dupe of the Minister of War, Stanton. Mr. Eisenschiml has further summed the matter up in another book entitled *In the Shadow of Lincoln's Death*, and a woman named Izola Forrester, who claims to be Booth's grand-daughter, adds fuel to the flames in her book called *This One Mad Act*.

These three publications have raised various points for consideration. If Booth did escape, it could only have been through the connivance of people holding sufficient authority to make his escape possible. It is claimed that the likeness of a man named Harry Stevenson, Booth's widow's son, who was born in 1869, to Booth establishes that he was alive after 1865. It is claimed that the solution to the mystery might come from the comparison of the cavalry boot on the body buried in Greenmount Cemetery, Baltimore, with the other boot found at Dr. Mudd's house, and now preserved in Washington. This might settle the question whether the body is that of Booth, who undoubtedly left the boot at Dr. Mudd's house, or that of the Confederate soldier named John Howard Boyd. But officially the case of Booth is closed and no authority will give permission for the exhumation of the body.

By various writers on the subject over a dozen strong reasons have been put forward to support the belief that Booth escaped and lived on for many years after the date of his supposed death. Lincoln was inadequately guarded at Ford's Theatre, although it was known that a Southern plot was in existence to kidnap him. The Secretary of War refused to appoint an adequate bodyguard. The policeman, who was supposed to be on guard outside the box, slipped off for a drink at the time of the assassination, but he was neither reprimanded nor dismissed.

Four years later, when Edwin Stanton resigned from the War Secretaryship, this policeman was immediately dismissed on the grounds that he had been found asleep on his beat.

It had been arranged that General Ulysses Grant, the victorious Northern General, would accompany the President to the theatre. Yet Grant, usually the most punctilious of men, left Washington that afternoon, giving the flimsy excuse that he desired to visit his children. The failure of the hero of the hour to accompany the President on such an occasion seems strange.

Within minutes of Lincoln's assassination a tight censorship was clamped down on all telegraph wires round Washington, save the one wire operated by the Department of War. Almost immediately this telegraph wire was put out of operation by, it was stated, a fault in the main batteries.

Although everybody knew the name of the man who had assassinated the President, his name was kept out of the papers and from all government despatches for five hours and by this delay the escape of Booth was facilitated. The responsibility of catching the assassin belonged to the Secretary of War, who possessed wartime powers of censorship.

Within an hour of the murder, thousands of soldiers were mobilized to guard every possible escape route, except the obvious one to the south which Booth took. Although there were many soldiers stationed on that route to Richmond, the Confederate capital, no attempt was made to close it until seven hours later. By that time it was clear that Booth must have passed the spot at least six hours before. No attempt was made to warn the military guard on the Navy Yard Bridge, by which Booth and his companion crossed, until 7 A.M. When he passed over Booth gave both his own name correctly and the correct counter-sign. But no report was made that he had left the city by that route.

When it became clear that Booth was travelling southwards, six separate parties of soldiers were sent to look for him but they did not co-operate, and in fact appeared to be in competition to gain the huge reward which had been offered. Because of the injury to his leg, Booth was forced to leave the direct route and seek shelter at the house of Dr. Samuel Mudd, and it has always been uncertain whether or not Mudd recognized Booth whom he had met previously. Although Mudd immediately notified the authorities of the visit of two strangers to his house, the clue was not followed up until 18 April. Secret service men, under the command of Lieutenant Baker, a subordinate of Stanton's, were secretly despatched to follow Booth. When Baker's force of twenty-five men was joined by a mysterious Colonel Condor, he was given command because of his superior rank.

Booth crossed the Potomac into Virginia on 22 April, where he was befriended by three Confederate soldiers who conducted him to Garretts Farm where the owner, some days later, swore that the man brought to him was a soldier named John Howard Boyd. Learning that Federal soldiers were looking for him, this man, whether he was Booth or Boyd, took shelter in a tobacco shed near the farm.

When Baker and Condor reached the farm they were told that the men they sought were in the tobacco shed and those within the shed were called upon to surrender. Booth's companion, Herold, came out and declared that the man still inside was Booth. While this conversation was taking place, Colonel Condor went round to the back of the shed and set it on fire. A shot was fired and when the soldiers entered the shed they found a man wounded in the head. According to Condor he had shot the man himself. But since then a sergeant named Corbett has been credited with killing Booth. He said he shot the man he saw inside through a crack in the woodwork.

Lieutenant Baker thought that Condor had fired the shot and he later testified that he had said to the colonel: "What on earth did you shoot him for?" "I didn't shoot him," replied Condor. "Then the idea flashed through my mind that if he did it, it had better not be known," stated Baker. The man in the shed, who died three hours later, according to Baker, need never have been shot for he could easily have been taken prisoner. The body was identified as that of Booth by a photograph. But some of the soldiers in the party stated their belief that the man was not Booth, and it has been said that there was a side door to the shed by which Booth could have escaped into the woods where a horse may have been hidden. There may have been three men in the shed, Herold, Boyd and Booth.

Booth's diary was found in the shed and it was given by Colonel Baker to Stanton but it was not heard of again until after Baker had been dismissed from the Service. By that time eighteen pages had been torn from it. Colonel Baker stated that when he told Stanton "we've got Booth" the Minister of War was speechless until he added that Booth was dead.

Booth's diary was later found to contain the strange statement: "I have almost a mind to return to Washington and clear my name which I feel I can do." As has been pointed out, he could have cleared his name only by disclosing those of his accomplices.

The greatest force which is given to the theory that Booth escaped is provided by the identification of the body and its disposal which are so confused that it is difficult to learn who identified what. The man shot at the farm was dressed in the uniform of a Confederate soldier, yet four days previously Booth had been seen wearing a black suit and four years later, when the body was handed over to his family, it was still clothed in this black suit. The soldiers stated that the man shot in the barn had fair or red hair but the body brought to Washington had black hair, as had Booth.

When the body was brought to Washington it was taken on board a warship where a commission was convened to identify it. The commission identified the body as Booth's by the damaged leg, by tattoo marks on the right hand and scars on the neck, all marks carried by Booth in his lifetime. But there seems to be considerable doubt whether the commission found the scar on the right or left side of the body's neck. One doctor declared that the right leg of the body had been fractured whereas it is known that Booth suffered that injury to his left leg. When this doctor was shown the body he stated it was a body which revealed no resemblance to the man he had known in life. He said at once to General Barnes: "There is no resemblance in that corpse to Booth, nor can I believe it to be that of him." But this Doctor May seems to have immediately changed his views. He had performed the operation which left the scar on Booth's neck and he stated:

"The body being turned, and the back of the neck was examined, and my mark was unmistakably found by me upon it. And it being afterwards, by my request, placed in a sitting posture and looking down upon it, I was finally enabled to imperfectly recognize the features of Booth. But never in a human being had a greater change taken place, from the man whom I had seen in the vigour of life and health, than in that of the haggard corpse, which was before me, with its yellowed and discoloured skin, its unkempt and matted hair, and its whole facial expression, sunken and sharpened by the exposure and starvation it had undergone."

Several separate and different stories of the disposal of the body have been recorded. It seems probable from these accounts that the body was first buried under a slab in the cellar of the Arsenal building in Washington but was later reinterred. After a lapse of four years it was handed over to the Booth family and inspected by a number of people. Booth's brother, Edwin, was present at the identification of the body and he accepted it for burial in the family lot. A chart of Booth's teeth, received from his dentist, was checked against those of the body by a non-dentist and declared to identify the body as Booth's.

In 1903 Basil Moxléy, the door-keeper at Ford's Theatre who had known Booth all his life, and was a pall bearer at the re-interment declared:

"I have never cared much for talking in regard to the truthfulness of the statement that John Wilkes Booth was buried in Greenmount Cemetery, for there has always been a certain amount of doubt existing as to whether or not the assassin of President Lincoln was ever captured, killed or even shot, but in order that I might clear up at least one supposition, I'll tell you positively that his body is not, and never was, buried in this city to my knowledge.

"Certainly the body buried in Greenmount Cemetery was not that of Booth, for I was one of the pall bearers, and I can safely say to you that there never were any two things in this world which resembled each other less than that body did John Wilkes Booth.

"I had known Booth all my life . . . I saw the body several times, and examined it, and I don't hesitate to say that the hair on the dead body was of a reddish brown colour, while Booth's was as black as a raven's wing.

"However, that mere detail made no difference, for we all knew at that time that the body was not that of John Wilkes Booth. You see, the whole affair was planned by friends of the family, and was done for a purpose which they deemed imperative."

Moxley suggested that it was incumbent upon the Government to furnish a body to make good their statement that Booth had been killed and that is just what they did. As a result, according to Moxley, the family were supplied with a red-headed man who looked no more like Booth than he did himself. "We all knew well that the body we buried was not Booth," stated Moxley. At Greenmount Cemetery, the body was interred twice, first on 19 February and again on 26 June, 1869.

Many years later some of the soldiers who had been present at Garretts Farm stated that they would not have recognized the body as that of Booth whom they had previously seen. They declared that they had been ordered to say nothing but in the first press release of the news of his death it was stated none of the party who were present was sure of his identity. A strange declaration came in 1908 from General O'Beirne, the Provost Marshal.

"I can tell you something that has never been published on this case, and never even mentioned, something you will never find on any record. There were three men in the barn and one of them escaped. Don't ask me who it was, because I won't tell. But use your imagination—think of how that place was padlocked carefully, and the key mislaid up at the house. It was never brought out at the testimony that there was another exit from the barn, but there was. Opening on the lower level at the rear was a small door which gave direct access to the ravine and woods. This was apparently overlooked while attention centred on the locked door in front. This is all I'm going to tell you at this time, and you can draw your own conclusions, but I am speaking the truth . . . we were all pledged to secrecy in those days."

From these accounts and reports it does not appear to have been established with any certainty that the man shot at Garretts Farm was Booth or that the body subsequently identified and buried was his. It seems possible that the body was accepted as that of Booth's but there seems to have been great confusion as to which leg had been damaged and the exact marking of the tattoos on the right hand. The Booth family may have been satisfied to accept the body for reinterment because by this fact the rumours that Booth was still alive might be stifled.

The belief that Booth was alive after 1865 and was seen and spoken to is based on a mass of hearsay and rumour. In effect claims have been made that two people were he. Izola Forrester refuses to accept the body of David George as that of her grandfather. The advocacy of E. L. Bates in his book for the recognition of the mummified body as John Wilkes Booth led to its examination by the Reverend Clarence True Wilkinson who seems to have been the first person to have hinted at the existence of a plot against Lincoln inside his own Cabinet. Wilkinson declared that if the mummy was authentic it should bear three distinguishing marks, a cut on the right eye, a deformed right thumb, and a scar on the back of the neck. The mummy appeared to satisfy all these conditions, but there were no tattooed initials on the right hand. This difficulty was overcome when a friend of George's said that he had these tell-tale initials removed in New Orleans. An X-ray examination has failed to disclose any scar on the neck of the mummy and, in 1924, the man who embalmed it declared that the eyes were blue while Booth's were black. When the mummy was X-rayed in Chicago in 1933 a metal object was disclosed and when it was removed it was found to bear the letter "B". Had Booth swallowed his signet ring? it has been asked. The story was told that David E. George, before he committed suicide, called at a theatre to see Blanche Booth, a niece of John Wilkes Booth. The card he sent in bore the inscription "John Wilkes Booth" but she refused to see him.

Izola Forrester, Booth's long unrecognized granddaughter, points to a totally different man as having been Booth, who, according to her, lived until 1879. She records the hitherto unknown fact that Booth was secretly married in 1859 to a woman called Izola Martha Mills and that the daughter born to them became Miss Forrester's mother. According to her, Mrs. Booth in 1868 travelled to California with a family friend named John H. Stevenson who handed her over to Booth in San Diego. Booth and his wife then went on to San Francisco where his brother Junius Brutus Booth was the manager of a theatre, and it is claimed that the remark of a San Francisco newspaper at this time which referred to "a mysterious stranger in our midst" may be significant.

Mrs. Booth gave birth to a son in 1869 who was named Harry Stevenson, and photographs of Harry as a young man suggest that he was the living image of John Wilkes Booth. On his death-bed he declared he was Booth's son. According to the story preserved in the family, Booth, after leaving California, crossed the Pacific to India. He was recognized by a Confederate soldier in 1873 in the Caroline Islands in the Pacific, and Booth asked him not to reveal his secret for "the world would not believe you. I have lost my identity and I have a new existence," he declared. Miss Forrester relates that amongst her grandmother's most cherished possessions was a box of sea shells which correspond to similar shells found "only in the Islands of the Caroline group".

Other stories collected by Miss Forrester refered to Booth's movements immediately after his supposed death. Prior to the assassination of the President, Booth had been in Canada and had shipped his trunks to the Bahamas. The wife of a ship's captain informed Booth's grand-daughter that he had been carried in her husband's ship, in May, 1865, to England via the Bahamas, and he was still lame from his accident.

According to Miss Forrester, Mrs. Booth declared that her husband had been the "tool of other men". An actor friend of Booth's told her that Booth had tried to bring him into the kidnapping plot, saying that there was no chance of failure "as there were parties on the other side who were ready to co-operate with him".

There is no doubt that John Wilkes Booth shot Lincoln. He escaped southwards, and he or another man was shot at Garretts Farm. The official reports of his death and the identification of the body are highly confusing and they certainly give rise to the belief that some other person may have been identified and buried as Booth. This belief may have arisen solely from the extreme carelesssness shown by those who captured Booth and by the commission appointed to establish the body's identity. Those who were involved may not have considered it necessary to be meticulously careful in their identification.

No case can be made out against Edwin Stanton as the organizer of a plot within Lincoln's Cabinet. But his actions were sufficiently strange to give rise to the suspicion that people in high places might have connived at Booth's escape.

The extraordinary circumstances under which Booth's accomplices were arrested and tried has given rise to the belief that there was far more in the theory that people in high places were concerned, not to bring out the truth, but to obscure it. Throughout their imprisonment and during the trial these accomplices had their heads covered with tight-fitting canvas bags which made it impossible for them to see, hear or speak. None of the people (except Dr. Mudd who was convicted as one of the conspirators) who gave Booth shelter during his flight or harboured him, were put on trial. The chief purpose of the trial was to make out that the assassination of Lincoln was a Southern plot, but this was never proved. Booth and his wretched accomplices may have been madmen, or they may have been dupes of people in high places who desired to get rid of the one man who could quickly and surely bring about resumption of peaceful realtions between the Northern and Southern States.

John Wilkes Booth left his mark on American life. He has gone down in history as one of the world's most terrible assassins. Whether or not he escaped his richly deserved fate will never be known with certainty, but, as the matter stands, there must always be some doubt and some mystery about his death.

* * *

The case of the foundling boy of Nuremberg, Kaspar Hauser, beset the thoughts of our nineteenth century ancestors. His identity has never been established, though dark hints have been dropped, probably with little foundation. The controversy as to the boy's identity started on Whit Monday, 26 May, 1828, when a shoemaker named Weichmann in the Unschlitt Platz came across a boy who appeared to be either drunken or idiotic. He handed the shoemaker a letter which was addressed to "The Captain of the 4th Squadron of the 6th Regiment of Cavalry in Nuremberg".

Unable to get any information from the boy the shoemaker led him to the captain's house where he left him. The servant who took the boy in stated that he had handed him a letter which read "I want to be a soldier as my father was" and he refused or would not answer any questions. He indicated that his feet hurt him and he appeared to be hungry. He was offered a meal of meat, bread and beer which he rejected but he ate bread and drank water as if he were starving. The captain, unable to get any further information from the boy, took him to the nearest police station. Even then he would say no more than that he wanted to be a soldier but, given a piece of paper and pencil, he wrote the name "Kaspar Hauser".

The letter he carried appeared to be the only clue to the boy's identity; it read:

"Honoured Captain, I send you a boy who is anxious to serve his King in the Army. He was left at my house, 7 October, 1812, and I am only a poor day-labourer. I have ten children of my own. I have enough to do to bring them up. His mother left this child for me to take care of; but I do not know who she was, and I did not tell the police that the child was left at my door. I thought I must take him as my own son. I have brought him up as a Christian.

"I have not let him go out of the house since 1812. No one knows where he was brought up, and he himself does not know the name of the town, nor where my house is: you can question him as much as you like, but he cannot tell you anything.

"I have taught him to read and write, and when he is asked what he wants to do, he says he wants to be a soldier like his father. If his parents had lived he might have been well educated, for if you show him anything he can do it right off. I have taken him as far as Newmarkt; he

182

must go the rest of the way himself. I have told him that, as soon as he is a soldier, I will come and bring him home, otherwise I could not have got rid of him. Good Captain, you must not punish him to make him tell where he came from, for he really does not know. I carried him away in the night, and he could not possibly find his way back. Your Obedient Servant. I do not sign my name for fear of being punished. The boy has no money for I have none to give him. If you do not want to keep him you can kill him, or hang him up the chimney."

As well as this letter there was a note, which appeared to have been written by the child's mother in 1812, oddly enough in the Latin language, which read:

"This child has been baptized. His name is Kaspar. You must give him a surname, and take care of him. His father was a cavalry soldier. When he is seventeen years old, you must send him to Nuremberg, to the Sixth Cavalry Regiment; his father used to belong to it. I beg you to keep him until he is seventeen years old. He was born on 30 April, 1812. I am a poor girl and cannot take care of my child. His father is dead."

Neither of these letters gave the police any real clues to the identity of the boy who appeared to be about seventeen years of age and was broad-shouldered and well built. His eyes were blue, his hair a light brown, his complexion fair, and his hands and feet were small. His feet were the strangest things about him for they were as soft as a baby's, yet were badly blistered as though he had only just walked for the first time. He smiled like an innocent child and when he tried to walk he stumbled like a child learning to walk for the first time. He did nothing more than sit staring into vacancy.

When questioned he made the same answers as before and kept crying "horse", "horse". The only time he showed any emotion was when he was given a wooden toy horse; he cried and fondled it, bedecked it with ribbons and kept it at his bedside at night. Placed in the care of a policeman's wife, he showed no embarrassment when he was bathed and he continued to eat only bread and water. Meat made him ill at once and he became sick at the smell of liquor or cooking. Given a lighted candle he put his finger in the flame and drew it back with a cry of pain and amazement.

Taken through the streets of Nuremberg to see if he could

recognize where he had entered the city, he greeted all humans with the cry of "boy", and all animals he called "horse". His actions were observed carefully and it was noted that when he was given a plaster horse he tried to make it drink and could not seem to understand when the plaster melted in the water. On another day he spent hours trying to force a bridle into the closed mouth of a wooden horse. Slowly he learnt to speak German with the assistance of the children of the policeman's wife.

After some months he was able to explain that all he remembered was that he had lived in a cell six to seven feet long, four feet wide and five feet high, its floor being made of earth. When he awoke each morning, he found a jug of water and a piece of bread by its side. Sometimes the water had a bitter taste and he fell asleep after drinking it. When he awoke he found that his clothes had been changed and his nails cut. He had no recollection of any other life, but he recalled playing with toy wooden horses and he never saw anyone except on one occasion when he made a noise; he was struck on the arm with a piece of wood. Then, just before he arrived in Nuremberg, a man came into his room and taught him to write the words "Kaspar Hauser" on a piece of paper and instructed him to repeat over and over again the words "I want to be a soldier as my father was". Then the man came and took him out and carried him up a hill. The next he knew he was wandering in the city.

A number of notable people from all over Europe came to visit Kaspar whose fame had spread. The first was the famous German criminologist, Anselm Ritter von Feuerbach, who was convinced to the end of his life that Hauser was no imposter.

About eighteen months after Kaspar was found in Nuremberg, he was visited by the English Lord Stanhope, who appears to have had some strange interest in the boy's identity. Stanhope, a notorious adventurer, the stepbrother of the famous Lady Hester Stanhope and a nephew of William Pitt, the British Prime Minister, saw Kaspar and then had a number of talks with the ducal family of Baden and another strange individual, Major Hennenhofer, who had at one time been an official at the ducal court.

Shortly after Lord Stanhope's visit, Kaspar Hauser started to suffer from what his partisans declare was the first attempt to murder him. His detractors claim that it was the first attempt to take his own life, which ended successfully. Kaspar was found unconscious, his face covered with blood, on the floor of the cellar in the house in which he lived. He said he had been attacked by a man as he went to the lavatory. Clearly the deep wound in his head had been made by a knife. There seemed some semblance of truth in his story, for he described his attacker as wearing a dark coat, black pantaloons, leather gloves, and polished black shoes. A man answering that description had been observed in the vicinity of the house.

Kaspar was placed under guard, and considerable attempts were made to establish his identity, one theory being that he was a Hungarian by reason of certain words in that language which he appeared to understand. None the less, the rumour had spread that he was the illegitimate or unwanted child of some well-known German family and gossip connected him with the Grand Ducal family of Baden.

Other attempts to identify him linked him with the illegitimate child of the daughter of an innkeeper and a priest, but this was soon shattered when it was disclosed that their child had been born with a hare lip. Rumours were rife, and they were heightened by Lord Stanhope's visit to Baden. On his return to Nuremberg, Stanhope made great efforts to persuade everyone that Kaspar Hauser was a Hungarian and had no connexion with the Ducal family of Baden. He was allowed to adopt the boy and take him away from Nuremberg to the town of Ansbach, where he placed him in the care of a tutor, Doctor Meyer, and under the protection of a police officer named Lieut. Hickel.

Most of our information about Kaspar Hauser is derived from the memorandum drawn up by von Feuerbach, who reported to Queen Caroline of Bavaria, who had been a princess of the Royal House of Baden. Shortly afterwards von Feuerbach died mysteriously but this document was found in his papers. It read:

1. Kaspar Hauser is not an illegitimate, but a legitimate child, as is proved by the great care taken to keep his birth secret. The means are out of all proportion to the end, supposing him to be illegitimate, no matter of how high parentage.

2. The persons entrusted with the secret were possessed of extraordinary power and means for the carrying out of their criminal undertaking.

3. Kaspar Hauser must be a person upon whose life or death great interests are centred, as is shown by the recent attempt to murder him.

4. It is evident from the circumstances that crime against Kaspar Hauser's liberty was not prompted by hatred or revenge, solely by selfish interest.

5. He must be a person of high birth, of princely origin.

To sum up, von Feuerbach wrote:

"Kaspar Hauser is the legitimate son of royal parents, and was put out of the way in order to open the succession to other heirs. As no such child is known to have disappeared, it follows that he is supposed to be dead. The only royal house upon which such suspicion can fall is the House of Baden, wherein all the heirs of the regular line died within a short time, and under highly suspicious circumstances, leaving the crown to the offspring of a 'morganatic marriage'."

Von Feuerbach wrote a book about Kaspar Hauser which, while it posed no definite information as to its origin, hinted at official secrets.

Kaspar Hauser was either murdered or he took his own life on 14 December, 1833. He went to walk in the park in Ansbach, according to him having been invited to meet a man who he had spoken to in the street. In the park another man stabbed him in the heart, but he was able to reach home where he collapsed and died three days later. The doctors who examined him reported that the deep wound in his stomach which had grazed his heart could not have been self inflicted, but Lord Stanhope asserted that he had taken his own life.

The belief that Kaspar had been attacked and murdered was corroborated by his possession of a purse, and various objects which had never been seen in his possession before that day. The post-mortem examination corroborated his story that he had been confined in his youth in a sitting position, for his unusually large liver and small lungs and the distorted state of his legs indicated this. A doctor who asserted that the wound had not been self-inflicted reported afterwards that he had been offered a bribe to change his opinion. Before he died Kaspar said, "I didn't do it myself" and "Many cats are the sure death of the mouse".

It was widely believed in Germany that Lord Stanhope had been responsible for Kaspar Hauser's death. He and Lieut. Hickel were summoned to the presence of King Ludwig of Bavaria who was reported to have said he was convinced they were responsible for the boy's murder.

A flood of books and pamphlets spread all over Europe dealing with the mystery of Kaspar and his extraordinary end. It is claimed that great efforts were made to prevent the circulation of these books within the Duchy of Baden and it was frankly stated that Kaspar had been a prince of the Ducal house born on 29 September, 1812. It was said that his supposed mother, the Grand Duchess Stephanie, had wept when she was told of his death.

Some substance had been given to the theory that Kaspar was a child of the Ducal house of Baden by the somewhat strange facts which have emerged from the history of that family.

Karl Frederick, the Duke of Baden, and his wife Caroline had three sons, Karl Ludwig born 1751, Frederick born 1756, and Ludwig Wilhelm born 1763. On the death of his wife Caroline in 1783, the Duke married again, morganatically, a girl aged nineteen named Louise Caroline Geyer. Rumour declared that she was the mistress of her new husband's youngest son by whom she had five children.

We are concerned with the Duke's eldest son, Karl Ludwig, who had a son also named Karl who became, on his father's death in 1801, heir to the dukedom. His wife was named Stephanie Beauharnais and he succeeded his grandfather in 1811. A son born to him and his wife on 29 September, 1812, died two weeks later. Kaspar Hauser is supposed to have been this boy.

According to the theory which links him with the Ducal family of Baden, the first duke's morganatic wife, in order to secure the succession for her children, smuggled into the palace the dead child of a peasant woman and got rid of the baby prince. The true heir was smuggled out by Major Hennenhofer who put him into the care of a governess who was told he was the illegitimate child of a Court lady. Rumours that the true heir had been murdered were revived in 1816 when a second son died suddenly. When the old Grand Duke died in 1818 the way was clear for the succession of the children of the morganatic marriage.

The story of the substitution of a dead child for the true prince and the fate of the boy who became Kaspar Hauser is supposed to have been disclosed at a secret Council of State held on 30 March, 1830, when the Baden Minister of Foreign Affairs declared the true heir was living in ignorance of his rights. Major Hennenhofer is stated to have admitted that the boy known as Kaspar Hauser, found in Nuremberg two years previously, was the son of Karl Frederick, born in 1812. Taken from the care of the governess in 1816 he had been placed in the custody of an ex-soldier named Kaspar Muller by whom he had been kept in an underground cell until it was believed no one would suspect his identity. Then he was abandoned in Nuremberg. When the reigning Grand Duke declared his determination to restore Kaspar to his rights, he was persuaded, by fear of scandal, to let the matter drop.

There is no corroboration of this story, but it is claimed that pictures of Kaspar Hauser disclosed a striking likeness to the Ducal family of Baden. On the other hand when, later in the century, the Grand Duke threw open the family archives for inspection, to refute the story, nothing was found to support it. In 1851, on Major Hennenhofer's death, all his papers were seized and his heirs compensated for their loss.

The Kaspar Hauser mystery is one to which there is no solution. But there must have been some dark secret to be hidden.

* * *

The exact location of the bee farm in Sussex to which Sherlock Holmes retired in 1914 is shrouded in mystery. This is right and proper. Clearly the authorities, including the Post Office, were seeking only to preserve Holmes in his venerable old age from curious sightseers. Little else about his life and work is a mystery. It can be reconstructed from the sixty case histories faithfully recorded by Dr. Watson, who made Holmes' lean, hawk-like face, his pipe and deerstalker cap, and, above all, his methods, known all over the world.

Dr. Watson's meeting with Holmes is described in the *Study in Scarlet*, their first case together. Both men were seeking inexpensive lodgings, and a mutual friend brought them together. We can arrive at the date with some exactitude. Watson had been wounded at "the fatal battle of Maiwand" in Afghanistan, which we know took place on 27 July, 1880. Watson was invalided home and stayed for some time at an hotel in the Strand. The Lauriston Gardens mystery, which Watson named the *Study in Scarlet*, started on 4 March, some weeks after Holmes and Watson had taken Mrs. Hudson's rooms in Baker Street. We can date the Holmes-Watson meeting, therefore, some time in January, 1881. From this first fixed date we can trace Holmes' career backward and forward. Holmes' first case, *The Musgrave Ritual*, had occurred some two to three years previously, because we are told that Holmes had established for himself "a considerable though not a very lucrative connexion" and he refers also to "all those months of inactivity". A clue to the year in which Holmes commenced his career comes from Watson's statement in 1903 that "Mr. Sherlock Holmes was in active practice for twenty-three years". If we allow for the break of three years between 1891 and 1894 when, after the "Moriarty" incident, Holmes was considered dead and out of practice, this takes us back to the year 1878.

We can go even farther backwards. When Reginald Musgrave consulted Holmes in 1878, Holmes had not seen him for four years, since they were at college together. Young Musgrave could hardly have gone down later than 1874, for he had been managing his estates since his father's death and had become the "Member for the district" by 1878, which must have taken him at least four years to achieve. Eighteen seventy-four must also have been Holmes' last year at college, for he and Musgrave were clearly undergraduates of the same year. Musgrave would not otherwise have known about Holmes and his methods, which Holmes declares he fabricated during his last years at the university.

It is clear that Holmes must have taken a post-graduate course and travelled on the Continent between 1874 and 1878 because he acquired considerable knowledge of medicine and familiarity with at least three European languages. This reconstruction places Holmes' matriculation, at the age of eighteen, in 1871, and his birth in the year 1853, which is confirmed by the description of him in 1914 as "a tall gaunt man of sixty".

Holmes seems to have been reticent about his life, and previous education, before 1871. He merely told Watson that his ancestors had been country squires of no particular distinction and his grandmother was a Vernet, a sister of the French painters of that name, one branch of whose family had settled in England where the name had been changed to Verner. A member of that Anglo-French family, a distant relative of Holmes, bought Watson's practice in Kensington, in 1894, with money advanced by Holmes. We know also that Holmes had an elder brother named Mycroft who was in government service and who was at times "the British Government itself". It has been suggested that Holmes may have been born in America, or at least spent part of his youth in that country. Since that was long before the days of passports and of minute personal documentation it is impossible to check this thoroughly.

Returning to the year 1874, it seems strange that Dr. Watson omits to state clearly at which university Holmes had been educated. It is clear that Holmes was up at either Oxford or Cambridge, for Reginald Musgrave, who is described as "the scion of one of the very oldest families in the kingdom", would have been at one or other of the senior universities and Holmes himself refers to attendance at chapel and that athletics were a major interest of university life, which indicates that he was at one or other of these two universities, but which?

There are a number of conflicting clues. The first is the incident of the dog in the *Gloria Scot* case. Holmes tells Watson that he was never a very sociable fellow at college and that Victor Trevor was the only man he knew "and that only through the accident of his bull-terrier freezing on to my ankle one morning as I went down to chapel". It has been claimed that such an incident could not have taken place inside the college as dogs were not allowed inside. But of course the dog may have escaped from Trevor and entered Holmes' college.

From this clue the crime writer Miss Dorothy Sayers deduces that Holmes must have been at Cambridge. He was living out of college and was bitten by the dog on his way to chapel. This is, of course, not certain, for Holmes may have stepped outside the college for a moment on his way, which is expressly stated to have been *down* to chapel. If, however, he was living out of college when he met Trevor he would either have been in his last year at Oxford, where undergraduates live in college for the first two years, or in his first years at Cambridge, where undergraduates often have to wait one to two years to obtain rooms in college. As Holmes does not appear to have known anyone at the university when he met Trevor the incident appears to point to Cambridge, where he was in his early years. Other equally cogent grounds seem to point to Oxford, which was favoured by the late Father Ronald Know, an enthusiastic investigator of the Holmes legend.

He points to the fact that the scene of *The Missing Three-Quarter* takes place at Cambridge but it does not appear that Holmes had ever been in that city before and he is ignorant of the surrounding countryside. He does not know, as surely as any undergraduate should have known, that there was a late train from London to Cambridge, of which he speaks as "this inhospitable town" indicating, it is suggested, the opinion of a member of the rival university, Oxford, which he calls "this charming town".

Another clue comes from Holmes' statement to Watson: "You are not familiar with Cambridgeshire scenery, are you?" for it suggests that the scene of an earlier case, *The Three Students*, which had taken them to "one of our great university towns", must have been Oxford where Holmes describes Hilton Soames, the tutor and lecturer at the college of St. Luke's as "an acquaintance" presumably of his undergraduate days. It is significant, too, that Soames says to Holmes "you are aware that our college doors are double". Would Holmes have been expected to know that fact unless he had been up at Oxford? Holmes also shows knowledge that there are four stationers' shops in Oxford, which again suggests that that must have been his university.

Miss Sayers refuses to be shaken in her belief that Holmes was at Cambridge and she has gone deeply into the question of which was his college and what was the nature of his studies. She declares that he must have been aiming at an Honours degree, and by a process of elimination she suggests that the Natural Sciences were his particular line of study, which, Holmes tells us "was quite distinct from that of other fellows". Miss Sayers has discovered that in 1874 only seventeen students at Cambridge took this examination, one each from Clare, Pembroke and Sidney Sussex, the latter of which she selects as Holmes' college as being small, inexpensive and as offering special scholarships and prizes for this particular line of study. She has even discovered a "P. S." Holmes at Sidney Sussex who matriculated in 1871 and became a B.A. in 1875. She believes that it is possible that his Christian names "Thomas Scott" may have been incorrectly recorded owing to the university custom of writing names in Latin. But this T. S. Holmes became Chancellor of Wells Cathedral, and could not have been our Sherlock.

This brings us to the thorny question of the site of Mrs. Hudson's establishment at 221b Baker Street. There are a number of theories. On one point there is general agreement, for all the evidence indicates that the house was on the west side of the street although, in *The Cardboard Box*, there is a disturbing reference to the sun shining in the morning on the house opposite, which may, however, have been a house at the back seen from the rear of Holmes' rooms. That 221b was on the west side of Baker Street is clearly shown by the course of events in *The Empty House* in which Holmes and Watson approach the rear of the house opposite their own from the east. The choice of the site narrows down to three places, Abbey House, 109 Baker Street, farther south between Marylebone Road and York Street, or somewhere in the blocks above or below Blandford Street.

Abbey House is supported by the fact that it now occupies Nos. 219-223 Baker Street, but one of the strongest points against its choice is that, until 1930, that part of the street was called "upper" Baker Street. This, however, may in fact be corroboration for its choice as we find in Conan Doyle's notebook, at the time when he was editing the first of Watson's MSS, that the address is given as 221b Upper Baker Street, wherein he may have meant perhaps only to make clear that the house was in the upper rather than the lower part of the street. That Abbey House is directly opposite the Metropolitan Station is claimed both in support and against its selection as the site of Holmes' rooms. In *The Beryl Coronet* Watson notices the distracted banker approaching from the station and he arrives breathless after running hard which suggests that Holmes' rooms were farther from the station than Abbey House.

The attempt to identify "109" Baker Street as the site is believed to be discredited on the grounds that, until 1921, that part of Baker Street was called "York Place". But the selection of "109" turns on a most interesting piece of evidence. The clue comes from the case known as *The Empty House*.

Approaching Baker Street from the east, Holmes and Watson traverse narrow passages and find themselves in the rear of "Camden House" from which they can see directly into their own rooms across the street. Searching for the site on the clues provided by this evidence, and following the passages indicated, Dr. Chandler Briggs of St. Louis came upon the rear of a house in which he found himself exactly opposite 109. Then, on going round to the front of the house in which he found himself, he saw to his amazement that over the door was the sign "Camden House", which clearly indicated that 109 was the original 221, on the first floor of which Holmes and Watson had occupied rooms. To make doubly sure Dr. Briggs counted the steps of the staircase and found that they numbered exactly seventeen as is stated in *The Scandal in Bohemia*.

After such an amazing piece of detective work the consideration of other possible sites hardly seems necessary but it may be remarked that a most ingenious theory has been put forward to link Holmes with No. 27 Baker Street, occupied by "Hudson Bros., Grocers", it being suggested that Mrs. Hudson, Holmes' landlady, may have left the house to her sons, who set themselves up as grocers.

The documentation of Holmes' friend and chronicler, Dr. John H. Watson, is no less authentic. Watson tells us that he took his degree of Doctor of Medicine at London University in 1878, and became a House Physician at "Barts" before joining the Army Medical Service and going to Afghanistan where he was struck in the shoulder by a bullet which shattered the bone, grazing his subclavian artery, a wound which within six years became transferred, rather strangely, to his leg.

Watson lived with Holmes until 1887 when he married Miss Mary Morstan, whom we meet in *The Sign of Four*, and then set up as a general medical practitioner, buying a practice in Paddington which later he sold in order to purchase a better one in Kensington. It can only be assumed that Watson's wife died, for by 1896 he is back at Baker Street apparently single. He must have married again for in 1902 Holmes speaks of Watson having "deserted me for a wife". Watson indicates that his father must have been well off for he owned a watch worth fifty guineas and he says that his elder brother, who inherited it, was a drunkard for the key had made many scratches round the winding hole. We know that Watson played rugger for Blackheath and that as a boy he had been in Australia, for he speaks of Ballarat as if from personal experience. Competent doctor though he obviously was, he was always ready to leave his profession when Holmes beckoned. That Watson makes a number of chronological errors in his recordings of Holmes' cases suggests there were so many of them that his memory became vague. Or his notes, written in the usual medical hand, may have been untranscribable. His habit of recording Holmes' cases out of order may have led to inaccuracies, but he succeeds, perhaps intentionally, in cloaking the true identity of a number of Holmes' clients. After seventy years, for example, the identity of Holmes' *Illustrious Client* is still cloaked in mystery. The date of Watson's first marriage, to Miss Morstan, is clearly the key to the whole structure of the Holmes chronology for certain cases are referred to as having occurred before or after Watson's marriage.

The exact dating of Holmes' cases, as recorded by Watson, is fraught with difficulty. Clearly there are some chronological errors, which may never be fully explained. Watson obviously met his first wife during the case known as *The Sign of Four,* but he must have mistaken her reference to "about six years ago—to be exact, upon 4 May, 1882," which indicates that the loss of the Agra treasure took place in 1888, for what is related in two other cases makes it clear that the mystery of *The Sign of Four* took place in 1886 and that Watson was married in June, 1887. At this time Watson may have been under considerable emotional excitement for he clearly indicates that he fell in love "at first sight" which may understandably account for these strange inaccuracies.

The date of Watson's marriage is clearly indicated from two cases. At the date of *The Reigate Squires,* which occurred in April, 1887, Watson is still in Baker Street but during Holmes' investigation into *The Naval Treaty,* which is dated July, 1887, Watson describes it as immediately succeeding his marriage. During the case of *The Five Orange Pips,* which occurred in September of that year, Watson is back in Baker Street while his wife is visiting her aunt. Six months later Holmes is able to point out to Watson that he has put on seven pounds in weight as a result of marital happiness. There can be little doubt, therefore, that Watson was married in June, 1887.

Holmes retired in 1903, according to Watson, for the case of *The Creeping Man,* which took place in September, is described by Watson as being "one of the very last cases handled by Holmes". We know that Holmes was brought out of his retirement in 1914 to handle a case called by Watson *His Last Bow,* in which we finally take leave of Holmes and Watson. We find them gazing out over the moonlight sea at Harwich, in intimate converse, as the Great War of 1914 breaks out.

While Watson may have been guilty of many inaccuracies, it is possible to date a number of Holmes' cases from internal evidence. For example, the case of *The Bruce-Partington Plans* can be dated in 1886 from the reference to Lord Bellinger as being twice Premier of Britain, clearly indicating that this was an alias for Lord Salisbury, who was Prime Minister for the second time from 1886 to 1892. While the description of this "Lord Bellinger" seems to apply with greater force to Mr. Gladstone, who was Prime Minister for the second time from 1880 to 1885, it is thought that Watson would not have so clearly disclosed the incognito. Watson indicates that the reference refers to the first year of Lord Salisbury's period of office, when there was a separate Foreign Secretary, as he indicates in the story. After that date Lord Salisbury combined the Ministry of Foreign Affairs with the Premiership.

The emotional turmoil in which Watson found himself when he fell in love with Miss Morstan during *The Sign of Four* is disclosed from a minor inaccuracy. According to Watson the letter received by Miss Morstan on the morning of her visit to Baker Street was dated 7 July, but Watson a few hours later speaks of it being a "September evening" and the time of year is confirmed by the statement that they enjoyed a supper of grouse and oysters before setting out on the chase down the river. Another chronological clue comes from the case of *Silver Blaze*, in which the racehorse of that name is described as being of Isonomy stock. A check of the records has disclosed that Isonomy went to stud in 1881, and as the case clearly occurred before Watson's marriage, and *Silver Blaze* was certainly more than three years old, the disappearance of the favourite for the Wessex Plate must have occurred in the year 1886.

Watson is clearly muddled in his dating of *The Hound of the Baskervilles*, which he implies occurred in 1889. Internal evidence indicates that 1899 is the earliest possible date on which this case could have occurred, from the mention of an article in *The Times* on free trade which certainly could not have been published long before the year 1900. Other internal clues show also that it must have occurred after the death of Mrs. Watson for the Doctor is back at Baker Street and we note the deferential attitude of Lestrade, the Scotland Yard Inspector, who we recall is somewhat offhand with the more juvenile Mr. Holmes in *The Study in Scarlet*. By 1889 he would have treated him with greater respect. Two other of Holmes' famous cases have been dated from researches in the public records. *The Missing Three-Quarter* must have occurred in 1887, as is shown by the records of the varsity rugger match and *The Beryl Coronet* took place on 28 February, 1886, as is disclosed by information obtained from the Meteorological Office about snowfalls in London.

Watson appears to have been completely muddled by the "Moriarty" incident. The problem of exact dating is so difficult that it has even been suggested that Holmes created a fictional Professor, the "Napoleon of Crime", to disguise and obscure from Watson a long series of failures as did in fact occur, we know, in the cases of *The Five Orange Pips* and *The Engineer's Thumb*. It seems possible that Holmes' mental powers may have broken down from overwork. Either way, Watson seems to have known very little of

Holmes' activities during this period. Watson, who was told by Holmes of "Moriarty" for the first time in 1891, accompanies Holmes to Switzerland where, having been decoyed away, Watson returns to find that Holmes and Moriarty have gone over the Reichenbach Falls locked in a life and death struggle.

Three years later Holmes reappears to inform Watson that he escaped and spent two years in Tibet, paid a visit to Mecca, and called on the Khalifa at Khartoum. Although he left his friend Watson in the belief that he was dead, Holmes appears to have kept Scotland Yard informed of his continued existence, for we find Lestrade greeting him with the understatement "it is good to see you back in London, sir". It has been suggested that Holmes' failure to reassure Watson may have been due to his intention to protect his friend from such dangerous knowledge while members of the Moriarty gang were still at large. That Moriarty, unknown to Watson, must too have escaped is clear, unless there were two James Moriartys, for he springs up again in 1889 at the head of a gang in *The Valley of Fear* which clearly took place in that year. Yet Watson indicates that it took place in the year 1891 when as we know from *The Final Problem*, he had not then heard of Moriarty. Watson's complete confusion about Holmes' movements at this time is shown by his dating of *The Wistaria Lodge Case* in 1892 when, as he should have known, Holmes was at the bottom of the Reichenbach Falls.

That Watson was not an accurate chronicler, or possibly that he was hoodwinked by Holmes, is suggested by his description of the great man as a drug addict. He describes Holmes as "a self poisoner by cocaine and tobacco". Watson states that though he had done his best to wean Holmes from the drug habit, it persisted until 1897 and he gives many statements which corroborate his belief that Holmes took drugs for many years. A learned correspondent to *The Lancet*, on 26 December, 1936, suggests that Holmes was pulling Watson's leg. The bottle from which Holmes injected himself contained water not cocaine for it is quite impossible that if he had persistently taken cocaine his mental powers would have been as keen as we are led to believe they were.

Apart from recording the details of Holmes' many famous cases, Watson supplies a great deal of other information about him, that he was the compiler of a great Index of Crime, a composer of music, a performer on the violin, an art lover, a researcher into old English charters, an excellent linguist and an expert marksman. Watson is not blind to Holmes' imperfections for he records at least one case of burglary and another of trespass and, in the case of Sir Henry Baskerville, he jeopardizes his client's life so that Baskerville is allowed to have the hound's fangs almost in his throat before Holmes could intervene. He allows criminals to escape, thus becoming an accessory to their misdeeds and he clearly recognizes revenge as being justifiable.

He even makes incorrect deductions, as in *The Reigate Squires* where he falls into the error of assessing a man's age from his handwriting, which is now known to be impossible, and in another case he concludes from a large hat that it was obvious that its owner was a person of extreme intelligence. While Watson makes reference to a number of the famous monographs composed by Holmes, he is maddeningly reticent about them. Clearly the science of detection has been maimed by Watson's omission to give the details of Holmes' conclusions "on the Distinction between the ashes of the Various Tobaccos, in which he enumerates one hundred and forty varieties". What would Scotland Yard today give for the knowledge clearly contained in the monograph "the Influence of a Trade upon the Form of a Hand"?

On the other hand, Watson supplies numerous examples of amazing mental powers and the science of deduction which Holmes instituted, certainly in the science of criminal investigation.

Clearly there were a number of other cases which Holmes refused to allow Watson to chronicle: he was allowed only to deposit his notes in a travel-worn and battered despatch box in the vaults of the bank of Cox and Company at Charing Cross, where they still presumably lie, awaiting permission for publication. We are left to imagine what must have occurred and how Holmes dealt with such cases as *The Singular Tragedy of the Atkinson Brothers at Trincomalee, The Little Problem of the Grosvenor Square Furniture Van, The Adventure of Ricoletti of the Club Foot and His Abominable Wife*. We know nothing either of *The Case of Wilson the Notorious Canary Trainer* or *The Repulsive Story of the Red Leech*, or of *The Giant Rat of Sumatra*. Even more maddening is Holmes' refusal to allow Watson to record *The Strange Case of Isadora Persano* who is described as being found stark staring mad with a matchbox in front of him which contained a remarkable worm stated to be unknown to science.

Holmes is immortal. Watson has supplies us with sufficient information to detail his career with extraordinary accuracy. To those who doubt the actual existence of the most famous detective of fiction, we need only to quote Holmes' maxim "that when you have eliminated the impossible, whatever remains, however improbable, must be the truth".

*　　*　　*

In an ex-army hut in the Black Forest in Germany lives an elderly woman called Anna Anderson, who for forty years has claimed to be Anastasia, the youngest daughter of the last Czar of Russia, born at St. Petersburg on 4 June, 1901. Nicholas II, his wife, his heir, and his four daughters are supposed to have been murdered by the Bolsheviks at Ekaterinsburg in the Ural Mountains on 18 July, 1918, and there can be no doubt that the Royal Romanoffs were shot in the cellar of their prison house on the orders of the Urals Soviet as White Russian counter-revolutionary forces approached the town.

There have been numerous rumours that one of the daughters, Anastasia, escaped and it is claimed she might have been rescued in the confusion which followed the massacre when the bodies were hurriedly thrown into a lorry to be driven to a disused mine outside the town and burnt. It is said that one body was unaccounted for and a wide search was made for one of the daughters, believed to be Anastasia. It is not beyond the bounds of possibility that this happened, and it is quite impossible to verify such rumours behind the Iron Curtain.

The woman Anna Anderson who claims to be Anastasia first appears in Western records when she was fished out of a canal in Berlin on 12 February, 1920, taken to a hospital and later transferred to an asylum. From that moment her career is well documented and her claims were made known to the world in her book, *I Anastasia*. published in 1958, and by two films based on her life story.

Is her claim true? Since 1957 her claim against the acknowledged Romanoff heirs, the near relatives of the late Czar, has been proceeding in the Hamburg Courts and on 15 May, 1961, the Court rejected her claim to be recognized as Anastasia. The Court rejected also the counter-claim of Barbara, Duchess of Mecklenburg, representing the Romanoff family, against whom Anna Anderson brought her case, that Frau Anderson was really a Polish land worker named Franziska Schanzkowski. Passing judgment, the President of the Court said that Frau Anderson had failed to prove her identity with Anastasia. Frau Anderson, he said, had made herself available for questioning for a very limited period and she had answered a few questions in a "completely inadequate way". The Court complained it had received no opportunity to establish the scars Frau Anderson claimed she suffered. Her knowledge of Russian was, stated the President, a "great riddle". Although urged to speak Russian "the plaintiff preferred to run the risk of being considered a swindler than speak one single sentence of Russian". The fact that she knew of conditions at the Russian Court was impressive, but it was pointed out that this could have been picked up from memoirs.

How can such a person prove identity? History shows the difficulties to be overcome. Naundorff failed, or was given no chance, to prove he was Louis XVII of France. To establish identity a person believed dead must primarily tell from the start a convincing story. He must show knowledge of people, places and events which could be known only to him. He must provide either documentary proof or show convincing physical marks or likeness. He can be expected to speak his native language fluently and he needs to be recognized by his alleged relatives or friends. How does Anastasia, as we may call her, measure up to these standards?

It seems, from her own story, that Anastasia has done a great deal to invalidate her claim but that is not necessarily against her, for it is clear that, particularly in the 1920's, she was a very sick woman, whoever she was. Her history since 1920 has been a terrible one. Most of her life has been spent in hospitals and asylums, though she has never been certified insane. She has been exploited and many of her friends and supposed relatives have blown both hot and cold. She has ignored or quarrelled with many of those people who might have helped her. Again, that is not necessarily against her for, if she is Anastasia, her experiences might well have turned her mind.

First, her escape story. She says that in the massacre at Ekaterinsbury she was knocked unconscious and the next thing she knew she was in a cart and was being carried across Russia by four people named Tcharkovski. In her book she has collected statements to corroborate this. Franz Svoboda, a former Austrian prisoner-of-war in Russia, is said to have stated on 12 December, 1938, that he followed the guards into the cellar and saw a soldier turn over one body. When the girl screamed, he hit her over the head with his rifle butt. Svoboda recognized the girl as Anastasia and he helped the soldier roll up her body in a blanket, put it in a cart and take it to a house. He then escaped himself to Vladivostock. Arthur Rohse declared, in November, 1956, that he was an officer in the advancing White Army and he heard a rumour that one of the Czar's daughters had escaped and that a search was made for her. Various other people are recorded by Anastasia as saying that one of the Grand Duchesses had escaped.

According to Anastasia, the journey in the cart to Rumania took months, which must have been true since the distance is fifteen hundred miles and the whole of South Russia was in the throes of civil war. Alexander Tcharkovski told her that he and his brother belonged to the Red Guard at Ekaterinsburg and, seeing that she was only wounded, took her to their cart and escaped with their mother and sister. Anastasia supplies the statements, recorded in 1927 and 1955, of two men, a German officer who was in the Ukraine, and an Armenian, who say that they knew that the cart they saw crossing the Dneister and Bug rivers in December, 1918, contained the Grand Duchess Anastasia.

In Bucharest, Anastasia had a child by Alexander Tcharkovski and married him there but he was killed. Her baby was taken away from her, and she was conveyed by his brother to Berlin. They went to an hotel and on finding him gone next morning she went out and slipped into the canal.

There is no further corroboration of her escape story. Checks in Rumania have failed to locate the child or to find any record of the marriage either under the name of Tcharkovski or under that of Miskhevitch, which is believed to have been the true name of the two brothers, inasmuch as two Polish brothers of that name are recorded as having been guards at Ekaterinsburg. Asked why she did not immediately go to her relative, Queen Maria of Rumania, Anastasia declared she could not go to her in a pregnant condition.

When she was questioned in hospital, Anastasia says she decided not to speak or to give her true name. The police report says she had no papers or means of identification. At the asylum to which she was moved she was recognized by another patient named Klara Peuthert, who had been dressmaker to various ladies at the Russian Royal Palace, as one of the Czar's daughters, but it seems that this woman believed that at first she was Titiana, the second daughter. It has been asserted by Anastasia's detractors at first she said she was Titiana, and then switched to Anastasia. Her recognition by Peuthert gave her the idea of posing as one of the Czar's daughters. Subsequently, Anastasia was released to the care of certain Russian refugees, and she was visited and inspected by members and close relatives of the Russian Royal Family. She says she refused to speak to these people but some of them recognized her, either confirming it, or rejecting it later.

One point is clear from the photographs of the Romanoff family and of Anastasia herself, which she publishes. Anastasia bears a strong resemblance to both "Anastasia" and to her alleged relatives, and it seems that many of the people who came to visit her recognized this likeness. One fact seems extraordinary. Anastasia either could not or would not speak Russian or English, both of which the Russian Royal children spoke fluently. She appeared to speak only German with which the children were not conversant. She says she refused to speak Russian because of the terrible experiences in Russia. A psychologist, Dr. Bonhoeffer, who examined her in 1926, remarked: "You cannot get any coherent account of her childhood and later experiences. She often evades detailed questioning by telling you it is too painful to talk about her memories."

In her book, published in 1958, Anastasia recalls memories of her childhood which appear to be convincing proof of her unique knowledge, but it needs to be borne in mind that she might have acquired this information from books of reminiscences or from the Russian refugees with whom she mixed for some years. It is quite impossible to sort out what she might have learned after 1920 from what may well be genuine memories. One statement she makes appears to represent information which could not have been known to other than a member of the Russian Royal Family. She says that in 1916 her German uncle, her mother's brother, the Grand Duke Ernest of Hesse, visited Russia on a secret peace mission. This the Grand Duke has denied, but various people have stated, according to Anastasia, that this visit did take place in great secrecy and that they saw the Grand Duke on his journey. If Anastasia could substantiate this statement it would be strong proof of her claim.

For and against Anastasia's claim is her alleged recognition by Glebe Botkin, the son of the Czar's personal physician and his sister, and by the Grand Duchess's former governess who, according to Anastasia, recognized certain body marks. On the other hand, Pierre Gilliard, their French tutor, who was with the family in Siberia and who visited Anastasia in Germany, is said at first to have been favourable to her claim and then suddenly to have become sceptical. We have only Anastasia's word for these distinguishing marks; so it is impossible to assess their evidential value. If what she says is true, she bears just those marks, such as a cauterized mole, as did the young Grand Duchess. Another strange fact was the refusal of the former Court dentist in Russia, whom she located in Paris, to identify her teeth.

All these "recognitions" and "rejections" are highly confusing, and it is difficult to assess their strength and weaknesses from Anastasia's story. All that can be said is that amongst the people who were in a position to recognize her, some did so, others did not, others were hesitant. Many of these people, however, appear to have seen at least some resemblance to their relative. According to Anastasia, her nearest relatives refused to recognize or see her because her established existence would jeopardize their claims to the funds supposed to have been deposited by the Czar in European banks. But this great treasure of the Romanoffs has never been located.

It is quite impossible to come to any firm conclusion about Anastasia. Her detractors claim that she is in reality a Polish peasant woman named Franziska Schanzkowski who was reported missing in Berlin in 1920. Anastasia declares that the police learned that this woman was murdered in August, 1921. According to Anastasia, when the two sisters of this woman were brought to see her in 1933 they failed to recognize her.

Anastasia does not put forward any convincing legal proof of her claim in her book. The Soviet authorities are hardly likely to supply evidence that one of these girls escaped from the terrible murder that was carried out quite unnecessarily. The murder of the Czar and of his entire family is a black episode in Russian history which the Soviet authorities are unlikely to re-open. Though on the face of it unlikely, it is not impossible that one of the daughters did escape, or was not killed at the time. In the confusion anything might have happened.

Would it be possible for such a girl to prove her flight across Russia to Rumania? Even if the Tcharkovskis still existed, it is doubtful if their word would be taken to corroborate the escape. If Anastasia is genuine it is understandable that she behaved, particularly in the 1920's, in a way completely inimical to her claim. Feeling that everyone's hand was against her, she may well have acted as she appears to have done. It would be quite understandable if her mind had "blacked out" under the experiences she went through. Then, resenting the scepticism she encountered, she heightened disbelief by her behaviour. There was no one to advise her how to set out to substantiate her claim in a quiet, well-ordered manner.

If she is genuine, then Anastasia is the world's most unfortunate individual. If she is a fake, then she has put up a highly convincing deception for forty years. The problem of her identity is perhaps the most extraordinary mystery of the twentieth century.

THE RUTHLESS MEN

FOR CENTURIES the stone statues of Easter Island have stared out into the Pacific, their inscrutable faces posing a problem which was apparently an impenetrable mystery. Clues had grown cold in the mists of time. Now the mask has been pulled away, partly at least. For over two hundred years, since the Dutchman, Roggeven, discovered and named the island on Easter Day, 1722, there has been intense speculation as to the statues' origin. Who carved and erected these colossal stone monuments on a tiny island in the Pacific, thousands of miles from anywhere, and why? Their cutting and erection constituted a vast unproductive work, requiring considerable time, a high degree of technical skill and intense determination. The people who spent their lives, generation after generation, carving and erecting these statues, must have been completely isolated from the world for centuries, for such a grandiose operation could have been conceived and carried out only by a people unhindered by the fear of aggression from without.

The statues of Easter Island, which portray in the far Pacific the faces of white Caucasian men, depicting all the characteristic features of a white Nordic race, are no longer a complete mystery, thanks to an imaginative and enterprising expedition as romantic as the story the hardy detectives have disclosed since 1947. While the mystery of the statue builders, who they were and from where they came, has been solved, a greater mystery remains. Who were the bearded white men who came from the east, from across the Atlantic to Central and South America during the first thousand years of the Christian era, long before the Norsemen reached Vinland, and long before Columbus sailed across the Atlantic?

While Europe and the Mediterranean world were in the grip of the Dark Ages, the thousand years in which inquiry, research and discovery were stultified by superstition and ignorance, white men crossed the Atlantic, visited the Mayas in Central America, progressed down South America to Peru and Bolivia, leaving behind them vast works in stone, unequalled elsewhere in the world for their size and technical excellence. Then having sojourned for some years, how many we do not know, they sailed across the Pacific in the direction of the setting sun to reach the islands we now call Polynesia. They settled there and spent their lives in feverish activity, and with complete singleness of purpose, erecting statues of their ancestors, men of hard, ruthless, scornful and pitiless faces, alien to the South Seas.

This is one of the world's strangest stories, a gigantic riddle which archaeologists gave up as hopeless, which no one thought would ever be solved.

Easter Island is no tropical paradise. A tiny dot in the ocean wastes thousands of miles from any other land, only thirty-five miles in circumference, its soil produces a meagre living for less than two thousand people. Volcanic in origin, it rises sheer from the Pacific breakers. Its only mammals are rats and men. Surely it is the last place to expect to find such magnificent works of art? So thought the early European voyagers who chanced upon them, and revealed to an astonished world that unknown men had been labouring for centuries in this far-away island carving literally many scores of gigantic stone statues, some of which were the height of a three-storeyed house. These statues were carved with nothing stronger than stone tools. Right from the start the mystery was deepened by the presence on the island, amongst a people of otherwise Polynesian racial type, of men and women so fair that they might be taken for Europeans.

These white people are found elsewhere in the eastern Pacific, as my own ancestor, Captain Tobias Furneaux, himself noticed in 1767, when he landed as the first European on the island of Tahiti. Throughout the islands of the Society group and the Marquesas, as well as on Easter Island, there were and are still today, a number of men and women as fair as northern Europeans. Roggeven and his successors, Captain Cook and the Frenchman, La Perousse, found some Easter Islanders as white as themselves who had fair or red hair, blue eyes and aquiline noses, with elongated ears like those of the strange statues which dominated the land. Pictures drawn by Captain Cook's artist show the islanders as having ears reaching to their shoulders and faces quite without those features, broad faces, squat noses and thick lips, which are now well known as characteristic of the Polynesian peoples. These strange white racial types were noticed both on Easter Island and on the other Polynesian islands before the European seamen had satisfied their lusts upon the not unwilling women of the South Seas.

The European exploration of the Pacific in the eighteenth century and its consequences, brought tragedy to the peoples of the South Seas. Diseases which were common to Europe but hitherto unknown in the South Sea islands, decimated their populations. In the case of Easter Island, a Peruvian slave raid in 1862 reduced the population of some two thousand to a few hundred. Yet even amongst those that remained, the strong white racial type still persists. From where had these people come? When they were first discovered the islanders had no more than a few tiny canoes.

As well as the statues which have made Easter Island world famous, there are massive walls and platforms cut from huge blocks of stone and fitted with meticulous exactness. It may be remarked that similar stone structures, walls, temples and burial places are found throughout the islands of the Marquesas group. The majority of the statues, which are of many different sizes, are found on the slopes of the volcanic mountain named Rano Raraqu. Within the crater of the volcano there are many others still part of the living rock from which they were being quarried. Other statues are found alongside ancient roadways, and on stone platforms, though many of these have been thrown down and broken.

There are at least one hundred completed statues and some one hundred and fifty more that are unfinished. One of the smaller statues is on view in the British Museum. The statues which are visible above ground have certain common characteristics. They are all of nude males. All have elongated ears hanging to their shoulders, thin noses and lips, large eyes, jutting chins, which probably suggests beards, and pronounced nipples. Their heads are huge, their legs tiny and stunted. The hands are laid on the stomachs, and the sole decoration is a belt carved around the stomach. Many of the statues originally had top-knots made from red volcanic stone and placed on the heads after the statues had been erected. All the top-knots have now fallen off.

One of the most remarkable aspects of the statue making on Easter Island is that it was suspended suddenly and never renewed. Many gigantic statues, half shaped, lie in the niches where they were being hewn from the volcanic rock inside the crater, and beside them scattered about lie the stone tools of their carvers. The Easter Island workmen cut the statues, some of which are over sixty feet high, from the actual rock. After the general outline had been decided, above and below each proposed statue gutters were made in which the workmen lay as they cut at the rock until the general outline of the statue emerged. At this stage the statue was still held to the rock by a keel or cord down the back. When the final stage was reached, stone wedges were rammed underneath and behind the statue to prevent it slipping away before a rampart of earth had been prepared on which to slide it down. Some unfinished statues still have the wedges in position. When a statue was finally cut away from the rock it was slid down to the lower slopes of the crater where the final touches were made and the details of the faces were carved. Then came perhaps the greatest work of all, transportation over miles of ground to the position where the statue was to be set up. As some of the statues found in different parts of the island weigh over sixty tons, their movement must have required the labour of at least five hundred people at one time. The islanders had neither wheeled transport nor beasts of burden and this suggests the employment either of slave labour, or of a fanatical religious zeal in the islanders themselves. The time which statues have stood in position is indicated by the silting up of earth and grass around them so that only the heads are visible. For this to happen must have taken centuries.

Many statues lie fallen beside the paved roads which lead from the mountain to other parts of the island; others lie broken and overthrown near the great stone platform.

The most remarkable features of the statues, apart from their size and weight, are their pitiless facial expressions, their red top-knots, which suggests that they were meant to depict men with red hair, and of course their elongated ears which are a salient feature of all the statues. The top-knot of red hair and the elongated ears came to be so admired by the successors of the statue builders that they are today considered as emblems of manly beauty in Easter Island.

Another remarkable feature of the statues is their balance. All had been cut so symmetrically that when erected they had perfect equilibrium. Yet how could they have been erected? That is another of the strange problems of Easter Island. Many statues were moved ten or twenty miles to where they were erected. Each statue had to be stood upright on its pedestal, and the large red top-knot dragged up and placed on the head. The work must have taken a very long time.

Written boards in the form of pictographs, the like of which can be found nowhere else in Polynesia, also were found on Easter Island. It seems unlikely that a written script would have been invented on so tiny an island where there could have been little need of written communication. No one now can decipher these pictographs; the last man who claimed to understand them died in 1914. Although the meaning of this script has been lost some of the islanders claim to associate certain traditions, stories and songs with particular pictographs. Whether this unknown script will ever be deciphered is very doubtful, for to their meaning there is no clue such as was found on the Rosetta stone in the case of the Egyptian hieroglyphics.

As well as the stone statues the Easter Islanders possess a number of tiny wooden images which depict people similar to the statues and which are supposed to represent their earliest ancestors who came to the island from elsewhere. It is significant that these wooden images all depict emaciated men with their ribs sticking out, suggesting perhaps the results of a long and arduous voyage.

It is with the islanders' traditions that we start to get clues as to the origin of the statue builders, the "long ears" as they are referred to by the present "short ears".

According to these traditions, which were noted by Europeans before the year 1888, the "long ears" led by a chief named Hotu-Matua had come to the island fifty-seven generations before. This takes us back to about the year A.D. 475. Hotu-Matua arrived after a voyage of a hundred and twenty days from a land in the east named Marae-toe-Hau, meaning "the burial place", the climate of which was so hot that at certain times of the year people died from the effects of heat and plant life was scorched. He had been preceded by his brother with six men whose voyage had taken sixty days.

In all some three hundred people came with Hotu-Matua. Driven from their homeland by a rebellion of their subjects, they had set sail in the direction of the setting sun. Tradition related that they brought with them sweet potatoes, other seeds and a written script. Twenty generations later true Polynesians, the "short ears", reached the island by island-hopping across the Pacific. These "short ears" were enslaved by the "long ears" who proved hard taskmasters, forcing them to work on the cutting, dragging and erecting of statues, generation after generation until at last the slaves rebelled. Then, about eleven generations back, or approximately in our seventeenth century, a great battle took place in which the "long ears" were overcome and slain. There was only one survivor, a man named Ororoina, who had many descendants, some of whom are still living today.

The rebellion of the slaves must have been sudden for the "long ears" precipitately abandoned their statue carving but it could not have been entirely unexpected for excavations at the eastern end of the island show that the "long ears" must have spent years, perhaps even generations, in making a very strong fortified position guarded by a great ditch which according to tradition they filled with wood and bushes with the intention of guarding themselves from attack by a flaming pit.

Apparently they were betrayed by the "short ear" wife of one of the "long ears". According to the story this woman, after the "long ears" had retired to their prepared position, sat herself by the cliff and gave a signal which allowed a number of the "short ears" to creep up along the cliff and secrete themselves behind the "long ears". When they were in position she gave the "short ears" army a signal so when the attackers swarmed up towards the trench, the first party of "short ears" attacked their "long ear" enemies from their rear and prevented them from setting fire to the brushwood. In a terrible battle, the last great stand of these amazing men, they fell victims to the slaves they had forced to labour on what must have been to them an unrewarding and quite unintelligible task. From the one survivor of the massacre emanates the traditions which are our strongest clue to the origin of the "long ears".

There can be no doubt that the "long ears" were the original inhabitants of Easter Island. Arriving there in the fifth century of our era they lived in peace and solitude for over thirty generations, perhaps for a thousand years, until suddenly out of the blue came Polynesian peoples in their canoes. There is no doubt that these Polynesians, people of the Malay race, progressed throughout the Pacific, often sailing vast distances out of sight of land. They did indeed reach the islands farthest to the east. Inevitably they must have reached Easter Island, and there perhaps they were at first welcomed by the "long ears" who saw in them, a primitive people, ideal subjects. But, as in other parts of the Pacific, where there are still examples of the white Caucasian type, the more prolific and simpler Polynesians in the end killed their masters and became their inheritors, though intermarriage between the two peoples led to fusion in many of the islands.

Other traditions recorded on the island refer to its original name. It was called Te-Pito-te-Henua meaning the "navel" of the islands, and by tradition the original landing-place of the "long ears" on the island was called the "golden navel". It was marked by a tooled sphere of stone. It is thought that the word "navel" in this connexion refers to the first landfall of the voyagers. The island is also known as Great Rapa, and there is another island to the west called Little Rapa which suggests that the original voyagers may have progressed to found a subsequent colony on the similar island. Easter Island had also another name, Mata-kite-Rani, which means "the eye which looks towards heaven", or, as has been suggested, towards the original homeland.

One of the most significant clues which we can derive from these island traditions is that the original voyagers, Hotu-Matua and his men, came, not in canoes, but on "wood bound together with ropes".

There have, of course, been many speculations about the origin of the statue builders of Easter Island. One of the first theories was that Easter Island had been at the end of a Pacific continent which may have sunk below the sea as a result of volcanic action. There is, however, no geological evidence that such a continent ever existed, at least within the period of human inhabitance of the earth. The other theory, long held, and still believed by many archaeologists, is that the Easter Islanders, both the "long ears" and the "short ears", were Polynesians, Malays. There are strong objections to this theory. The Polynesians, all of whom speak the same language, are part of the yellow-brown race and are of Asiatic origin, as are also the American Indians, who undoubtedly reached the American continents not more than twenty thousand years ago via the land bridge at Alaska, thereafter progressing slowly southward to the very tip of South America.

If the Easter Island statue builders were no more than Polynesians, how is it that these Polynesians, elsewhere in their progress across the Pacific, did not stop to build similar statues? Why should they suddenly blossom out as sculptors only at the extreme tip of the Pacific on Easter Island? There is no doubt that the peoples of South-east Asia two thousand years ago were prolific and expert workers in stone. They would have been capable of such work as we find on Easter Island; but the fact that they produced no statues between Cambodia and Easter Island five thousand miles apart seems to rule out the Polynesian theory. There is also another very strong objection to this apparently convenient explanation. The islanders of Easter Island, when discovered, were living in a Stone Age culture and knew not the working of iron or the use of the wheel. Yet both iron and the wheel had been used in South-east Asia for many thousands of years before any Polynesians who might have reached Easter Island set out from their original homeland.

For years the savants argued about the origin of the Easter Islanders. The problem appeared insoluable. Then in 1947 there appeared on the scene a Norwegian ethnologist named Thor Heyerdahl. He put forward a revolutionary theory. He stated his belief that the islands of the eastern Pacific, and in particular Easter Island, had been reached originally by American Indians sailing westward from Central and South America. There were many strong supports for his theory. Apart from the traditions which he himself had noted in eastern Polynesia, that the ancestors of the white type of peoples he had met had come from the east by voyaging westward, he found other clues, such as the name of the sun god Tiki, which was common to many peoples in eastern Polynesia and in Peru and Bolivia. Moreover, only in Peru and on those islands nearest to South America, in the Pacific, was found the sweet potato, a vegetable which has its origin in Peru. He found also six other plants common to both areas, but not found elsewhere in the world.

Coconuts grow both in Central America, South America and in Polynesia; they cannot survive a trip by water. If they had floated across, their "eyes" would have sucked in sea-water and the coconut would have been ruined. So it appeared probable that nuts had been taken from one place to the other by the agency of man.

Massive stone statues are found both in the Andean Highlands of Bolivia and on Easter Island. There were traditions, collected by the Spaniards after they had conquered Peru, of the arrival in that part of the world about the fifth century A.D. of bearded white men who had sojourned there and taught the natives the arts of agriculture and architecture. After a time these men moved down to the coast and, in the picturesque language of the natives, spread their wings and sailed away in the direction of the setting sun. This occurred at about the same time as, according to Easter Island tradition, Hotu-Matua arrived with his three hundred followers two thousand miles away in Easter Island.

Mr. Heyerdahl found the savants sceptical of his theory for one basic cause. How, asked these gentlemen, could the American Indians have sailed across the broad Pacific? No such voyage could have been undertaken in the canoes which existed at the time of the Spanish conquest. Thor Heyerdahl refused to be daunted by this challenge. He was determined that his theory was correct.

All the civilized world knows of the famous voyage of the Kon-Tiki balsa-wood raft in which in 1947 Heyerdahl and five companions of Scandinavian origin sailed across the Pacific and after ninety-seven days reached a far-flung atoll four thousand miles westward of Peru. Many people have read the book he wrote about the voyage, others have seen the films he shot. Against scepticism he proved that South American Indians could have done as he had done, constructed rafts of light wood and sailed, certainly half the distance he had done, to Easter Island following the Trade Wind and the currents which set permanently all the year round from the coast of South America to the islands of the South Seas. In Peru and Bolivia he found pictures and descriptions of rafts of balsa wood constructed by the pre-Inca Indians, and there were traditions of the use by the Incas of great fleets of balsa rafts, on which they sailed as far as the Galapagos Islands, hundreds of miles westward of the South America continent.

Heyerdahl and his companions set sail from the port of Callao, slightly northwards of the point of departure required for the currents to take him directly to Easter Island. Following a wide circle the raft slowly drifted well to the northward of Easter Island to the Pacific coral islands. Later, in a Norwegian whaler, accompanied by experienced scientists, Heyerdahl set out for Easter Island itself. Before we deal with his finds there it would be as well to explain something of the discoveries that have been made in Peru and Bolivia which go so far to strengthen the theory that the Easter Islanders, the "long ears", come from there.

When the Spaniards, under the leadership of Pizarro, conquered the Incas of Peru in the sixteenth century, they found there a highly developed civilization. While the whole of Peru and parts of Bolivia contain many majestic stone cities and monuments, we are concerned particularly with the ruined city of Tiahuanaco, which stands on Lake Titicaca, fourteen thousand feet up in the towering Andes. It is surely one of the last spots in the world where one would expect to find a majestic city, yet this may well have been the place from which the people of Easter Island came.

Tiahuanaco poses more questions than can be answered. It was already a ruin when the Incas dominated Peru in the century or so before the Spaniards arrived. In the traditions of the local Indians, recorded at the time of the Spanish conquest, the city was built by bearded white men before the Flood. Apparently its culture had no past, no long and evolutionary period. It bloomed suddenly on the Andean plateau, but no one knows from where the seed came.

The builders of Tiahuanaco were the most expert workers of their day in stone in the world, cutting huge blocks to mathematical exactness with tools of stone. They transported over great distances without the aid of wheels or draught animals, huge stones, some weighing more than a hundred tons, and they set these stones up in position.

When the Spaniards arrived on the scene, the city, although already desolated, was in a far better state of preservation than it is now. Unfortunately, the Spaniards wrecked it still more.

There are only three great structures left, the Akapana or fortress, the Kalasaya or temple, and the Palace of the Ten Doors. Excavation has shown that there were two separate culture periods. It is surmised that the first builders of Tiahuanaco were defeated, for their structures collapsed. The town was rebuilt by the survivors perhaps stimulated by outside influences. They reached an even higher degree of skill before they, too, passed from the scene.

Both the Spaniards and the Incas did damage to the ancient city, for both wished, for different purposes, to eradicate memories of the past. In the case of the Spaniards it was the traditions of pagan gods, and in the case of the Incas the suggestion that there had been in Peru people cleverer than they.

The Akapana is a pyramid-like structure, in which a natural mound has been shaped and faced with stone. It is seven hundred feet long and five hundred feet wide rising to fifty feet above the plain. Its summit, which covers three hundred thousand square feet, was once reached by a stone stairway. In the temple, approximately four hundred and fifty feet square, upright stones show that they must have once supported a roof. Some of these stones are fourteen feet high, four feet wide, and two and a half feet thick.

A great feature of the temple is the Gateway of the Sun which is formed of one block of stone fifteen feet long, eleven feet high and two feet thick, and is the largest single block of cut stone in the world, weighing two hundred tons. The nearest quarry is twenty-five miles away across both lake and land. Above the doorway is a carved representation of the Supreme God of the Universe, Viracocha. On the reverse side of the Gateway, on each side of the door are rectangular niches, cut so accurately that it is not possible to find a deviation of more than one fiftieth of an inch in their angles and surfaces.

Near the temple is the one statue that remains of the many hundreds that tradition accords to Tiahuanaco. Known as the "Friar" or the "Bishop" this statue appears to be holding something which seems to be a book. Two smaller heads taken from the ruins now stand by the village church, and one of the earliest Spanish visitors, Ciaezade de Leon, refers to two other statues both eighteen feet high which no longer exist. Another visitor in the year 1878 noticed other structures, including a hall of justice, which are no longer to be seen.

Another Spanish visitor at the time of the Conquest, a priest named Diego de Alcobasco, refers to many other stones carved in the shape of men and women. He stated that they looked so natural that they appeared to be alive; some were drinking with cups in their hands, others sitting, others standing, others walking in the stream which flowed by the walls.

Although the past history of Peru had been blotted out by the Incas, some traditions remained amongst the Indians as to the people, their own ancestors, who had built this unique city.

From some of the ancient legends recorded by the early Spanish Conquistadores it appears that a primitive culture grew up around Lake Titicaca in the first three centuries of our era. Then came a great influx of alien peoples from the north. These people came down the coast on balsa rafts and in canoes. With them they brought a far more advanced culture and it appears their arrival took place some time before the year A.D. 450. They themselves were replaced during that century by a further wave of invasion of similar peoples whose empire lasted until about the eighth century of our era.

The first wave of this alien invasion is associated in native tradition with an individual who became deified as the god Viracocha, who is always described in the legends as "white, bearded, dressed in flowing robes, and of imposing mien". He is remembered as the chief of a "large-eared" people who were the builders and first inhabitants of Tiahuanaco.

A Spanish writer named Betanzos, writing in 1551, says:

"When I asked the Indians what shape this Viracocha had when their ancestors had seen him, they said that according to the information they possessed, he was a tall man with a white vestment that reached to his feet, and that this vestment had a girdle, and that he carried his hair short with a tonsure on his head in the manner of a priest, and that he carried in his hands a certain thing which seemed to remind them of the breviary that the priests carried in their hands."

By breviary the Indians meant a book such as the Spanish priests carried. According to the legend, Viracocha and his men taught the natives the arts of agriculture and architecture.

Kon Tiki Viracocha, as he was known, and his men were defeated on an island in Lake Titicaca, in a rebellion of their subjects. He left the city and with his men sailed away from the coast, on what appear to have been rafts, in the direction of the setting sun.

Who these apparently white men of Nordic race were nobody knows. There are equally strong traditions of the arrival of similar white strangers from the direction of the rising sun, from across the Atlantic, amongst the Mayas of Yucatan and the Aztecs of Mexico. Amongst the former their leader was known as Kukulcan and by the latter he was called Quetzacoatl.

So strong was the memory of these white strangers, who brought benefits to the peoples of Central and South America, that when Cortez arrived in Mexico and Piazarro in Peru, the natives were convinced that their ancient gods had returned. As a result, at first they put up no great resistance against the Spanish Conquistadores. The appearance of these bearded white men in Mexico and Peru is such a vivid memory that it must represent an historical event.

The point of importance in the mystery of Easter Island is that bearded white men of Nordic type arrived in Peru, sojourned there for some time, built gigantic stone monuments, and erected statues in their own image; then in the fifth century of our era departed suddenly by sea westward in the direction of the setting sun.

About the same time the first inhabitants of Easter Island arrived, coming by sea from the east. They are described in local legend as being "white". They erected gigantic statues in their own image. Even more significant is the fact that these white strangers in Peru were called "large ears" and in Easter Island "long ears", and the statues they built depicted just such ears.

There are many other circumstantial links between the men of Easter Island and Tiahuanaco. Sweet potatoes, bottle gourds and coconuts grow in Easter Island as in South America. The statues of Easter Island and Peru have many common characteristics, such as stunted legs, lack of neck, and having the arms pulled back. There the distinct resemblances end, but we must recall that, by the time the Spanish had finished their vandalism around Lake Titicaca, there were very few of the ancient statues left to act as a comparison.

The raft trip of the Scandinavians across the Pacific had caught the imagination of the world and had focused attention on the mystery of Easter Island. Mr. Heyerdahl's next step was to visit Easter Island itself. This he did in 1955 in a Norwegian whaler in which he was accompanied by a number of scientists, each a specialist. There he saw for himself the great statues, the massive walls of which the stone blocks fitted with mathematical exactness, and he heard at first hand the traditions which had been passed down for generations amongst the natives. He found direct descendants of the "long ear" Ororoina, one of whom, named Pedro Atan, the Mayor of Easter Island, was the eleventh generation from the lone survivor of the great massacre. There were at least eighty to ninety other Easter Islanders of the pure "long ear" blood. The party made many new discoveries, and carried out a number of tests and experiments.

Amongst the descendants of Ororoina they found a number of islanders with white skins, red hair and blue eyes, people who could have passed without notice in Scandinavia or northern Europe. They excavated the site of Hotu-Matua's house, which according to tradition he had built on his arrival. They excavated the bases of many of the statues which had become silted up and almost buried. They noted a most remarkable resemblance between the temple building, known as the Ahu, on Easter Island with the Peruvian mural constructions of massive stonework in which great blocks of stone were fitted with equal mathematical exactness. On Easter Island gigantic blocks of hard rock had been cut and fitted without a crack or hole. They had been worked entirely with stone tools.

Heyerdahl and his companions learned that the natives, particularly the descendants of the "long ears", had retained the tradition of the cutting of the statues, the method of dragging them across the island, and of how they had been erected. Parties of natives demonstrated exactly how these operations were done, and in the case of the cutting of the statues, Mr. Heyerdahl was able to work out that the rate of progress would have required some twelve or fifteen months to cut a single statue from the rock. Then five hundred natives demonstrated how a statue was dragged across the island on a stone and wooden sledge.

"How were the statues erected into a standing position?" asked Heyerdahl. With eleven men the mayor set out to show exactly how their ancestors had done this. They built a stone ramp and slowly pulled a statue up on to it so that it was levered into position and finally tipped over and slid down to finish upright on its legs. Then, the red top-knot brought from another part of the island was rolled up the ramp and fixed on top of the statue's head. The whole operation took eighteen days. The statue, as in the case of all the others, but been cut so symmetrically that when it finished upright on its legs it had perfect equilibrium.

Another test was made to check the tradition of the last stand of the "long ears". Across the eastern promontory of the island lay the ditch, in which the "long ears" were supposed to have proposed to burn wood to make a fiery furnace through which their enemies could not come. Was this a natural or man-made ditch? When test-holes were dug by the expedition, they showed, each at the same level, a strata of burnt ash, demonstrating that the tradition was a true one. There was a broad red and black stripe of ashes in three layers which upon being tested showed carbonized wood. Tested for radio-activity the charcoal indicated that the fire had taken place about three hundred years earlier, somewhere about the year 1650. When the ditch was fully excavated it showed that it had been dug initially about the year A.D. 500. Tools, bones and artefacts were found.

One important link remained to be discovered. While the statues of Easter Island showed a general resemblance to the stone-work of Peru, there were no exact parallels with the Andean statues. The Easter Island statues represented a completely new departure in the form of sculpture. All the statues were of the same type; characteristic of Easter Island and of nowhere else in the world. Each face had the same ruthless mien, the same elongated ears, and the same general shape; each statue had stunted legs and the significant red top-knot. Surely, if as had been surmised, the Easter Islanders came from Peru, they would have started at first by reproducing statues similar to the ones they had left behind them? Soon the scientists discovered a number of far older and smaller statues which had been completely covered by the earth or had been walled up in buildings. These were far more typical of the South American art form. They had a fully developed body with complete legs, they were posed in a kneeling position, with the hands on the knees, and were wearing a short cloak or "poncho", as did the statues Heyerdahl had seen in Peru and Bolivia. They were not naked like the others. Their heads were round, they had goatee beards and expressions quite alien to those of the statues which were found above the surface. Apparently when the "long ears" first arrived they had set about cutting and carving small statues, representing their ancestors, of exactly similar type to those at Tiahuanaco. Then suddenly they had switched to a new form, that of the pitiless inscrutable faces with the elongated ears. The older statues had been abandoned, the entire community concentrating on producing the new type. As they gained experience the statues increased in size, becoming larger and larger until the final one which lay still unfinished in the quarry, still adhering to the solid rock, measured nearly seventy feet. For centuries the work of statue building went on, until the revolt of the "short ears" stopped it and ended the reign of the "long ears".

In the months in which the expedition remained on the island more and more pieces of the puzzle were fitted into place. As the descendants of the "long ears" worked on cutting a fresh statue, dragging it into position and erecting it, they sang songs which reminded Mr. Heyerdahl of the songs of the Pueblo Indians in New Mexico. Then came the greatest discovery of all. Slowly the scientists gained the confidence of the natives. They learned that all over the island there were secret caves belonging to the families of the descendants of the "long ears". In these caves, which members of the expedition were allowed to visit, were found numbers of small carved stones. These represented birds, animals and snakes all unknown on Easter Island, but all common on the South American continent. One carving was of a penguin, a bird which is found only in Antarctica and on the Galapagos Islands, which according to tradition the pre-Inca peoples of

Peru had visited in voyages. Another find in the caves was that of a carved lion or puma, an animal found in the South American jungles. Another link with South America were the reed boats made by the Easter Islanders. The reeds from which they were built grew in the crater lake, and were exactly the same type of reed as grew in Lake Titicaca in the Andes where the Indians made exactly similar boats.

Seldom has proof of a theory been so conclusive. The original inhabitants of Easter Island could have come from Peru and from nowhere else. They had arrived about the time in which South American tradition placed the departure of similar men from their shores. They could easily have navigated the Pacific in balsa rafts or reed boats, being carried by the current exactly to Easter Island and to several other islands farther on in the eastern Pacific. They reproduced at first similar statues to those they had erected at Tiahuanaco. Then came a new architect, a genius, who had perfected a new art form. They had made small carvings of birds and animals which were found only in South America. They grew sweet potatoes and other plants, which had their origin in that part of the world only.

The tradition of the fate of the "long ears" had been proved to be true. The recollections of the descendants of the "long ears" were accurate. The traditions as to how the statues were cut, dragged into position and erected, had not been lost. The history of Easter Island had been disclosed.

Somehow about the year 475 a party of three or four hundred American Indians, the "large-eared" people who had arrived in Peru not long before, reached Easter Island. There they had lived and increased for centuries, spending all their leisure in statue building. Suddenly came the canoes of the Polynesians. Allowing these people to remain, the "long ears" turned them into slaves. Then about the year 1600 of the Christian era the slaves had rebelled and killed their masters. But they revered and remembered them, passing down their traditions and their memories from generation to generation. Amongst them remain descendants of a distinct Nordic type quite alien to the South Seas.

These men, whoever they were, had gained immortality by their statues. Century after century their scornful, ruthless faces had stared out across the Pacific. We can trace them back to Central and South America in the early fifth century of our era. Beyond that their origin is a mystery. They came from somewhere outside the American continent, probably from Europe or the Mediterranean. They were men of high intelligence, of complete singleness of purpose, and of ruthless determination. We know that they were great navigators and seamen, sun worshippers, and magnificent builders in stone. Yet they had no knowledge either of the wheel, or of the working of iron, both of which had been in use in Europe and in Asia for thousands of years before the earliest time at which these people arrived in Central and South America.

At first they were popular amongst the people with whom they sojourned. They taught them the arts of agriculture and architecture, but in each case, in Tiahuanaco, the great city they built in the Andes, and in Easter Island, their subjects eventually turned against them, driving them away from the Andes, and massacring them in Easter Island. Their singleness of purpose and determination were too much for the easier-going peoples amongst whom their lot was cast. We know the names of some of them: Kon Tiki Viracocha, Kululcan, and Quetzacoatl, and Hotu-Matua. Of the presence of these white men in South America direct evidence has been found in graves, where long skulls, and scalps of fair or red hair have been found. The traditions of their arrival in Central and South America is certainly a matter of fact.

Yet there is no link to connect them with any of the white or fair peoples of Nordic type of whom we have knowledge. It is thought possible that Europeans may have preceded Columbus across the Atlantic to the West Indies and Central America, but, as they did not return, there is no tradition of their voyages. Certainly Columbus did not venture out completely into the "blue". He knew more of what lay ahead of him than has yet been generally supposed. The Norsemen who undoubtedly reached the shores of the north-eastern part of the North American continent about the year 1000 did not, as far as we know, progress any farther. Their traditions speak only of voyages to Vinland on that coast. Even if they had progressed farther down the coast the time was at least five hundred years later than the arrival of the mysterious white men in the South American continent. Thus, the clearing up of the mystery of Easter Island, the putting together of the pieces of the puzzle, while it solves one of the world's greatest historical mysteries leaves behind it a mystery more impenetrable.

ARTHUR OF BRITAIN

SEEKING A HERO, the medieval troubadours of England and France lighted upon a sixth-century British general and turned him into a mythical King Arthur, the founder of the Order of Knighthood of the Round Table, the personification of twelfth-century ideas of knight-errantry, courtly love and chivalry. Yet in the legend Arthur is a shadowy figure, a mere stage prop by which the deeds of his knights are introduced and the quest of the Holy Grail, the vessel which received Christ's blood on the Cross, becomes the dominant theme.

The legend of Arthur and his Knights of the Round Table is as follows:

The enchanter Merlin arrives at the Court of King Uther Pendragon at Carduel where he establishes a Round Table for the knights who attend the Court. A special place is reserved for the knight who by his purity can recover the Holy Grail. King Uther falls in love with Yguerne, the wife of Gorlois, who locks her up in his impregnable fortress at Tintagel. By Merlin, Uther is changed into the form of Gorlois and is smuggled into Tintagel where Yguerne receives him as her husband. Gorlois is killed in battle and Yguerne, now free to marry Uther, yields to his passion. The birth of their son, Arthur, is kept secret and he is given to Merlin to bring up. When Uther dies, apparently without an heir, Merlin makes known Arthur's lineage and he is hailed as king. Under Merlin's guidance he conquers twelve kings, one after another.

In another variation of the story, Merlin allows Arthur to make his kingship known by drawing from an anvil, after all the other knights have failed to move it, a sword which can be wrenched free only by the true king. King Arthur defeats those whose jealousy has been aroused but in doing so his magic sword is broken.

Standing by a lake bewailing his loss Arthur sees a white-draped arm holding a jewelled sword rise from the water. This sword he secures and names "Excalibur". With it he wins many victories against Saxon invaders. He invades Brittany and returns to marry Guinevere who brings in her dowry the Round Table which Arthur sets up at Camelot where he found his Order of Knighthood. Two seats are left to be filled, one by the knight who secures the Holy Grail and the other by him who shall be absolutely pure.

One of the knights, Sir Lancelot, falls in love with Queen Guinevere but Arthur suspects nothing and Sir Lancelot is healed of the madness of his love by a magical sight of the Holy Grail. Other knights enter the story and among them is Sir Galahad who takes the seat reserved for him who shall be absolutely pure without incurring the awful penalties destined for an imposter. The knights vow themselves to the Quest of the Holy Grail, but it is seen only by Parzival and Sir Galahad.

Knowing themselves unworthy of so great a boon the other knights return to Court where there are jousts and tournaments in honour of the ladies. Arthur's jealousy is aroused by Sir Lancelot who goes to Brittany where Arthur follows him, leaving his wife and kingdom in the care of his nephew Modred. Learning that Modred has betrayed his trust, Arthur hurries back, kills Modred but is himself wounded unto death. He orders that his sword Excalibur shall be cast back into the lake and he is rowed to the island of Avalon to be cured of his wounds so that he can one day return. Other versions relate that he was buried at Glastonbury.

How Arthur, a real sixth-century historical figure, became the symbol of romance to the feudal Courts of twelfth-century Europe is one of the strangest oddities of literature, one yet to be completely unravelled. The troubadours found their hero in the Welsh bardic poems and spread Arthur's fame all over Europe, the first impetus coming from the Court of Henry II of England and his Queen Eleanor of Acquitaine.

How far can Arthur be resurrected from the myth and legend which surrounds his name? Examination of ancient British and medieval English chronicles and of the Welsh poems discloses the true Arthur, the last great leader of Roman and Celtic Britain in the dark days of the Saxon conquest. That Arthur was a popular British hero is evident from the widespread association of his name with many parts of the British Isles and Brittany, from Cornwall and Wales, the last refuge of those who revered him.

Saxon tribes, impelled westward by the invasion of Europe by the Huns, had been attempting settlement and conquest for some years before the Roman legions were finally withdrawn from Britain in the year 410, on the collapse of the empire. For four hundred years a Province of Rome, the Romanized British and their Celtic allies were forced to fight on two fronts and to resist the invasion of the Picts from the north and the Saxons, Angles and Jutes on the east. While the British were stopping the northern floodgate, waves of Saxons landed in the east. By the year 465 Kent had been overrun by Hengist and Horsa, and by 500 the eastern and southern coasts were under Saxon control. —

In face of the common danger the British chieftains vested unity of command in Ambrosius Aurelianus "the great King amongst the Kings of Britain", a man of Roman-British descent who is credited with kinship with Roman emperors. He died about 490, leaving a number of sons and a brother named Uther Pendragon, who is believed to have succeeded him. Though the British were not sufficiently powerful to thrust the Saxons back into the sea, the Saxons were not strong enough to break into the British redoubt in Wiltshire, Gloucester and Somerset. But by A.D. 500 the Saxons were well established in the Thames Valley, which became a dangerous salient in the British line.

Arthur, we believe, succeeded Ambrosius as Commander-in-Chief of the British forces, and he achieved a great victory over the Saxons at Badon which, if it had been followed up, might have ensured independence for Britain.

Our first source of information about this period consists of the contemporary history of Gildas, a learned monk, who wrote a book entitled *De Excidio et Conquesti Britanniae*. Gildas does not mention Arthur by name as the victor of Badon, which he places in the year 517, probably for reasons which will be gone into later. Gildas, we note, does not mention anyone by name in his history between the years 388 and 540, about the year he wrote. He says that the British victory at Badon, after forty-four years of fluctuating strife, put an end to the Saxon war but not the civil war which led to the disintegration of the British in the face of a Saxon revival.

We hear first of Arthur in the 10th and 11th century manuscript copies of the chronicler Nennius, who edited earlier material and died in the year 811. He was a disciple of the Bishop of Bangor in North Wales and he probably collected together genuine traditions.

He speaks of a period of revival of British fortune, culminating in the victory of Badon, and he describes Arthur as *dux bellorium* and supreme King of the Britons "though many were more noble than he". Nennius gives a sketch of Arthur's campaign and names some of his battles, the obscurity of the location of which suggests that they could not have been invented.

Nennius relates:

"Then Arthur fought against them in those days with the Kings of the Britons, and it was he who led their battles. The first battle was at the mouth of the river which is called Glein. The second, third, fourth and fifth were upon another river, which is called Dubglas and is in the region of Linnuis. The sixth battle was upon the river which is called Bassas. The seventh battle was in the wood of Celidon; it is Cat Coit Celidon. The eighth battle was on the Castle Guinnion, wherein Arthur bore the image of St. Mary the ever-virgin upon his shoulders, and the pagans were turned to flight on that day and there was a great slaughter of them. The ninth battle was fought in the City of the Legion. He fought the tenth battle on the bank of the river which is called Tribruit. The eleventh battle was on the mount which is called Agned. The twelfth battle was on the Mount of Badon, wherein fell nine hundred and sixty men in one day at a single onset of Arthur; and no one everthrew them but he alone, and in all the battles he came out victorious."

Considerable controversy has raged as to the actual sites of these battles. That Nennius was drawing upon true traditions is suggested by the detail he supplied, for example, that the first battle took place on the River Glein and it was fought at its mouth. A convincing case has been put forward to show that the battles which preceded Badon represent a series of campaigns in Scotland and eastern England in which Arthur defeated the invading Picts and Saxons who, as they were driven off in one place, tried elsewhere.

Arthur's first recorded battle was at the mouth of the River Glein and four battles on the River Dubglas in the region of Linnuis followed. The sixth took place on the River Bassas. The seventh in the wood of Celidon and the eighth on the Castle Guinnion. The ninth battle took place in the City of the Legion, the tenth on the River Tribruit, and the eleventh on Mount Agned. It is possible to locate some of these sites.

The seventh battle, Coit Celidon, clearly refers to "Silva Caledonia", the Wood of Scotland. The Firth of Forth was a favorite Saxon landing place and from this clue we can suggest that the area of his first campaign was south-eastern Scotland where the Lammermuir Hills offered a strategic line of defence against the invader. Suggestively, at the end of the defile of Cockburnspath, through which the Saxons would have had to make their way, runs a river named Dunglass near by the village of Linton, which may have been the site of four of these battles.

It seems reasonable to assume that Arthur, having foiled a landing at the mouth of the Tweed by a battle in the glen, near to which is a ford still named Arthur's Steps, turned north to resist an even stronger invasion on the River Dunglass, where four battles were fought for the defile of Cockburns-path. In pursuit of the retreating Saxons, Arthur defeated them again at an unknown stream named Bassas and finally in the Great Wood, south-east of Edinburgh.

Guinnion is assumed to be the Roman Gariannonum or Yarmouth on the "Saxon shore", which is stated by Nennius to be a Roman fortified post. Next we learn of Arthur gaining another great victory at the City of the Legion, possibly Chester, or even York. If this was at Chester it suggests that the Saxons may have thrust westwards. If, as we think, Tribruit was the Celtic name for the Tweed, it indicates that Arthur returned to the north. The site of the eleventh battle, Mount Agned, cannot be determined.

Location at the site of the crowning victory of Badon is difficult. Several places in southern England have been identified as the site of the battle, but the most probable key is the current military situation. The strategic aim of the Saxons was to push westward to the Bristol Channel so as to divide their enemies to the north and south. To carry out such a campaign would have required concentration of forces from the eastern shore and from southern England, to co-operate with a thrust from the Thames Valley, where the Saxons were well entrenched.

It is not surprising that neither the Venerable Bede, who wrote in the eighth century, or the Angle-Saxon Chronicle of the ninth century, mention Arthur although they refer to the battle of Badon. Their authors were representative of the Saxons Arthur defeated. Our next source of information, the Annales Cambriae of the tenth century, refers to the battle of Badon and gives the additional information for the year 539 "the battle of Camlan in which Arthur and Medraut fell".

This brings us to a number of Welsh poems, both clerical and secular, about which historians are doubtful. Clearly these Welsh poems enshrine ancient traditions. That some at least of the traditions of Arthur were true is suggested by the poets' disrespectful treatment of the national hero. That they treat Arthur with a certain lack of sympathy, even with mixed feelings, may arise from their very origin. They suggest that Arthur was an able military upstart who, though he re-stored British fortunes, managed to offend both the Church and the petty chieftains of Wales. Nennius tells us that Arthur fought "alongside the Kings of Britain". According to these poems he was not a king himself but rather a "tyrannus" or an all-powerful general, to whom authority had been given by various kings in Britain. The Welsh poems suggest that Arthur was a West Countryman, possibly a man of Roman-British descent, which would have rendered him rather suspect in Celtic eyes. It is significant, however, that the poets appear to assume that their readers would know who Arthur was.

The life of St. Cadoc, of the Abbey of Llancarfan, makes two mentions of Arthur, and suggests that he made a habit of requisitioning Church property. The life of St. Padarn refers to "a certain tyrant by the name of Arthur". Caradoc's life of St. Gildas, the chronicler, says that Arthur was a *rex rebellius,* who rose to supremacy all over Britain". It is not perhaps surprising that a book about Gildas should have been unfriendly to Arthur because Gildas was related to families in Scotland defeated by Arthur. This book also states that King Melwas of Somerset kidnapped Guennuvar and imprisoned her at Glastonbury, which was besieged by Arthur commanding the armies of Devon and Cornwall, and he rescued his wife.

The Welsh secular poems, consisting of the Red Book of Hergest, the Black Book of Carmarthen, the Book of Aneirin, and the Book of Taliesen, also supply information. The Book of Aneirin makes the earliest allusion to Arthur, about the year 600, describing a warrior as "although he was no Arthur, his valour was great". The Black Book of Carmarthen refers to Arthur's son and calls Arthur "Emperor". It gives a long list of his knights and refers to "Arthur's men", which suggests that after his death some such corps continued to exist. It suggests, too, a hint of secrecy about the location of Arthur's grave.

Other Welsh poems, known as the Triads, refer to Arthur's feud with Modred. Modred invades Arthur's fortress at Kelliwic in Cornwall and raises his hand against Arthur's Queen Guinevere. In retaliation Arthur attacks Modred's fortress. Later Modred betrays Arthur to the Saxons and this leads to the great battle of Camlan in which both Arthur and Modred fall. We learn, too, that the Highland chieftains of Wales co-operated with the Romanized remnant of the British in their war against the Saxons. The poems stress Arthur's unique fame, and imply that he was a bold adventurer risen from lowly beginnings. He possessed a court and his knights were famed for their prowess. He sails for Ireland in quest of the sacred cauldron, a miraculous vessel. If these traditions are older than the medieval period, they show that some part of the Arthurian legend was original in its inception. They suggest that Arthur was the leader of some special order of soldiers and this implied that they were cavalrymen, or knights.

From these Welsh poems we gather the information that Arthur rose by his own valour from quite ordinary beginnings to be given military authority over the forces of several petty kings; that he was the leader of a corps of mounted men who owed obedience to him and to no one else. His doings centred in the West Country, probably in Cornwall. He was the commander-in-chief, or "dux bellorium" of the British forces and it is hinted that he was proclaimed "emperor".

This brings us to the medieval chroniclers. The great difficulty lies in isolating original traditions from the accretions of the Arthurian myth which grew up about this time. The references to Arthur by these chroniclers indicate that his name had never been forgotten in Celtic Britain, and was suddenly revived in the twelfth century, when his fame spread all over the continent through the songs of the Welsh troubadours. This interest in Celtic traditions is believed to have been inaugurated by the Anglo-Norman discovery of the ancient church and abbey at Glastonbury.

Welsh traditions implied that Arthur was still alive and might come again to lead them against their enemies. It was therefore of importance to the Anglo-Normans to establish his death with certainty. These medieval chronicles concerned are the works of William of Malmesbury, Henry of Huntington (which is little more than a paraphrase of Nennius), and Geoffrey of Monmouth's *History of the Kings of Britain*. William of Malmesbury, who wrote about 1120, made two visits to Glastonbury which brought him in touch with the Arthurian legends. He describes Arthur as a military leader and supplies the new information that he was a lieutenant of Ambrosius and "one who sustained his tottering country, and gave the shattered minds of his countrymen an edge for war".

Geoffrey of Monmouth describes Arthur as a king who was victorious over the Saxons, against whom he carried a campaign on to the continent. He holds court and presides over an Order of Knighthood. He fell at Camlan, as a result of the revolt of his nephew, Modred. It seems possible that Geoffrey drew upon ancient Celtic legends, and he refers to "an ancient book in the British language" which he was given by Walter, Archdeacon of Oxford. Though this book has never been found, it seems unlikely that Geoffrey would have invented its existence. Geoffrey's description of the battle of Badon suggests that he must have drawn upon some contemporary account, or one derived from an ancient source. He says:

"Stationing his companies, Arthur attacked the Saxons who were ranked in wedge-wise battalions. All day long they stood their ground while the Britons delivered assault after assault. At sundown the Saxons occupied (or retreated to) a hill close by. At sunrise Arthur and his army climbed to the top of the hill, albeit in the ascent he lost many of his men for the height was in favour of the Saxons. Putting forth all their strength, the British gained the top and closed with the enemy, the Saxons striving with all their strength to hold their ground. When much of the day was spent Arthur, waxing wroth at the stubbornness of their resistance and the slowness of his own advance, drew forth his sword Caliburn and thrust himself forward into the thickest press of the ranks of the enemy, who, after a great slaughter, took to flight".

Thus according to Geoffrey the battle took place in two stages. After a day-long battle the defending Saxons fell back and offered battle next day in a new position and the Britons made a dawn attack. The descriptions of Badon supplied to us by Nennius and Geoffrey of Monmouth provide evidence by which we can seek to identify Arthur's victory. Badon has been variously identified with Badbury Camp in Berkshire, with Badbury Rings near Wimborne in Dorset, and with Liddington Camp Hill, which is nine hundred feet high, which lies near another Badbury, four miles south of Swindon on the Marlborough Downs. It seems certain that Liddington Hill was the actual site of the battle, for it represents the ideal point of concentration for three Saxon contingents coming together from Kent, from the Thames Valley, and from East Anglia.

The late Colonel Alfred Burne, in his *Battlefields of England* (1950), reconstructs the scene as follows: Surprised by Arthur, the Saxons took up a position at Badbury in order to protect their line of retreat. Worn out by the charges of the British heavy cavalry, the Saxons withdrew overnight to Liddington Hill on which was an ancient fortification. Arthur's decision to attack again at dawn showed judgment worthy of a great general for the Saxons were in what was apparently an impregnable position on the crest of a steep hill up which the Britons would have to struggle. Arthur, thinks Colonel Burne, had been fighting the Saxons successfully for many years and his great victory was achieved as a result of a correct estimate of their morale. The Saxons had retreated and were dispirited. Arthur staked all on a brilliant thrust. His judgment was proved correct and he won a great victory which gave the British a respite for fifty years.

According to Geoffrey of Monmouth Arthur fell at the battle of Camlan in 538. Camlan has been identified both with the River Camel in Cornwall, where there is a "Slaughter Bridge", and with the River Cam in Somerset near Glastonbury. Various indications suggest that the latter may be the true site. Slaughter Bridge in Cornwall is believed to mark the site of a far later battle between the Saxons and the British. According to the legend Arthur died in "civil strife", which may well be true because he does not appear to have fought the Saxons again after Badon.

Various clues suggest that Arthur died and was buried at Glastonbury. The Welsh book of Carodoc refers to the siege of Glastonbury, and the Welsh traditions are obscure as to the site of his burial. Geoffrey of Monmouth says that after the battle of Camlan Arthur was borne away to the Isle of Avalon, the description of which fits Glastonbury, to be healed of his wounds, but he makes no reference to Arthur's death.

In the year 1190, when King Henry II was traveling in Wales, he was told by a bard that the site of Arthur's grave was in the old cemetery at Glastonbury, between two pillars. The monks of Glastonbury were anxious to publicize their abbey. Clearly the location of Arthur's grave there would bring many pilgrims to the abbey. They set out to excavate the presumed site. Digging seven feet down in the old cemetery, we are told, they came across a stone slab on which was inscribed in Latin: "Here lies the renowned King Arthur in the Isle of Avalon." Nine feet farther down they came across a huge coffin made out of a hollowed oak log, inside of which were the bones of a giant man, his skull being seriously damaged. After some years of exhibition these bones were re-interred by Edward I in front of the High Altar.

While all this may have been a pious fraud, two details in the story suggest that it may have been authentic and that the bones discovered actually were Arthur's. It would have been extraordinary for twelfth-century monks to have invented the story of an oak log coffin, for it would have been far more natural for them to have suggested a stone sarcophagus, then the method of interment. Only modern knowledge indicates that a hollowed-out log would have been a sixth-century method of burial. Then there is the depth at which the stone slab was discovered. Two hundred years before its discovery, St. Dunstan, a tenth-century Abbot of Glastonbury, covered the existing graveyard with a high mound of earth, in order to provide ground for further burials. An excavation in 1190 would have needed to have gone through this layer of earth to the site of the older Anglo-Saxon burials and it is quite likely that the monks would have needed to have dug for seven feet before reaching the stone slab. The coffin had been buried nine feet farther down, but did it contain the actual skeleton of Arthur?

It is considered significant that the Welsh traditions associated Glastonbury with Arthur's death, and that no challenge was made from Wales about the discovery of Arthur's grave in 1190. Indeed, the excavations confirmed old Welsh traditions. Glastonbury, near the River Cam, was a sacred place in Arthur's day and it is entirely possible that, mortally wounded in some battle in the year 538 near the Somerset Cam, Arthur was taken to Glastonbury where he died.

This does not entirely account for all the traditions which the medieval chroniclers may have drawn upon, before the Arthurian legend influenced their writings. But to accept all these traditions as genuine involves the danger that we are really drawing upon legends which arose after the time the Arthurian myth took shape in Europe. Many of these are too dangerous to employ, but it seems certain that these chroniclers knew Arthur as a king of Britain, Cornwall and Brittany, leader of a special corps of horsemen or knights.

Drawing upon these traditions the medieval troubadours turned Arthur into a great king, rather than a mighty warrior, the leader of a company who grouped themselves around the Round Table. Many of the traditions which became entwined in the Arthurian myth undoubtedly go back to early Celtic knowledge. It is significant that when two French priests visited Devonshire in the year 1113 they were told that they were in the land of King Arthur "who was still alive". The troubadours changed the tale, but they did not invent the basic core of the story. It was there ready-made in the ancient Celtic story of the British King Arthur, the *dux bellorium*, the tyrannus, even the *"imperator"*.

Before attempting reconstruction of the real Arthur from

myth and legend, the strange silence of Gildas about him may be remarked upon. Geoffrey Ashe, in his book *From Caesar to Arthur* (1960), puts forward the ingenious suggestion that the reason why Gildas does not mention Arthur as the victor of Badon was because he based his account of the battle and the strategic position in the war with the Saxons upon Arthur's last testament, given to Gildas by Arthur himself as he lay on his death-bed at Glastonbury.

Gildas could certainly have met Arthur at Glastonbury, which he is known to have visited, and he wrote soon after the year 538. If this suggestion is correct, it accounts for the strange omission of Arthur's name as the victor of Badon, inasmuch as Arthur himself in describing the battle and giving the final assessment of the campaign might have omitted his own name. Gildas' assessment of the position in respect to the invading Saxons is considered by Mr. Ashe to be exactly as Arthur might have envisaged the position.

From the history and legends, Mr. Ashe reconstructs the real Arthur as a man born in the West Country about the year 475, the son perhaps of a bi-lingual minor noble, one of the Roman-British families living in the Kingdom of Ambrosius. In his youth Arthur became the leader of a guerrilla band and his early victories, about which we know nothing, confirmed him as a leader of men. He joined forces with Ambrosius and became his lieutenant and his successor in the fighting against the Saxons. Learning of the success of regiments of heavy cavalry in the eastern Roman Empire, Arthur imported heavy horses from the Continent and formed a corps of heavy cavalry which carried all before them against the Saxon foot soldiers. In a land comprising many small kingdoms, Arthur led his cavalry corps to the aid of local contingents in their battles against the Saxons and was accepted throughout Roman Britain as the *dux bellorium*, the commander-in-chief in a military though not in a political sense. He drove the Saxon invaders back in the north-east and the south-east and then in 518 he succeeded in halting the Saxon advance. His well-disciplined cavalrymen defeated the Saxons and after the great victory at Badon Arthur was proclaimed "emperor" by his men in the same way as other Roman legions had acclaimed their generals, but it was a title of honour only.

With the danger from without lessened, the British petty kings quarrelled and civil war resulted. Arthur himself was mortally wounded in civil strife at Camlan. We know nothing of him between the victory at Badon in 518 and the year of his death 538, but it seems clear that there were no further battles with the Saxons. A great opportunity was lost. With Arthur's death resistance petered out and after Arthur "came the deluge". Writing in the year 540 Gildas states "even now the cities of our country are in a wretched state, deserted and wrecked". In 542 the Yellow Plague reached Britain, affecting the Britons, who by their insularity were possibly more subject to the illness than the invading Saxons.

In 550 the Saxons were on the march again, and in 557 the decisive battle was fought and they were able to thrust through to the Bristol Channel and finally to divide their foes. Britain became England, the land of the Anglo-Saxons.

We can look back upon Arthur as a great cavalry leader, the inventor perhaps of a corps of heavy cavalry, which six hundred years later became eulogized as an Order of Knighthood. As virtual commander-in-chief of the British forces, Arthur led his men up and down Britain in defence against the inroads of the Saxons which no one king could have resisted. If Arthur's victory at Badon had been followed up it might have been the end of the Saxon conquest, for there is some evidence from Roman records that they decamped from Britain in large numbers about this time. Arthur was a great leader amongst lesser men. The ancient traditions, rather than the medieval myths, testified to his popularity and renown as a great national hero, and there is no doubt that, particularly in the West Country, he was long remembered by his countrymen.

The real Arthur shines forth beneath the veneer of medieval legend as a true son of Britain. He can take his rightful place amongst the great military leaders of our history and we can best remember him as "one who long sustained his tottering country". He gave the shattered mind of his fellow citizens "an edge for war". But fortunately, or unfortunately for our history, the impetus he gave them was not sustained.

WHO WAS SHAKESPEARE?

THERE has been considerable controversy about the authorship of the plays and sonnets usually attributed to William Shakespeare of Stratford-on-Avon. Over fifty different Elizabethans have been identified as the true author. The subject has resulted in some six thousand publications written by English, French, Belgian, German, Italian, American, Argentinian and Russian authors. Several societies exist to further the claims made for particular contenders for the title of England's greatest dramatist. Everyone who writes about the authorship of the works attributed to Shakespeare is partisan: there is no neutral. No book considers the problem impartially.

To master the intricacies of the problem and to present an impartial summing-up would take a lifetime of study: it is possible only to present the different theories and consider some of the points presented for and against them. First, we must take notice of the evidence for and against the traditional view that the greatest plays in the English language were written by William Shakespeare of Stratford-on-Avon.

Many scholars accept Shakespeare as the author without question: they deny that there is any need to prove that he was the author of the plays and sonnets attributed to him. Yet no real proof exists that the actor-manager Shakespeare was indeed Shakespeare the dramatist. Other scholars dismiss Shakespeare as the author on a number of negative grounds and each advances what he claims are positive clues which prove that the author was someone else altogether.

No one denies that such a person as William Shakespeare existed and that he was an actor-manager, a man who was born and spent his childhood in Stratford-on-Avon and who returned there to die, a wealthy and an honoured citizen. Some point out that no one mourned the passing of the nation's greatest playwright. Shakespeare died unlamented and ignored by the people whom he had entertained with his plays; his friends at Stratford appear to have been unaware of his theatrical fame.

No one in Elizabethan England, Shakespeare included, ever claimed to be the author "Shakespeare". William Shakespeare's detractors assert that he was only a "front" for some noble who desired that his authorship of the plays and sonnets should be kept secret. The fact that, some years after Shakespeare's death, the plays were attributed to him is, they assert, no proof that he wrote them. None the less, there seems some indication that certain people, who should have been in a position to know who wrote the plays, considered William Shakespeare to be their author. It has been asserted that we know just enough of William Shakespeare to make his identification with the author possible.

William Shakespeare was baptized at Stratford-on-Avon on 26 April, 1564, the son of John Shakespeare and his wife Mary Arden. His father was a middle-class corn and leather merchant, perhaps also a butcher, who suffered various ups and downs of prosperity. He became an alderman in 1565 and Bailiff of the town in 1568 but between the years 1578 and 1579 he appears to have suffered some financial difficulties for we find him selling property and being unable to meet his commitments.

There is some doubt and considerable argument about the education William may have received. He could certainly have attended the free schools in Stratford but it is asserted that he may not have done so, because his father himself was not an educated man, which is supported by the fact that instead of writing his signature he made his "mark" on documents. It is claimed that, if John Shakespeare was a Roman Catholic as is sometimes thought, he might not have allowed his son to attend the Protestant school. If William did attend school he would have learned English grammar, Latin and some arithmetic. His detractors claim that, as there is no proof he did attend school, there is therefore no proof that he was educated at all.

According to Stratford tradition, William joined his father in business when he was thirteen years old. We next hear of him in 1582 when the banns were called for his marriage to Ann Hathaway on 28 November, plus the rather odd fact that on the day before they were entered for his marriage to an otherwise unknown woman named "Ann Whatley de Temple Grafton," which may have been a clerical error for Ann Hathaway. That William's marriage to a woman of eight years his senior was one of necessity is suggested by the birth six months later of a daughter who was baptized on 26 May, 1582. In February, 1584, twins were born of the marriage, a son and a daughter named Hamnet and Judith.

There follows a complete blank in Shakespeare's life until 1594, tradition saying only that he was accused of stealing deer belonging to Sir Thomas Lucy from Charlcote Park, it being suggested that this caused his flight to London where we find him next.

On 15 March, 1594, the Court Treasurer's accounts name Shakespeare, now aged thirty-two, as one of the actors paid for presenting "two severall comedies or interludes" before Queen Elizabeth, and in November of the same year a Writ of Attachment, to the Sheriff of Surrey, was issued naming him and three others, as sureties of the peace on behalf of William Wayte. Shakespeare was now a member of the Lord Chamberlain's company of actors. There was also a rival company known as the Lord Admiral's. In 1596 we find Shakespeare living on Bankside, and owning property assessed at £5. In the same year his son Hamnet died in Stratford-on-Avon.

At the end of that year William made an application at the College of Heralds on behalf of his father for a Coat of Arms, which was granted. In 1597 William purchased a large though somewhat dilapidated house in Stratford-on-Avon known as "New Place" with an acre of ground and he is described as "a gentleman and householder of Stratford". He paid £60 for the property. In London we find him appearing as an actor in Ben Johnson's play *Every Man His Humour*. In 1598 Shakespeare's son-in-law, Richard Quinney, wrote to him, the letter still surviving, asking for the loan of £30, and in 1599 his father John died.

Meanwhile, Shakespeare's affairs were prospering. In 1599 he became a one-tenth shareholder in the new Globe Theatre and in 1602 he bought more land in Stratford. In 1603 he acted in Ben Johnson's play *Sejanus* and he is given, amongst others, scarlet cloth as one of the king's (James I) servants. He attended the Spanish Ambassador as one of the Grooms of the Chambers.

In 1604 Shakespeare sued a Phillip Rogers, to whom he had supplied malt, for £1 19s. 10d., and for the return of a loan of 2s., and he bought various leases in Stratford for £440. There is evidence that he was now living with a wig-maker named Mountjoy in Silver Street, Cripplegate, and he was bequeathed the sum of 30s. by an actor to provide a memorial ring.

In 1608 Shakespeare became a one-seventh shareholder in the Blackfriars Theatre and he altered his share in the Globe Theatre to one-fifth and later to one-fourteenth. In 1609 he took legal action for £6 and costs against John Addenbrooke for malt and corn supplied, and in 1610 he bought more land in Stratford. These facts suggest that Shakespeare was carrying on his father's business in Stratford while he was managing and acting in London.

William Shakespeare died at Stratford-on-Avon and was buried on 25 April, 1616, aged fifty-two, having made a will, leaving estate and cash valued at £1,550, a very considerable sum for those days, with various small bequests, leaving "his second best bed" to his wife. He was buried in Stratford Church.

The thirty-six plays attributed to William Shakespeare are usually regarded as having been written between the years 1590 and 1613. Some, however, claim that these dates have been arbitrarily fixed by the Shakespearian scholars to fit in with his known lifetime and the dates in which he may have been living in London and acting in the theatre.

1590	Comedy of Errors.
1591	Two Gentlemen of Verona.
1592	Henry VI.
1593	Venus and Adonis.
	Titus and Andronicus.
	Love's Labour's Lost.
	Lucrece.
	Richard III.
1594	A Midsummer Night's Dream.
1596	Romeo and Juliet.
1597	Henry IV.
1598	The Taming of the Shrew.
	Much Ado About Nothing.
1599	Henry V.
	Merry Wives of Windsor.
	Julius Caesar.
1600	As You Like It.
	Twelfth Night.
	Hamlet.
1602	All's Well that Ends Well.
	Troilus and Cressida.
1604	Measure for Measure.
	Othello.
1605	King Lear.
1606	Timon of Athens.
	Macbeth.
1607	Anthony and Cleopatra.
	Pericles, Prince of Tyre.
1608	Coriolanus.
1609	Cymbeline.
	The Sonnets.
1610	A Winter's Tale.
	The Tempest.
1613	Henry VIII.
	The Two Noble Kinsmen.

It is considered strange that Shakespeare made no reference in his will to play properties or to any estate which they may have represented. Against this it is claimed that the rights in Shakespeare's plays would have been vested in the theatrical enterprises of which he was a shareholder.

The basis of the belief that William Shakespeare was the

author is derived from certain contemporary references to him, and to the statements of people soon after his death.

The first known reference to Shakespeare as a playwright comes from 1592 when he is spoken of in a tract by a writer named Robert Greene in rather a derogatory way. Greene himself was a disappointed playwright and his reference to Shakespeare is of no significance except for the fact that he refers to him at all in a sense which implies that he too was a playwright.

A reference, which may indicate Shakespeare, is found in the book of Edmund Spenser, *Colin Clouts Come Home Again*, written in 1594. Spenser is thought to have referred to Shakespeare by the name "Aetion" and to be referring to the well-known historical plays. He says:

"And, though last not least, is Aetion.
A gentler shepherd may no where be found,
Whose Muse, full of high thoughts invention
Doth like himselfe heroically sound."

Another contemporary reference comes from the *Scourge of Folly* by John Davies of Hereford who in an epigram refers to:

"To our English Terence, Mr. Will: Shake-speare.
Some say good Will (which I in sport do sing)
  Hadst thou not plaid some Kingly parts in sport,
Thou hadst bin a companion for a King;
  And Bene a King among the meaner sort.
Some others raile; but raile as they think fit,
  Thou hast no rayling, but a raigning Wit;
    And Honesty thou sowst, which they do reape;
    So, to increase their Stocke, which they do keepe."

Far stronger corroboration of the belief that Shakespeare was an author comes from the book called *"Wits Treasury"*, which was a review of all English literature by a clergymen named Frances Meres who declared, in 1598, that:

" 'the sweet witty soul of Ovid' lived again in Shakespeare's verse." He goes on to say: "As Plaustus and Senecca are accounted the best for Comedy and Tragedy amongst the Latins, so Shakespeare among the English is the most excellent in both kinds for the stage: for Comedy, witness his *Gentleman of Verona*, his *Errors*, his *Love*

Labours Lost, his *Love Labours Wonne*, his *Mid Sumers Night Dreame*, and his *Merchant of Venice*; for Tragedy his *Richard II*, *Richard III*, *Henry IV*, *King John*, *Titus Andronicus* and his *Romeo and Juliet*."

In 1599 a character in a comedy produced at Cambridge University is made to say:

"Oh Sweet Mr. Shakespeare. I'le have his picture in my study—I'le worship Sweet Mr. Shakespeare and to honour him will lay his *Venus and Adonis* under my pillow."

Two years later, in 1601, we find a very different reference to Shakespeare, one which may disclose an interesting aspect of his character. John Manningham writes in his diary for 2 February to 13 March the following:

"Upon a tyme when Burbage played Rich(ard) 3 there was a citizen gaen soe farr in liking with him that before she went from the play she appointed him to come that night to her by the name of Ri: the 3. Shakspere overhearing their conclusion went before, was intertained and at his game ere burbage came. Then the message being brought that Rich: the 3rd was at the dore, Shakespeare caused returne to be made that William the Conqueror was before Rich: the 3. Shakspere's name William."

Though amusing, this does not tell us more than that Shakespeare was conversant with the plays named.

In 1601 there occurred an incident which is taken by many as irrefutable proof that Shakespeare was the author of the plays attributed to him. In February, just before they marched into London, the Earl of Essex and his conspirators staged a performance at the Globe Theatre of *Richard II*. They hoped that the spectacle of King Richard II being deposed by his subjects might embolden Londoners to rise in support of Essex against Queen Elizabeth. The rising failed and the chief conspirators, the Earls of Essex, Southampton, and Rutland, were put on trial at which much was made of the special performance of *Richard II*.

All three earls are put forward as the true authors of the plays of Shakespeare, by various theorists who claim that Shakespeare himself was not proceeded against as the author because the Queen's agents knew well that he was only a cover for the true author, a member of the aristocracy. Exponents of the other point of view hold that it is significant that Shakespeare was not put to the "question" or made to confess who was the true author. They suggest that this shows conclusively that Shakespeare was the author and that he had written the play as one of a historical series without thought of contemporary application. If the Queen's agents had discovered that the author of the play was someone other than Shakespeare, a professional playwright, that person would have been proceeded against.

Before passing to references to Shakespeare made after his death, it may be remarked that Shakespeare's detractors claim that the silence of a number of people during his lifetime is significant. Why, they ask, did Phillip Henslowe, the actor-manager, make no reference to Shakespeare as the author of plays in his diary of his business transactions which he kept from 1591 to 1609? The answer is that Henslowe was the manager of the rival company to that to which Shakespeare belonged, and therefore it is not surprising that no reference is found to Shakespeare in his transactions.

The first concrete evidence of Shakespeare as the author comes in 1632, sixteen years after his death, when the First Folio of his Plays was published. The title page describes the contents as "Mr. William Shakespeare's Comedies, Histories and Tragedies, published according to the True Originall Copies" and the work is dedicated to "the Most Noble and Imcomparable Paire of Brethren," William Herbert, Earl of Pembroke and Phillip Herbert, Earl of Montgomery, who probably financed the work. To the Folio Ben Jonson, Shakespeare's rival and the other great dramatist of the age, writes the dedicatory lines "To the Memory of my beloved, the author, Master William Shakespeare, and what he has left for us." A picture of Shakespeare forms the frontispiece and under it appear the lines written by Ben Jonson, as follows:

"This figure, that thou here seest put,
    It was for gentle Shakespeare cut;
Wherein the Graver had a strife
    With Nature, to out-do the life:
O, could he but have drawn his wit
    As well in brass, as he hath hit
His face; the print would then surpass
    All, that was ever writ in brass.
But, since he cannot, Reader, look,
    Not on his Picture, but his book."

Ben Jonson is also credited with other references to Shakespeare. There can be no doubt that Jonson knew Shakespeare well, and would certainly have known whether or not he was the author of the plays attributed to his name. Jonson declared himself to be a lover of Shakespeare "this side idolatry" implying that other people may have carried their esteem too far. In 1619 Ben Jonson told William Drummond in Scotland that Shakespeare wanted "arte and sometimes sense." Jonson is supposed also to be referring to Shakespeare in his lines:

"Sweet Swan of Avon, what a sight it were
        To see thee in our waters yet appear,
    And make those flights upon the banks of Thames,
        That did so take Eliza and our James!"

Also on the First Folio there occur the lines written by Leonard Digges which read:

"Shakespeare, at length, they pious fellows give
        The world thy works; thy works, by which outlive
    Thy tomb thy name must: when that stone is rent
        And time dissolves thy Stratford monument."

To the Second Folio edition of Shakespeare's plays was affixed the poem written by Milton, who did not himself know Shakespeare and was interested only in his works.

"What needs my Shakespeare for his honour'd bones,
        The labour of an age in piled stones?
    Or that his hallow'd reliques should lie hid
        Under a star-y-pointed pyramid?
    Dear Son of memory, great heir of fame
        What need'st thou such weak witness of thy name?
    Thou in our wonder and astonishment
        Hast built thyself a live-long monument."

Perhaps the strangest evidence for Shakespeare the playwright comes from the monument erected in Stratford Church it is believed in 1631. This monument was clearly different in 1634 from what it became after 1725, for when William Dugdale, the antiquarian, in his *Antiquities of Warwickshire,* published in 1656, visited Stratford he drew a picture of the monument, which shows that it differs considerably from the one which we now know. In Dugdale's drawing

Shakespeare's hands rest upon what is clearly a sack, presumably containing wool or corn, and representing his Stratford business activities. In the existing monument the sack has become a cushion on which is lying a piece of paper and the figure of Shakespeare holds a pen. This suggests that when Shakespeare was buried in Stratford-on-Avon, he was remembered by his fellow townsfolk as a local business man, a maltster or corn merchant. But, when later on they became conversant with his national fame as a playwright, the monument was changed to conform with his profession as an author.

Shakespeare's detractors claim that the bust on the monument represents the face of a stupid man, one that could never have written the immortal works.

Before leaving the semi-contemporaneous references to Shakespeare the statement of Jonson towards the end of his life, and published after his death, may be remarked; he said:

"I remember the players often mentioned it as an honour to Shakespeare, that in his writing (whatsoever he penned) he never blotted out a line. My answer hath been, would he had blotted out a thousand. Which they thought a malevolent speech. I had not told posterity this, but for their ignorance, who chose that circumstance to commend their friend by, wherein he most faulted: and to justify my own candour: for I loved the man, and do honour his memory, on this side idolatry, as much as any. He was (indeed) honest, and of an open and free nature; had an excellent phantasy, brave notions, and gentle expressions; wherein he flowed with that facility, that sometimes it was necessary that he should be stopped: Sufflaminandus erat. His wit was in his own power, would the rule of it had been so too. Many times he fell into those things, could not escape laughter: as when he said in the person of Caesar, one speaking to him, 'Caesar, thou dost me wrong,' he replied, 'Caesar did never wrong but with just cause,' and such like; which were ridiculous. But he redeemed his vices with his virtues. There was ever more in him to be praised than to be pardoned."

One significant fact apparently has been overlooked. At his death Shakespeare left what was by contemporary standards a considerable fortune. Could he have acquired this, we may ask, solely by his acting and from his shares in various theatrical enterprises? Surely the popularity of his plays must have contributed?

The great difficulty in appreciating the complexities of settling the authorship of the writings attributed to Shakespeare lies in the necessity of a deep knowledge of the plays and the significance of countless allusions, biographical and political, which are advanced by the various theorists as the proof of particular authorship. It is claimed that many of these allusions could have been written only by some particular person who was not Shakespeare. This ignores the possibility, the very likely possibility, that as a great playwright, a genius, Shakespeare was putting words into his character's mouths which were, in his opinion, in keeping with the character he was portraying. It does not necessarily follow therefore that because a character makes a particular statement it means that that statement could have come only from a writer to whom the circumstances were applicable.

For example, it is concluded from the Shakespearian Sonnet 1-5 that the words "Weret aught to me I bore the canopy," must refer to the duties of the Earl of Oxford as Lord Great Chamberlain, whose responsibility it was to bear with the Earl Marshal the canopy over the head of the Queen. A great part of the various theories attributing the Shakespearian plays and Sonnets to a number of different aristocratic authors is based on just such allusions.

The claims made that Shakespeare did not write the plays, and that they were written by others, are based on both negative and positive factors. Negatively it is asserted that Shakespeare was incapable of being the author of the thirty-six plays and the Sonnets, which show considerable scholarship, and knowledge of European countries, of sports, of classical and continental languages, of legal affairs, and above all of Court life. It is asserted that only a nobleman, and a scholar at that, could have written such works. Shakespeare lacked the experience, and the knowledge required. It is pointed out that in his Will he made no reference to his plays and lays no claim to them as his property. Nor did he leave anyone any books, which is taken to suggest that he owned none, and therefore could not have made himself conversant with these facts from books. This is all negative proof, for a number of his contemporaries also omitted to mention their libraries in their Wills. By those who assert that the author was other than William Shakespeare, he is called a "money lending maltster", "the illiterate actor", and "a drunken Warwickshire rustic".

Many of the authors who have written books putting forward someone other than Shakespeare as the famous author have drawn up lists of the attributes which the author of the Shakespearian plays and Sonnets must have had. They claim that Shakespeare could not have filled these conditions and that their particular claimant did. One such list (Amphlett, *Who Was Shakespeare?* 1955) sums up the attributes as follows:

1. Shakespeare must have lived in the second half of the sixteenth century—with his highest producing powers in the 80s or 90s.
2. He must have been a man of deep learning, knowing Latin, some Greek, French and Italian, a little astronomy.
3. He must have been a lyric poet of very great distinction.
4. He must have been fond of music.
5. He must have had a clear understanding (bred of close study) of the law.
6. He had travelled and imbibed a love of Italy's culture and a knowledge of North Italian cities.
7. He had an equivocal attitude towards women.
8. He had Lancastrian sympathies.
9. He was a nobleman of ancient and honourable lineage, shown by his knowledge of hawking, hunting, heraldry, etc.
10. His character showed great insight into men's minds with a corresponding sympathy.
11. He suffered from some libellous attack which defamed his name.
12. He was interested in the drama not only as a writer but as a producer.
13. In money matters he was thriftless and lax.
14. The Sonnets refer to his being lame.

Historic doubts about the authorship of the Shakespearian plays are now two centuries old. The controversy appears to have been set off in 1759 by a play written by the Rev. James Townley entitled *High Life Below Stairs* in which a character is made to ask, "who wrote Shakespeare?" and the reply is given, "Ben Jonson". The character then says, "Oh no, Shakespeare was written by one Mr. Finis, for I saw his name at the end of the book." In an anonymous book published in 1769 entitled *The Life and Adventures of Common Sense: an historical allegory*, the hero says that in 1588 he wrote the plays which were passed off as his own by William Shakespeare. Quickly the doubt, the seeds of which had now been sown, spread and in 1785 the first attempt was made to suggest that the real Shakespeare was Francis Bacon.

The whole problem of Shakespearian authorship has been summed up by R. C. Churchill in *Shakespeare and his Betters*, in 1958, who sets out to criticize and debunk the theories which have found more than fifty different candidates for the Shakespearian authorship. Professor Churchill fails to examine the traditional claim that Shakespeare was in fact the author. He contents himself with examining and criticizing the various theories propounded during the last hundred years.

Professor Churchill deals first with the general theory that Shakespeare could not have been the author, and that the author of the plays must have been both an aristocrat and a scholar. As Professor Churchill points out, we know what Elizabethan Court life was like largely from the Shakespearian plays. There is no criterion therefore to judge whether the plays are correct or not in their representation of Court life. Shakespeare, as an actor who appeared in a number of plays given at Court, could have acquired at least a rudimentary knowledge of the language and behaviour of courtiers. Many plays of that period were set in palaces but it is not claimed that their authors must have been noblemen in order to have written about Court life. It is asserted that there was in existence in Shakespeare's time a Social Handbook, the Book of the Courtier, translated in 1561 from the Italian of Count Baldassare, which could have given Shakespeare an insight into the general thoughts and behaviour of the aristocracy.

It is agreed that the Shakespearian plays show a wide general knowledge of a number of arts and sciences and of life in European cities and courts. But no one knows just how accurate or inaccurate these Shakespearian references are. It does not follow necessarily, that the author of the plays must have been an expert, for example, on the law, Court life, military affairs, music, sports, and the natural sciences. Nor does it follow that the words placed in the character's mouths must necessarily represent the author's private opinions.

The Baconian theory is probably the oldest, and still the most widely known, of those which ascribe the plays of Shakespeare to other than William Shakespeare. Francis Bacon, Lord Verulam, Viscount St. Alban, died in 1626. Lord Chancellor of England, a notable lawyer, and a famous philosopher, he is believed by many people to have been the secret author of the Shakespearian works. This belief is based chiefly on what are known as the ciphers and cryptograms, which are reputed to have been found in the Shakespearian works. Perhaps the strongest grounds for identifying Bacon as the author lie in his knowledge of the law, and the knowledge of the law displayed in Shakespeare's works. It is claimed as irrefutable proof that Bacon was in fact the author that the plays contained so many legal allusions.

On the other hand, it is stressed by others that many of these legal allusions show laughable mistakes, which a man of Bacon's legal training could not have committed. He could not have committed the dramatic irregularities of the trial scene in *The Winter's Tale*, it is claimed.

The author Ignatius Donnelly, also the author of the first great work on mythical Atlantis, believed he had found a secret message contained in the Shakespearian plays which proved that they were written by Bacon. Donnelly's cryptograms are now discredited. It had been pointed out that the authorship of almost any book can be "proved" by ciphers. In fact one of Donnelly's ciphers can be made to read "Master William Shakespeare wrote this play". On the basis of various cryptograms it can be proved, as was pointed out by Father Ronald Knox, that Tennyson's *In Memoriam* was in fact written by Queen Victoria.

Bacon's works may show him to have been perhaps the greatest philosopher of the Elizabethan age but at least one of the worst dramatists and no more than a minor poet, hardly a man who could have written the immortal dramatic works and poems attributed to Shakespeare. In his *Seven Shakespeares* (1931) Gilbert Slater sums up the Bacon case as follows:

"To master the arguments, it would be necessary to begin the study of them at a very early age, and continue it steadily to the end of a long life."

Next we turn to the various group theories which attributed the plays of Shakespeare to a secret committee of aristocratic and scholarly gentlemen who preferred to remain anonymous. They combined together in order to write plays to educate the common man and to act as national propaganda. These group theories have found popularity because they seem to answer a number of awkward questions.

Nearly all the individuals who at one time or other have

been advanced as sole authors of the Shakespearian works have also been named as members of this "patriotic committee". The most favoured group theory suggests that this government committee was headed by the Earl of Oxford, and the historical plays were written as propaganda.

Against this convenient theory it has been pointed out that the propaganda value of the Shakespearian plays was very little. The committee could have found far more useful subjects in British history, for example the glorious deeds of the Black Prince rather than the revolt of the barons against King John and the revolt and deposition of King Richard II by his subjects. Surely the committee would have avoided themes which demonstrated civil strife? It is pointed out too that no suggestion has ever been made that the plays of Jonson or of Marlow were written in collaboration. According to these theories the authorship of the Shakespearian plays was a closely guarded State secret, cloaked by the name of the actor William Shakespeare, which was used as a nom de plume.

Other theories which have been advanced find Shakespeare in such people as John Florio, an Italian who lived in England, Lord Burleigh, Sir Walter Raleigh, Sir John Barnard, the Earl of Devonshire, the Earl of Stirling (who because he was in Scotland must have written Macbeth), the Earls of Essex and Salisbury (who were politicians and soldiers), Sir Anthony Shirley (a much traveled man), the Earl of Southampton (the only nobleman with whom Shakespeare is known to have had any connexion), Robert Burton (a student of theology and Rector of Segrave), the Earl of Rutland (who had traveled extensively in Italy and Denmark), and even Cardinal Wolsey and a group of Jesuits.

Others find feminine influence in the plays and attribute their authorship to various women, such as Queen Elizabeth herself, the Countess of Pembroke (mother of the two brethren to whom the First Folio was dedicated), to Shakespeare's own wife and to the mysterious Ann Whatley (the woman Shakespeare is supposed to have left on the altar steps the day before he married Ann Hathaway). There are at least some grounds for these theories, but generally they are all based on the assumption that the author of the Shakespearian works must have been a nobleman, or someone in close touch with Court life.

Sir Walter Raleigh, for example, is advanced as the author because he had knowledge of the sea and seamanship, which is shown in The Tempest. It is suggested, too, that the words in the Shakespearian Sonnet "I, made lame by Fortune's dearest spite" might refer to the wound Raleigh received at Cadiz in 1596 which rendered him lame.

The Countess of Pembroke, a highly educated woman, a patroness of literature, who certainly wrote poems and perhaps plays which were never published in her name, may be the person referred to by Jonson as "the Sweet Swam of Avon", because she lived at Wilton on the banks of a tributary of the Wiltshire Avon.

Another theory identifies Shakespeare as the famous Elizabethan playwright Christopher Marlowe, who was born in 1564, and is supposed to have disappeared mysteriously in 1593, the year before Shakespeare made his first appearance in London. But the report of the coroner's inquest has been found which proves that Marlowe was murdered in 1593, unless, as has been suggested, his death was faked because he was, in fact, a Government secret agent. It is contended that there are distinct resemblances of style between Marlowe's and Shakespeare's plays, and Marlowe was certainly a well-educated man. The Marlowe propagandists declare that he fled abroad in 1593 leaving his "Shakespearian plays" in the hands of Sir Thomas Walsingham. A search for clues in Walsingham's tomb in 1955 yielded no information.

Cases have been made out for the authorship of the plays by the Earls of Derby and Rutland. The claims for Derby are based chiefly on the discovery of certain documents in the Calendar of State Papers, Domestic Series, which refer to him as being "busyed only in penning comedies for the commoun players", and therefore being unsuitable to be drawn into the net of the Catholic anti-Elizabeth plots of the period. He was a much-traveled man who had visited the Court of Navarre, the scene of *Love's Labour's Lost,* and he knew France well. He was the patron of the company of players, which included the actor Shakespeare, which after Lord Derby's death became the Lord Chamberlain's Company. While there is nothing in the plays themselves to identify Derby as the author, the plays show the important part played by his family in the downfall of Richard III, and the accession of Henry VII.

Roger Manners, the fifth Earl of Rutland, is advanced as the author principally on the grounds that he had visited Verona and Denmark, the scenes of Shakespearian plays. It is suggested, too, that the theme of ill-feeling between brothers, which is demonstrated in some of the plays, may indicate Rutland as the author because he was on bad terms with his younger brother who may actually have murdered him. He was involved also in the attempted rising organized by the Earl of Essex in 1601, which was preceded by the special performance of *Richard II.*

The strongest case for an individual noble author has been made out for Edward de Vere, the Earl of Oxford, who lived from 1550 to 1604. He was put forward as the true author by J. T. Looney in 1920 who wrote a book entitled *Shakespeare Identified as Edward de Vere.* Of the de Vere case Gilbert Slater, in his *Seven Shakespeares,* says "we can hardly deny that a very strong case has been made out, nor can we be surprised that it has convinced so many scholars", and he stresses that no adequate reply to the Oxford case has ever been published. The chief ground for rejection of Edward de Vere as the author is the fact that he died in the year 1604, before eight of the Shakespearian plays had been written, according to the usual dating. Believers in the theory suggest that all these plays had been written before Oxford's death, and that they were perhaps rewritten into final form by others after his death. This, they suggest, would account for the marked change in style between the early and middle Shakespearian plays.

It is clear that the Earl of Oxford, more than any other individual, fits the requirements which have been laid down for the author of the Shakespearian works. He was a leading noble and a scholar of note, who was described by his contemporaries as the "best for comedy in his day". But no dramatic works written by the Earl of Oxford have survived unless they are those attributed to Shakespeare. A small but vital point is that the Earl of Oxford's coat-of-arms included a man shaking a spear. It is suggested that this emblem is the true derivation of the nom de plume "Shakespeare", which quite by chance became attributed to Shakespeare the actor-manager.

Many incidents in Shakespearian plays are taken to indicate Oxford as their author. He was a Lancastrian sympathizer, an enthusiast for Italian Court life, a lover of music and sport, and improvident in money matters. His attitude to women was conflicting and doubtful. He had traveled all over the Continent and was himself an enthusiast for the drama and for poetry. He was dangerously wounded in a duel which left him lame and he is the only individual who is known to have borne the canopy over Queen Elizabeth at the Armada celebration. This unique occasion is supposed to be recalled in the Shakespearian line already quoted.

It is considered extraordinary that from the year 1585 until his death the Earl of Oxford was paid the enormous sum of £1,000 a year from the Secret Service Fund, it being declared that this payment was made to him to write and organize the production of plays as national propaganda against the Catholic and Spanish cause.

Many statements found in the Shakespearian plays are declared to be autobiographical, and if so it is held that, from what we know of his life, they could have been written only by the Earl of Oxford. Another ingenious clue, linking Oxford as the true author, has been drawn from the publication of the Shakespearian Sonnets in the year 1609, which were dedicated to "Our ever living poet", which is taken to suggest that the author must have been dead, as Oxford was by that year. Such words could hardly have been employed to describe a still living author. It is considered significant that the Sonnets were published in the same year as his widow sold his house at Hackney, it being suggested that the manuscripts of the Sonnets then came to light, and they were published by a local Hackney man. The "de Vere" theory is undoubtedly the strongest of all those which find the author of Shakespeare as other than Shakespeare himself. It has been supported in a number of books, and it is the chief theory of the long-established Shakespearian Fellowship Society.

But the great question is, do we have to look further than the name of the traditional author as the originator of the plays and poems of William Shakespeare? Many scholars accept Ben Jonson's words as irrefutable proof that Shakespeare was the author. It seems difficult to accept any other interpretation of Jonson's statements, unless he, like anyone else, was completely fooled. Surely if anyone was in a position to know the truth of the Shakespearian authorship, it would have been the rival playwright?

MYTHICAL ATLANTIS

BELIEF in the one-time existence of a great Atlantean continent is based on the story related by the Greek philosopher Plato. In his *Timaeus*, written about 400 B.C., the lawyer Solon is told by a priest in Egypt the following story:

"Solon, Solon, you Greeks are all children—there is not an old man in Greece. You have no old traditions, and know of but one deluge, whereas there have been many destructions of mankind, both by flood and fire. Egypt alone has escaped them, and in Egypt alone is ancient history recorded: you are ignorant of your own past.

"For long before Deucalion, nine thousand years ago, there was an Athens founded, like Sais, by Athena: a city rich in power and wisdom, famed for mighty deeds, the greatest of which was this. At that time there lay opposite the columns of Hercules, in the Atlantic, which was then navigable, an island larger than Libya and Asia together, from which sailors could pass to other lands, and so to the continent. The sea in front of the straits is indeed but a small harbour; that which lay beyond the island, however, is worthy of the name, and the land which surrounds that greater sea may be truly called the continent. In this island of Atlantis had grown up a mighty power, whose kings were descended from Poseidon, and extended their sway over many islands and over a portion of the great continent. Even Libya up to the gates of Egypt, and Europe as far as Tyrrhenia, submitted to their sway. Even harder they pressed upon the other nations of the known world, seeking the subjugation of the whole.

"Then, O Solon, did the strength of your mighty republic become clear to all men, by reason of her courage and force. Foremost in the arts of war, she met the invader at the head of Greece, abandoned by all her allies, she triumphed alone over the Western foe, delivering from the yoke all the nations within the columns. But afterwards came a day and night of great floods and earthquakes; the earth engulfed all the Athenians who were capable of bearing arms, and Atlantis disappeared, swallowed by the waves; hence it is that this sea is no longer navigable, from the vast mud-shoals formed by the vanished island."

In another book named *Critias*, Plato gives further details of the destruction of Atlantis, about the year 9600 B.C., and he gives descriptions of its temples, palaces, bridges, canals, and its great wealth. It consisted of twelve islands each ruled by an independent king and its people were gentle and obedient to the laws. He says:

"The palaces in the interior of the citadel were constructed in this wise: in the centre was a holy temple dedicated to Cleito and Poseidon, which remained inaccessible, and was surrounded by an enclosure of gold. Here too was Poseidon's own temple, having a sort of barbaric splendor. All the outside of the temple, with the exception of the pinnacles, they covered with silver, and the pinnacles with gold. In the interior of the temple the roof was of ivory, adorned everywhere with gold and silver and orichalcum; all the other parts of the walls and pillars and floor they lined with orichalcum. In the temple they placed statues of gold: there was the god himself standing in a chariot—the charioteer of six winged horses—and of such a size that he touched the roof of the building with his head; around him there were a hundred Nereids riding on dolphins. Around the temple on the outside were placed statues of gold of all the ten kings and of their wives; and there were many other great offerings, both of kings and of private individuals, coming both from the city itself and the foreign cities over which they held sway."

Plato, it is claimed, was either perpetrating a gigantic hoax or he was himself the victim of a "tall story". On the other hand, he may have created a mythical story to illustrate the ideal political state: or he may have heard some vague rumor of lands on the other side of the Atlantic.

It is quite feasible that the peoples of the eastern Mediterranean may have known something of the peoples of the Americas. While no record of such voyages has survived, it is possible that Phoenician, Egyptian, or Greek sailors, who undoubtedly penetrated the Atlantic, may have been swept across it and returned.

The Greeks knew that the world was round and they must have assumed therefore that there was land on the other side of the Atlantic. Phoenicians and Greeks undoubtedly reached Britain and Iceland and they sailed far down the coast of Africa. They knew of the Sargasso Sea which lies on the American side of the Atlantic. As is shown by the voyages of Columbus, ships could be blown across the Atlantic in the autumn and could return by a northerly route in the spring. The Greeks believed that across the ocean lay the home of the Cimmerians, a people who dwelt in darkness in the house of the dead and far out in the Atlantic lay the Islands of the Blest. The story of Hercules is associated with the west and the hero is supposed to have reached the "far confines of the Ocean". A Greek historian of the fourth century B.C., Theopompus, describes a continent of immense greatness between Europe and Africa.

Whether or not Mediterranean voyagers reached the American continents, there was nothing there then to give rise to the story told by Plato. The great civilizations of Peru, Yucatan and Mexico were still to flourish. Their great days did not come until the first and second centuries A.D.

When travelers and archaeologists first visited the ruined cities of Central America and Peru they supplied apparent corroboration for the one-time existence of Atlantis. It was not at first realized that the civilizations of ancient Peru and of the Mayas flourished far later than was supposed. Then ancient Spanish records, written at the time of the conquests, were found. These recorded local legends derived from the Indians who spoke of bearded white men arriving from the east before the flood. These mysterious visitors brought with them the blessings of civilization and knowledge of agriculture and architecture, and they built pyramid-like structures, similar to those which existed in Egypt. An even stranger fact came to light. None of these American civilizations appears to have originated in the Americas. All seem to have had no evolutionary period but to have blossomed suddenly. Their cultures appeared to be fully fledged. Clearly, claimed the theorists, they had been founded by the survivors of lost Atlantis. But Atlantis, according to Plato, had sunk beneath the waves in 9600 B.C. A forlorn attempt was made to overcome this disparity in chronology by the suggestion that part of Atlantis, the island Antillia, survived until quite recent times.

The evidence supplied by the civilizations of the Mayas and of Peru is indicative not of the one-time existence of an Atlantean continent but more probably of the visit of strangers from the Mediterranean area. Many discoveries on the American side of the Atlantic confirm that such visitors did arrive from the east. Although three or four thousand years later in time, the American "Indian" civilizations paralleled those of the Old World in many ways. From where could they have acquired their knowledge?

The Mayas had a great understanding of astronomy. They knew the year consisted of three hundred and sixty-five days, and they added Leap Years and calculated eclipses. The people of both the north and south American continents knew creation and deluge stories very similar to those of the Old World. These beliefs may have been part of the common heritage of mankind, acquired by the American Indians, really Mongols from Asia, before they crossed into Alaska and migrated southwards.

Whereas many factors would seem to suggest that the people of the New World had a knowledge of the civilization of the Old World, they knew nothing of the wheel, an Old World invention which was at least three thousand years old at the start of the Christian era, and they were ignorant of the use of iron. It seems strange that if people did visit them from the Mediterranean or from Europe they did not teach the use of either the wheel or the making of iron tools and weapons.

Those who believe in the former existence of an Atlantean continent point to the strange affinities of flora and fauna on both sides of the Atlantic. Many animals, birds, insects, fish and plants are common to both shores. Remains of prehistoric and extinct animals are found on both sides of the Atlantic and also in Asia and Africa. On the other hand, such useful plants as the potato of Peru and the tomato of Mexico were not found in the Old World, nor were they introduced to Europe until after the voyages of Columbus.

At first sight the configuration of the bed of the Atlantic between Bermuda and Spain appears to confirm the former existence of Atlantis. Depth sounders carried westwards from Spain disclose first a valley three thousand feet in depth, the sea bed then rising perpendicularly to the summits of the Azores which are in effect the tops of a high mountain range which runs under the sea north and south in the Atlantic. The ocean bed then drops to another valley two thousand feet deep and rises steeply again to the island of Bermuda, another mountain top. It appears, therefore, that the Azores represent the last remaining outposts of Atlantis. But geological surveys of the ocean bed have disclosed that, if any subsidences took place, they occurred at a date a hundred thousand years or more before the time of the supposed loss of Atlantis.

The story of Atlantis is an ancient myth, a human dream conjuring up the greatness of its past. We now know too much about human history to give credence to the belief in its existence. Yet those who believe in Atlantis cling to their theories, and many of them are busy trying to find Atlantis is places other than in the central Atlantic. It has been located in the North Sea and another theory locates Plato's mythical continent in Libya, still another in Crete.

Yet it is clear, from a careful reading of his works, that Plato set out to do no more than to tell an allegory, in order to illustrate his conception of the perfect political state. He created two political systems and shows them locked in a life and death struggle. He pointed the moral, but it has been ignored. His purely mythical conception has been preferred. He may have known something of the peoples of the other side of the Atlantic. That is the only basis for believing that he wrote about reality rather than myth.

If we forget mythical Atlantis we can, however, learn something from Plato's allegory of two worlds locked in strife, a battle which results in the sudden and entire destruction of one world. We can hope only that there will not be some future Plato who will be forced to record the actual destruction of one part of the world by another. Plato attributed the cause of the destruction of civilization to man's own folly. Unlike other contemporary writers he did not attribute natural disasters to the anger of the gods.

BIBLIOGRAPHY

THE MONEY PIT.
    Harris, R. V.   The Oak Island Mystery, 1958.

THE MAN OF THE MASK
    Furneaux, R.   The Man Behind the Mask, 1954.

THE LOST EXPLORER.
    Fawcett, P. H.   Exploration Fawcett, 1953.
    Fawcett, Brian.   Ruins in the Sky, 1958.
    Dyott, G. M.   Man-hunt in the Jungle, 1930.

WRIT ON ROCK.
    Minnesota Historical   Collections XV.
               Society.
    Holland, H. R.   Westward from Vinland, 1940.
                            America, 1355–1364, 1946.
    Means, P. A.   Newport Tower, 1942.

EGYPTIAN MYSTERIES.
    Petrie, Sir F.   Pyramids and Temples of Gizeh, 1883.
    Edwards, I. E. S.   The Pyramids of Egypt, 1947.

DAUPHIN AND DUCHESS.
    Madol, H. R.   Shadow King, 1930.
    Lenotre, G.   The Riddle of the Temple. 1932.
    Maeckel, O. V.   The Dunkelgraf Mystery, 1929.

FORGOTTEN SCRIPTS AND SCROLLS.
    Allegro, J. M.   The Dead Sea Scrolls, 1956.
    Cleator, P. E.   The Lost Languages, 1959.
    Burrows, M.   The Dead Sea Scrolls, 1956.
    Bruce, F. F.   Second Thoughts on the Scrolls, 1956.
    Dupont-Sommer, A.   Jewish Sects of Qumran, 1954.
    Wilson, E.   The Scrolls from the Dead Sea.

A GENTLEMAN OF SUSSEX.
    Vere, Francis.   The Piltdown Fantasy, 1955.
    Weiner, J. S.   The Piltdown Forgery, 1956.

RUMOURS OF MONSTERS.

Heuvelmans, B.   On the Track of Unknown Animals, 1958.

Issard, R.   The Abominable Snowman, 1955.

Stonor, G. R.   Sherpa and Snowman, 1955.

THE PLATE OF BRASS.

California Historical Society.   Special Publications.

Wagner, H. R.   Sir Francis Drake's Voyage Round the World, 1926.

BUILDERS IN STONE.

Atkinson, R. J. C.   Stonehenge, 1956.

Pavre, V.   Zimbabwe, 1957.

BIBLICAL MYSTERIES.

Peake, H. J. E.   The Flood, 1930.

Lucas, A.   Route of the Exodus, 1935.

Jack, J. W.   Date of the Exodus, 1952.

DOUBTFUL IDENTITIES.

Bates, F. L.   The Escape and Suicide of John Wilkes Booth, 1908.

Eisenschiml, O.   Why was Lincoln Murdered? 1937.
In the Shadow of Lincoln's Death, 1940.

Forrester, I.   This One Mad Act, 1937.

Evans, E. E.   The Story of Kaspar Hauser, 1892.

Anderson, A.   I, Anastasia, 1958.

Botkin, Gleb.   The Woman Who Rose Again, 1938.

THE RUTHLESS MEN.

Means, P. A.   Ancient Civilizations of the Andes, 1931.

Posnansky, A.   Tiahuanaco, Cradle of American Civilization, 1914.

Heyerdahl, T.   The Voyage of the Kon Tiki.
American Indians in the Pacific, 1952.
Aku Aku, 1959.

ARTHUR OF BRITAIN.

Chambers, E. R.   Arthur of Britain, 1927.

Ashe, G.   From Caesar to Arthur, 1959.

WHO WAS SHAKESPEARE?
  See full bibliography
  printed in
      Churchill, R. C.   Shakespeare and His Betters, 1958.

MYTHICAL ATLANTIS.
  Donnelly, I.   Atlantis, 1885.
  Bramwell, J.   Lost Atlantis, 1937.